Breaking Free from Toxic Leadership

A Guide to Navigating Manipulation and Thriving in Your Career

MARKUS ZEHENTNER

CLAUDIA SCHWINGHAMMER

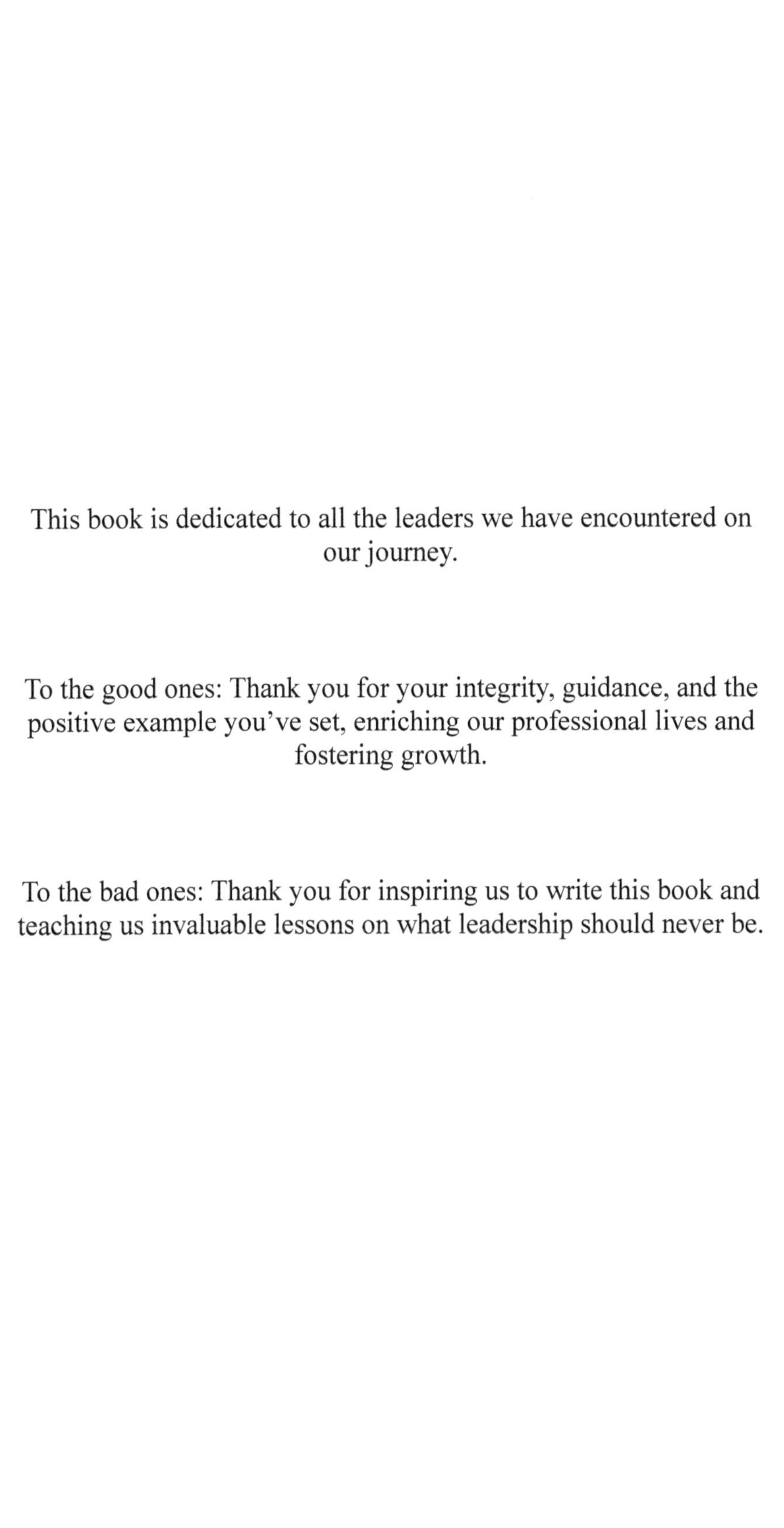

This book is dedicated to all the leaders we have encountered on our journey.

To the good ones: Thank you for your integrity, guidance, and the positive example you've set, enriching our professional lives and fostering growth.

To the bad ones: Thank you for inspiring us to write this book and teaching us invaluable lessons on what leadership should never be.

Disclaimer

This book is inspired by true events and experiences encountered in various professional environments. We have changed all names, locations, and identifiable details to protect privacy and maintain confidentiality. Any resemblance to actual persons, living or dead, companies, or specific events is purely coincidental and not intended by the authors.

The examples and stories shared within these pages are intended to illuminate the challenges posed by toxic leadership in the workplace and to offer insights and strategies for navigating such environments. They are not meant to pinpoint culpability or to defame any individual or organization. Instead, they serve as a foundation for discussion, reflection, and, ultimately, empowerment for those who find themselves in similar situations.

Our goal is to foster a deeper understanding of toxic leadership dynamics and to provide practical advice for individuals seeking to thrive in their professional lives despite these challenges. This book should be seen as a guide for personal and professional development rather than a critique of specific individuals or entities.

We encourage readers to use the information and narratives in this book as tools for growth and resilience. The strategies and advice offered herein are based on the authors' experiences and professional knowledge and are meant to support readers in their journey toward a healthier work environment.

While we strive for accuracy and relevance in our discussions and advice, we acknowledge that every individual's experience with toxic leadership is unique. As such, readers should consider their personal circumstances when applying the insights from this book.

Table of Contents

Preface

Life, at times, feels like a high-wire act without a safety net. It doesn't take much to unbalance us, and sometimes, it's the unexpected gusts of wind that throw us off track. That's what happened to me, Markus, a lawyer by profession and now author of this book.

A few years ago, I found myself walking that high wire, trying to balance my career, my family life, and a serious medical crisis that threatened to send me plummeting. My first son was diagnosed with a severe form of epilepsy at the age of 5 months, leading to countless days in hospital, rehab stays, and a whirlwind of appointments with doctors, therapists, and authorities. The fight to ensure a hopeful future for our son was exhausting and stressful and left little room for anything else.

During this turbulent time, work became a battleground instead of a refuge. My environment was steeped in toxicity, and a new boss, manipulative and demanding, joined the fray. Even as I reduced my working hours to have more time for my family, the workload piled up, causing an immense strain on my already overstretched resilience.

It all came to a head during my annual appraisal, where I was hit with a harsh review and accusations that held no basis in truth. Moreover, all the extra tasks I had taken on — often in my personal time — my efforts to foster team spirit and mentor young colleagues, and the excellent feedback from other managers I worked with outside of my division were all dismissed. This appraisal felt like a punch in the face, well, actually even worse than that; it was an emotional pummeling that attacked my core values and completely disregarded the extra miles I went to demonstrate my commitment to the company, the division, and last but not least, to my boss. Reeling from the shock, I decided to take a week off to regroup and shake off the experience, planning to return to work as if nothing had happened. However, my body succumbed to illness — a lung infection that kept me bedridden for another week. And when I revisited my doctor, he quickly realized that my malaise wasn't only physical.

The stress and pressure from the ordeal at work had breached my defenses. I was fixated on the events 24/7, trapped in a cycle of relentless internal dialogues, negotiations, and conflicts that I couldn't escape. Poor sleep, troubling dreams, and waking up fatigued became my daily reality. This mental turmoil impaired my ability to function at home, and the mere thought of returning to work and facing my bosses triggered an overwhelming physical shutdown.

I found myself unable to continue; thus, my sick leave was extended. Eventually, thanks to my exceptional practitioner, I embarked on a 6-week rehabilitation program, which changed everything.

Because, as they say, every cloud has a silver lining. In rehab, I met my now co-author Claudia, a Psychotherapist, Trainer, RTT® Certified Hypnotherapist, and the founder of SPARK, an award-winning company committed to enhancing mental health within businesses through workshops, training programs, and personalized support services. Her expertise and compassion not only helped me navigate my struggles but also sparked an idea that was to change the course of both our lives.

We saw a pressing need for a guide to help people navigate toxic work environments, a manual to help them avoid the pitfalls that had pushed me to my breaking point. We wanted to equip people with the tools to understand, cope with, and hopefully triumph over manipulative behavior in the workplace.

Thus, this book was born. It's a collaboration born from personal adversity, professional expertise, and the shared belief that knowledge can empower and protect. We hope that our experiences and insights can provide you with guidance to steer clear of the hazards of toxic leadership and help you thrive in your career.

While the journey to get here wasn't easy, the lessons learned were invaluable. With Claudia's help, I've not only escaped the clutches of manipulative leadership but also regained my joy and motivation for my work. Today, I'm well-equipped with skills that protect me from becoming prey to such destructive management behavior ever again. This book is a testament to that journey, a beacon for anyone struggling in a similar situation.

And just in case you were wondering, my son Theodor, despite all odds and a severe diagnosis three years ago, is now thriving, filling our lives with the joy and strength that inspires me every day.

Remember, we all wobble on that high wire at times, but with the right strategies and inner resilience, you can keep your balance, no matter how strong the winds. I hope that through our experiences, you find your footing, reclaim your power, and walk ahead with newfound confidence.

Welcome to our journey. Now, it's time to start yours.

Markus & Claudia

> "When setting out on a journey, never seek advice from those who have never left home."
>
> *- Rumi*

About this Book

Welcome to "Breaking Free from Toxic Leadership – A Guide to Navigating Manipulation and Thriving in Your Career." This book is an insightful exploration into the complex dynamics of workplace manipulation and toxic leadership. It will equip you with the tools, techniques, and strategies you need to recognize, resist, and overcome manipulative behavior.

This guide is designed to support a broad range of readers. If you're an employee dealing with a manipulative boss, you'll find strategies for coping and techniques for confronting the issue. HR professionals can gain insights into managing workplace dynamics and fostering healthier environments. Therapists and counselors will find a comprehensive exploration of manipulation in the workplace that can be useful for client support. Business leaders and managers will find guidance on creating positive work cultures free from toxic leadership, while students entering the workforce can equip themselves with invaluable knowledge to handle potential — and unfortunately not unlikely — future scenarios.

Our book is divided into several parts, each focusing on a unique aspect of toxic leadership. After exploring why an alarmingly high number of bosses fail to be effective leaders, we delve into the psychological underpinnings of manipulation. Later sections focus on detecting manipulative tactics, dealing with manipulative bosses, and self-care and stress management strategies. The book concludes with chapters on emotional intelligence, responding to manipulative behavior, and advocating for a healthier workplace culture.

To make the most of this book, we suggest taking the time to reflect on the concepts and strategies presented in each chapter and perhaps even making notes or journaling your thoughts and experiences related to the material. Consider how the scenarios, tactics, and solutions discussed align with your experiences and use these insights to inform your actions. It's not just about reading; it's about engaging, reflecting, and applying the lessons learned in your context.

While we have organized this book to build upon each chapter, we recognize that your needs and interests may vary. Therefore, we've designed it in a modular fashion, allowing you to navigate directly to the sections most relevant to your situation. There's no need to read it from cover to cover — although we generally recommend doing so for a more comprehensive understanding. Feel free to dive into any chapter that speaks to you and use it as a resource to consult whenever you need guidance or support.

As you embark on this journey, remember that the purpose of this book is to empower you. As you navigate the pages of this guide, we hope you'll gain not only a deeper understanding of manipulation and toxic leadership but also the tools and confidence to stand up for yourself and promote a healthier, more respectful workplace.

We are delighted to have you on this journey. Let's take the first step together.

Extend Your Discovery

With the QR code below, you're welcomed to sign up for exclusive bonus content on **toxicleadership.info**. Before you deep dive into the chapters ahead, know that additional insights on Jung's typologies, legal and ethical considerations in confronting toxic leadership, enriching case studies, and resourceful links are prepared to further your exploration.

This portal is continually expanding and offers a quiet space for you to enrich what you're about to learn, providing supplementary tools and narratives to accompany your journey through this book.

Moreover, we invite you to share your own experiences. If you've navigated through toxic work environments and wish to offer your insights, consider contributing a guest blog post. Your story could be a beacon of support and guidance for others facing similar challenges. Together, we can foster a community of learning, support, and empowerment.

Welcome to Your Journey

As we embark on this insightful journey together, let's look ahead to the pivotal lessons we will explore. In this book, Claudia and I will guide you through the complex terrain of workplace manipulation, revealing strategies to identify, understand, and address such challenges.

Understanding Manipulation: We will differentiate between influence and manipulation, shedding light on the subtle yet profound ways manipulation manifests in the workplace.

Psychological Insights: Delving into the psychology of power and manipulation, we will unpack the role of personality traits, cognitive biases, and power imbalances in creating manipulative environments.

Strategies Against Manipulative Bosses: We will uncover tactics used by manipulative bosses and provide tools to counteract them, from recognizing gaslighting to dealing with emotional exploitation.

Empowerment and Defense: The book will arm you with strategies to detect and defend against manipulation, emphasizing the importance of establishing boundaries and developing resilience.

This journey will equip you with the knowledge to not only recognize and withstand manipulative behaviors but also to thrive and foster positive change in your professional environment.

Empowerment Through Knowledge

This is not just an introduction to the challenges ahead but the start of an empowered path forward in your professional life. This book is more than a guide through the hidden complexities of workplace manipulation; it's a transformative expedition that will equip you with the knowledge and insights to face workplace challenges with new-found confidence and perspective.

Harnessing Insight for Empowerment

The insights you gain from understanding manipulative tactics and the psychology behind them will transform you from a passive observer to an informed and active participant in your workplace. This knowledge is your power, arming you to recognize and counteract manipulation and to navigate complex interactions with a clear, discerning lens.

Awareness and Preparedness: Your Shields

Awareness and preparedness are your first lines of defense. Recognizing manipulation, understanding power dynamics, and identifying toxic behaviors are steps towards safeguarding your well-being. These strategies will equip you to engage more effectively with workplace dynamics, whether it's setting boundaries, asserting your rights, or seeking support.

Facing Challenges with a Growth Mindset

As you step into your professional world, view challenges not as obstacles but as opportunities for growth and positive change. The road ahead is filled with potential for learning and development. Embrace this journey, not just with the tools and strategies you'll acquire but also with a mindset geared towards continuous learning and adaptation.

Adapting to an Ever-Evolving Workplace

The professional landscape is dynamic, and so should your approach to it. Commit to continuous learning through various means like reading, workshops, or professional development. This commitment to staying informed and adaptable is key to navigating and influencing the evolving world of work.

This is your invitation to begin a journey of empowerment and transformation, equipped with the insights and strategies from this book to make a meaningful difference. Let's embark on this path together, stepping confidently into a future where you not only cope with workplace challenges but thrive amidst them, fostering a culture that values and nurtures its members.

Career
Leadership Skills

1

Why Are So Many Bosses Bad Leaders?

Introduction

If you've ever found yourself dreading the start of another workweek, not because of the job itself but because of who leads you, you're not alone. Many of us have experienced the sinking feeling that comes with being under the thumb of a leader who, rather than inspiring us, drains our enthusiasm and stifles our potential. This chapter is for you — the one who has endured the frustration of being led by someone who fails to recognize your value undermines your contributions, and, perhaps without even realizing it, transforms what could be a fulfilling role into a daily test of endurance.

"Bad leadership" is not just a phrase — it's a reality for countless employees who navigate their workdays under leaders who lack the essential qualities of empathy, fairness, and vision. These leaders might excel in achieving targets and pushing for results, but at what cost? If you've ever felt belittled, overlooked, or unfairly criticized, you know the cost all too well. It's the loss of motivation, the erosion of trust, and, ultimately, the diminishing of workplace morale.

This chapter aims to dive deep into the heart of why so many bosses fail to be good leaders. It's about understanding the gap between mere management and true leadership. But more importantly, it's about acknowledging your experiences, validating your feelings, and beginning the journey toward healing and empowerment. So, as we explore the characteristics of toxic leadership and its impact, remember: Your feelings are valid, and change starts with recognition.

In today's fast-paced and highly competitive work environments, the prevalence of toxic leadership is alarmingly high. In their pursuit of quick results and efficiency, organizations often inadvertently promote individuals who prioritize results over people. This short-sighted approach has led to a significant number of workplaces being dominated by leaders who, while perhaps effective in driving numbers, fail miserably at fostering a positive and supportive work culture.

The costs of such leadership are profound and far-reaching. Beyond the immediate impact on individual employees' mental health and job satisfaction, the ripple effects extend to organizational performance. High turnover rates, decreased productivity, and a tarnished company reputation are but a few of the consequences that can arise. The paradox is clear: in the quest for achieving outstanding results, the very essence of what makes a team or organization thrive — trust, collaboration, and mutual respect — is eroded under toxic leadership.

Recognizing the widespread nature of this issue and its detrimental effects is the first step towards catalyzing change. This chapter not only aims to shed light on why bad leadership is so common but also to explore the tangible and intangible costs associated with it. As we delve into these discussions, it's crucial to remember that while the situation may seem bleak, understanding is the foundation upon which improvement is built.

Just a Bad Leader or a Toxic Boss?

In the realm of workplace dynamics, not all leadership shortfalls are created equal. The distinction between a bad leader and a toxic boss is crucial, not just in terms of terminology but in their impact on individuals and organizations.

Bad leaders, at their core, are often individuals who lack the necessary skills, awareness, or willingness to guide their teams toward success effectively. Their leadership deficiencies might manifest as poor communication, indecisiveness, lack of vision, or simply the inability to motivate and support their team members. While these shortcomings are typically a result of a gap in competence or experience rather than malice or intentional harm, it's essential to recognize that the cumulative effect of such leadership deficiencies can also lead to a toxic work environment. This occurs as team frustration, confusion, and disengagement grow over time, eroding team morale and productivity.

Characteristics of bad leaders may include:

- A lack of clear direction or goals for the team.

- Inconsistent feedback or communication.

- Difficulty making decisions or delegating tasks effectively.

- A tendency to micromanage or disengage entirely from team oversight.

Toxic bosses, on the other hand, represent a more severe problem. These individuals not only exhibit poor leadership skills but also engage in behaviors that are damaging to the mental and emotional well-being of their employees. Their approach, characterized by a pattern of abusive behavior, manipulation, and a blatant disregard for others' dignity and rights, directly contributes to creating a harmful and oppressive environment. The immediate and significant impact on employees' mental health and job satisfaction further exacerbates the toxicity of the workplace.

Characteristics of toxic bosses include:

- Manipulative or deceitful behavior.

- Use of fear or intimidation to control others.

- A persistent pattern of undermining or belittling team members.

- Discrimination, harassment, or other unethical conduct.

The distinction: The key distinction lies in the intent and impact. While bad leaders may inadvertently lead to a toxic work environment through their lack of skill, toxic bosses actively create a harmful atmosphere. However, it's essential to recognize that both can significantly contribute to the development of a toxic work culture. Addressing the challenges presented by both types of inadequate leadership is crucial for fostering a healthier, more productive workplace.

The obvious question now, of course, is: if these individuals are bad leaders or even toxic bosses, how do they so frequently ascend to and maintain positions of leadership within organizations? So, let's have a closer look at that.

The Challenges of Leadership Selection

In many organizations, the criteria for selecting leaders are often misaligned with the qualities that define effective leadership. This misalignment not only hampers the development of a supportive and productive work environment but also perpetuates a cycle where leadership positions are filled based on flawed metrics.

Promotion Criteria vs. Actual Leadership Qualities

Traditionally, criteria for leadership roles tend to emphasize technical expertise, tenure, and professional connections over genuine leadership skills such as emotional intelligence, the ability to motivate and inspire effective communication, and conflict resolution. While expertise and connections are valuable, they do not necessarily translate into leadership prowess. The overvaluation of these aspects can lead to the elevation of ill-equipped individuals to foster a positive team dynamic and guide their team towards achieving collective goals.

The Discrepancy Between Valued Attributes and Leadership Needs

This discrepancy creates a significant challenge within organizations. On one hand, there's recognition of the need for leaders who can navigate complex interpersonal dynamics, drive innovation, and create an inclusive culture. On the other, the selection process often defaults to tangible but less relevant metrics such as years of experience in a specific domain or the ability to deliver short-term business results. This approach overlooks critical leadership competencies, such as adaptability, strategic thinking, and empathy, which are crucial for long-term success and sustainability. To address this gap, many organizations would have to fundamentally rethink their criteria for leadership selection.

The Challenge of Measuring Leadership Skills

Assessing leadership potential is a complex endeavor that challenges many organizations. Unlike technical skills or professional knowledge, which can be quantified through certifications, tests, or demonstrated experience, leadership skills are nuanced and multifaceted. They encompass a range of interpersonal, strategic, and emotional competencies that are not easily measured. This complexity poses significant challenges for organizations seeking to identify and nurture potential leaders.

One of the primary difficulties in measuring leadership skills is their inherently subjective nature. Leadership involves influencing others, making strategic decisions, and fostering a positive work culture — abilities that are challenging to quantify. Traditional evaluation methods, such as interviews or performance reviews, can provide insights but often rely heavily on the evaluator's perceptions, introducing a degree of subjectivity that can skew results.

Further, there is no universally accepted framework or tool for assessing leadership potential. While many organizations use leadership competency models or psychological assessments, these tools vary widely in their approach and effectiveness. The absence of standardization makes it difficult to compare leadership qualities across different contexts or to benchmark progress over time.

While the quest to accurately measure leadership skills remains daunting, numerous organizations are indeed venturing beyond traditional methods, adopting more intricate approaches such as 360-Degree Feedback, Behavioral Event Interviews (BEIs), and comprehensive Leadership Development Programs. These innovative techniques aim to shed light on a candidate's interpersonal, strategic, and emotional competencies by gathering diverse perspectives and focusing on demonstrated behaviors and outcomes.

However, the efficacy of these advanced methods is not without question. Critically, there's a growing concern that such practices may sometimes serve more as a facade for a company's hiring and promotion strategies rather than as genuine tools for identifying and nurturing leadership talent. The application of sophisticated assessment tools can sometimes veer into the territory of "greenwashing" the leadership selection process — portraying an image of fairness and modernity while obscuring the actual, perhaps more traditional, decision-making processes. This skepticism highlights a crucial gap between the potential of these methods to contribute to objective leadership assessment and their implementation in a manner that genuinely reflects the organization's commitment to identifying and supporting true leadership potential.

Experience in Leading vs. Quality of Leadership

The Misconception of Experience as a Leadership Qualifier

In the quest to appoint leaders within organizations, a common criterion that often takes precedence is the experience of leading. At first glance, it seems logical to equate years of leadership experience with a high leadership quality. However, when used in isolation, this metric is grossly inadequate for gauging true leadership capabilities.

The Fallacy of Experience Equating to Competence

The reliance on leadership experience as a primary qualifier implies the assumption that past leadership roles have endowed an individual with the skills necessary to inspire, guide, and support a team. However, this assumption fails to account for the complexity and diversity of leadership roles. Just because someone has held a leadership position does not necessarily mean they have done it well or developed the skills necessary to lead effectively in different contexts. Leadership experience, without reflection on and learning from past successes and failures, can lead to the repetition of past mistakes and a lack of growth in essential leadership qualities.

When I, Markus, worked in legal consulting, I encountered a colleague named Aaron who, despite not being formally promoted, was tasked with leadership responsibilities by his superiors. Unfortunately, this newfound authority did not suit Aaron. His approach to leadership was marked by yelling at colleagues, speaking negatively about them in their absence, and offering insincere apologies that barely went beyond, "Sorry, but that's just how I am." Such admissions unwittingly highlighted his unsuitability for any leadership role. Despite Aaron's behavior contributing to a toxic and detrimental work atmosphere, his resume misleadingly boasted "x years of leading experience," seemingly qualifying him for even higher positions. For years, Aaron's detrimental behavior was overlooked, with his superiors turning a blind eye to the burgeoning toxicity. It wasn't until top management became aware of the significant negative impact Aaron's leadership was having that they decisively removed him from any further leadership duties.

Using experience as the sole or primary metric for leadership selection is inherently flawed for several reasons:

It Overlooks Potential: Many individuals possess the innate qualities of great leaders but may not have had the opportunity to hold formal leadership positions. Over-reliance on experience can exclude these potential leaders from consideration.

It Ignores Context: The challenges and requirements of leadership roles vary significantly across different organizations and industries. Experience in one context may not translate to effectiveness in another.

It Neglects Soft Skills: Leadership involves a significant amount of interpersonal interaction. Skills such as empathy, communication, and conflict resolution are critical, yet these are not necessarily developed through experience alone.

Quality leadership is characterized by a combination of emotional intelligence, strategic thinking, adaptability, and the ability to foster an inclusive and motivating work environment. These attributes enable leaders to navigate the complexities of modern organizational life, including managing diverse teams, driving innovation, and handling crises. Unlike mere experience, which is quantifiable, the qualities that make for effective leadership are nuanced and require a deeper level of evaluation. Regrettably, such comprehensive evaluation frameworks are scarce across many organizations, and when they do exist, their implementation is often nominal and limited to procedural compliance rather than genuine analysis and improvement.

Career Success vs. Leadership Effectiveness

In the landscape of modern organizational hierarchies, a prevalent paradox emerges: the trajectory of career advancement often diverges significantly from actual leadership ability. This paradox underscores a fundamental misalignment between the metrics used to gauge career success and the qualities intrinsic to effective leadership. Career advancement, typically measured by titles gained, projects led, and financial results delivered, does not necessarily equate to the capability to inspire, guide, and support a team towards achieving collective goals.

The corporate world, with its emphasis on tangible achievements and quick wins, inherently favors careerism — the pursuit of advancement in one's career as a primary objective, often at the expense of developing genuine leadership potential. This systemic bias manifests in selection processes prioritizing the visible markers of success (such as sales figures or project completions) over less quantifiable leadership qualities like empathy, communication skills, and the ability to foster a positive work culture. As a result, individuals who excel in self-promotion and navigating corporate politics may ascend to leadership positions despite lacking the necessary competencies to be truly effective leaders.

Let's be honest — we've all encountered colleagues who may not be the brightest bulbs in the chandelier but excel remarkably at self-promotion. They possess an uncanny ability to navigate the intricate maze of corporate politics, knowing precisely who to suck up to for their career advancement. In the unfortunate event, they become your boss, be prepared for a leadership style that not only thrives on self-aggrandizement but also skillfully deflects responsibility. Such bosses are adept at taking all the credit for successes while conveniently placing the blame for failures on others. This behavior not only highlights their toxic nature but also exacerbates the challenge of fostering a positive and collaborative work environment. Awesome, right?

The Rise of Bad Leaders

The ascent of bad leaders can be traced back through history, yet it has taken on new dimensions in modern organizational life. In the past, leadership was often a result of lineage or battlefield prowess. Today, it's increasingly a matter of navigating corporate hierarchies and the subtle art of office politics. The dynamics of globalization and the digital age have further complicated leadership, introducing challenges that demand not just expertise but emotional intelligence and adaptability — qualities that are often overlooked in favor of more tangible achievements.

Organizational culture plays a pivotal role in either fostering or hindering the rise of bad leaders. Cultures that prioritize short-term results over long-term growth and that value compliance over creativity are especially prone to elevating individuals who may achieve immediate targets but do so at the cost of team cohesion, morale, and ethical standards. In such environments, the qualities that make a good leader are often undervalued, leading to a cycle where bad leadership is not only tolerated but, in some cases, rewarded.

Psychological Factors

Toxic Personality Traits & the Dunning-Kruger Effect

The presence of toxic personality traits in leadership — such as narcissism, Machiavellianism, and psychopathic — can have devastating effects on an organization. Leaders with these traits are often more concerned with their success than the well-being of their teams or the ethical implications of their decisions. Their leadership style can foster an environment of fear, stifle innovation, and lead to ethical breaches that tarnish the organization's reputation.

The Dunning-Kruger effect, which refers to a cognitive bias in which people with limited knowledge or competence in a domain overestimate their own ability, plays a significant role in the rise of bad leaders. This effect can lead individuals to pursue and attain leadership positions without the self-awareness to recognize their limitations, preventing them from seeking improvement or valuing the expertise of their team members.

A vivid portrayal of the Dunning-Kruger effect in a workplace setting can be observed in the popular TV show "The Office" (US version), particularly through the character of Michael Scott, played by Steve Carell. Michael's overconfidence in his managerial skills, despite clear evidence of his incompetence, offers a humorous yet insightful look into how the Dunning-Kruger effect can manifest in leadership. His actions often lead to awkward and problematic situations, highlighting the potential consequences of overestimated self-assessment in professional environments.

One memorable example is the "Scott's Tots" episode where Michael promises college scholarships to a class of third-graders, only to realize years later that he cannot fulfill this promise due to his misunderstanding of his financial situation. This scenario not only encapsulates the essence of the Dunning-Kruger Effect but also underscores its potential to create chaos and disappointment in professional settings. Michael's misplaced confidence in his financial acumen and generosity sets the stage for a series of uncomfortable revelations, vividly showcasing the pitfalls of overestimating one's competence in real-world situations.

If you haven't yet had the pleasure, **I, Markus,** highly **recommend** watching **"The Office"** to see these dynamics in action. This hilarious show provides not only entertainment but also a valuable lens through which to examine and understand the complexities of workplace relationships and leadership challenges.

Watching the series a second time during a period when I was navigating a toxic work environment myself, I viewed the show through a different lens. It unveiled parallels to my own experiences that I hadn't noticed on the first watch, offering a form of comic relief that made it easier to not take certain aspects of work too seriously. Besides, as we all know, laughing has its own benefits for our mental health.

A less humorous but significantly more consequential example of the Dunning-Kruger effect manifested during the COVID-19 pandemic. Overnight, individuals with no background in virology, epidemiology, or public health miraculously transformed into authorities on vaccines, respiratory diseases, and, most impressively, elaborate global conspiracies. These newfound experts, fueled by an internet connection and an overestimation of their Google-fu skills, boldly led charges against real scientists and health professionals. They spun tales of doom, featuring villains like the pharmaceutical industry, finance moguls, and political elites — with Bill Gates often cast as the mastermind in a grand scheme to oppress the masses, presumably for the sheer thrill of it. Because, of course, who needs years of research and study when a few hours at YouTube university and a hefty dose of confirmation bias can make you a sage on how to save humanity from these nefarious vaccine plots?

Okay, /sarcasm off. If you're nodding along because you've had to endure dinner table lectures from these newly minted "experts," you're not alone. Indeed, the Dunning-Kruger effect has never been more vividly or painfully illustrated, giving us all a front-row seat to the spectacle of overconfidence crashing into reality.

The Peter Principle

The Peter Principle, a concept introduced by Laurence J. Peter in his 1969 book, presents a paradox within organizational hierarchies: individuals are promoted based on their performance in their current role rather than their abilities relevant to the intended role. This ascent continues until they reach a position where they are no longer competent, leading to a stagnation where they neither excel nor qualify for further promotion. This scenario underscores a critical systemic flaw in traditional promotion strategies — assessing potential leaders by their current job performance without considering their suitability or skill set for higher-level responsibilities.

> "In a hierarchy, every employee tends to rise to his level of incompetence."
>
> *- Laurence J. Peter*

This principle not only illuminates the prevalence of ineffective leadership but also serves as a commentary on the structural inadequacies in recognizing and nurturing leadership qualities. It reveals a common oversight in organizational development strategies: the failure to distinguish between technical proficiency and leadership capability. While an individual might excel in a technical or specialized role, this does not inherently equip them with the skills needed for effective leadership, such as strategic thinking, empathy, communication, and team motivation.

Moreover, the Peter Principle suggests a misalignment between promotion criteria and role requirements, often leading to a cascade of productivity and morale issues within an organization. As individuals ascend to levels of incompetence, their inability to perform effectively can demoralize subordinates, stifle innovation, and perpetuate a cycle of inefficiency. This situation is exacerbated in environments where there is a lack of continuous training, mentorship, and leadership development programs aimed at preparing individuals for the complexities of leadership roles.

Why it Matters to You

Understanding the root causes of the rise of bad leaders and distinguishing between ineffective leaders and toxic bosses is essential for you, even if directly changing your work environment might be beyond your immediate control. This knowledge empowers you to understand the underlying mechanics of leadership behaviors, offering insights into why some leaders act the way they do. While it's not about sympathizing with toxic behavior, this understanding can help you take such actions less personally. This shift in perspective is a crucial first step towards safeguarding your well-being and forms a foundation for navigating challenging workplace dynamics with resilience and strategic insight.

Moreover, recognizing the difference between merely ineffective leaders and genuinely toxic bosses is crucial, particularly as it allows us to maintain hope — especially for the former. Leaders who exhibit signs of poor leadership, yet possess a willingness to self-reflect, accept constructive criticism, and demonstrate a genuine commitment to enhancing their leadership skills may indeed transform into effective and inspirational figures over time. This evolution, however, is distinctly unattainable for truly toxic bosses. The inherent nature of their toxicity — characterized by manipulative, self-serving, and destructive behaviors — makes meaningful internal change highly unlikely. Nonetheless, even in the shadow of such toxicity, strategies exist not to change these individuals but to mitigate their negative impact. Developing skills to navigate, neutralize, and withstand toxic leadership and manipulation is essential, serving as a crucial support system until the toxic influence is removed or a new opportunity emerges. This insight is invaluable, offering guidance to safeguard your well-being and flourish in even the most difficult situations.

Key Takeaways

- Bad leaders lack basic leadership skills, while toxic bosses exhibit manipulative and abusive behaviors; both can lead to a toxic work environment.

- Leadership roles are often awarded based on technical expertise or tenure, not leadership qualities.

- Poor leadership can lead to high turnover, decreased productivity, and a damaged company culture.

- Personality traits such as narcissism and Machiavellianism are linked to manipulative or toxic leadership behaviors.

- Leadership skills are challenging to measure, leading to promotions based on visible achievements rather than true leadership capabilities.

- Emotional intelligence and soft skills are critical for leadership but are frequently undervalued in selection processes.

Manipu
lation
Basics

2

About Manipulation

Influence or Manipulation?

In the movie "Jerry Maguire," sports agent Jerry (played by Tom Cruise) is attempting to convince his client Rod Tidwell (played by Cuba Gooding Jr.) to stay with him after he loses his job at a prestigious agency. Jerry passionately explains how he can help Rod advance his career, emphasizing that he genuinely cares about his client's success ("Help me help you! Help me help you!!"). They go on to form a strong partnership, with Jerry working tirelessly to secure a better contract for Rod.

In contrast, in the movie "The Devil Wears Prada," Miranda Priestly (played by Meryl Streep), the editor-in-chief of a top fashion magazine, uses subtle but powerful tactics to control her assistant, Andy Sachs. Miranda sets high expectations, often without explicitly stating them, and uses her authority to push Andy to her limits. Andy, desperate to please her boss and succeed in the fashion industry, eventually adopts some of Miranda's ruthless ways to advance her career.

Both scenarios involve characters influencing the behavior and actions of others, and it is pretty apparent which one is an example of positive influence and which one demonstrates manipulation.

The answer lies in the intentions and methods behind each character's actions. In "Jerry Maguire," Jerry's influence stems from his genuine belief in his client's potential and a desire to help him succeed. He uses positive reinforcement and encouragement, ultimately benefiting both parties. On the other hand, Miranda Priestly's methods involve subtle manipulation, using her power and authority to control her assistant's actions and decisions for her own benefit, often at the expense of Andy's well-being.

Now, let's consider this workplace scenario: a boss calls one of his employees, let's call her Sandy, to his office and assigns her a challenging project, saying, "I believe this project is an excellent opportunity for you to showcase your talents and take on new responsibilities. You have proven your qualities in the past, and I'm absolutely positive you can handle this." Sandy walks away with tons of documents in her hands and a smile on her face. She is happy that her time has come. She is dedicated to putting all her effort into absolutely smashing this project. So, has Sandy been influenced? Or has she been manipulated?

Well, the truth again lies solely in the intentions or inner thoughts of the boss and not in his actions or words, which are the same either way. In one scenario, the boss could genuinely believe in Sandy's capabilities and assign the project with the intention of helping her grow professionally and showcase her skills. In another scenario, the boss could have a hidden agenda – he hopes Sandy will fail, allowing him to justify replacing her or taking credit for fixing the project.

In both cases, the boss's actions and words are the same – assigning a challenging project to the employee and expressing confidence in her abilities. However, the intentions behind these actions are drastically different. In the first scenario, the boss is using their influence positively, aiming to empower the employee and contribute to their professional growth. In the second scenario, the boss is engaging in manipulative behavior, setting the employee up for failure to serve their own interests, and – on top – instilling a potentially harmful belief in Sandy that her worth as a person is tied to her professional achievements.

Influence can be a powerful force for good, persuading, encouraging, or inspiring people to make choices that benefit themselves and others. However, when influence turns into manipulation, it becomes a negative and unethical practice that can harm individuals and create toxic work environments.

In this book, our focus is on manipulative tactics and their negative consequences in the workplace. We aim to provide you with a clear understanding of what constitutes manipulative behavior and help you differentiate between ethical and unethical influence in the workplace. By recognizing and addressing manipulative behavior, you and your organization can create a healthier and more supportive work environment for all.

Manipulative bosses can create a toxic work environment, negatively impacting employee morale, productivity, and mental health. Understanding the characteristics and tactics of manipulative bosses is essential for employees to recognize and navigate such situations effectively. This book will explore the rise of manipulative bosses, their various tactics, the role of workplace culture in fostering manipulative behavior, and how to detect and address these situations in the workplace.

Understanding Persuasion Techniques

Persuasion is a psychological mechanism often used to influence others' opinions, attitudes, or actions. While manipulation tends to have a negative connotation, persuasion is typically viewed as more benign or positive. The critical difference lies in the transparency and intention behind the act: Persuasion is open about its aims and seeks a mutually beneficial outcome. At the same time, manipulation is covert and primarily serves the manipulator's interest.

Persuasion techniques are numerous and vary in their subtlety and impact. They can range from logical reasoning and presenting clear arguments to the use of emotional appeals, storytelling, and the creation of cognitive dissonance (making someone aware of an inconsistency in their beliefs or attitudes).

Take, for example, a supervisor, Susan, who wants her team to adopt a new software tool. Instead of ordering the team to use it or implicitly threatening them with consequences if they don't (which would be manipulative), she uses persuasion. She demonstrates how the tool will make their work easier, shares testimonials from other teams who've successfully used it, and addresses the team members' questions and concerns. Susan is using persuasion techniques to achieve her goal in a respectful and transparent way.

Understanding persuasion techniques offers distinct advantages. Firstly, it enhances your ability to communicate more effectively, advocate for your ideas, and foster productive relationships in the workplace. Additionally, it equips you with the critical ability to identify when these techniques are being used on you, enabling you to make more informed decisions about whether to accept or resist the influence being exerted.

The Prevalence of Manipulation in the Workplace

"I need you to go through the files and find every piece of research we have on sugar."

"Sure, Don. Can I ask what it's for?"

"I'm working on a pitch for a new client. I need all the information I can get."

"Of course. Just one thing, though: I'm already swamped with work. Do you think I could get some help, or maybe an extension on the other assignments?"

"Peggy, if you want to succeed in this business, you need to learn how to prioritize. Sometimes, that means putting in extra hours. Do you want to be a secretary forever, or do you want to become a real copywriter?"

This dialogue from the popular television series "Mad Men" illustrates a situation where a boss uses flattery, appeal to ambition, and pressure to manipulate their employee into taking on additional work without complaint.

In the world of work, manipulation is a complex issue that's deeply embedded in how people interact. Back in the 1980s, researchers like David M. Buss and others started to uncover the different ways people manipulate each other, identifying tactics like charm, silent treatment, and coercion (1987). Their work shows just how nuanced manipulation at work can be. More recent studies, like those by Förster, Mauleon, and Vannetelbosch (2014), dive into how manipulation can change the dynamics of trust within social networks, affecting leadership and influence. Then there's Krause's work (2012), which highlights the emotional toll manipulation can have on employees, affecting their feelings and how they relate to one another.

All this research points to a common theme: manipulation is a significant force in workplaces, shaping interactions in obvious and subtle ways. It can range from the more visible tactics like gaslighting and emotional blackmail to the subtler forms like neurolinguistic programming, all of which have a profound impact on the atmosphere at work and how employees feel.

By educating ourselves about the different types of manipulation, we can develop the necessary skills and strategies to counteract them, fostering a more positive and supportive work environment for everyone involved.

The Psychological Background of Manipulation and Power Dynamics

Manipulation in the workplace is often rooted in the complex interplay of psychological factors and power dynamics. As someone who might have experienced or witnessed manipulative behavior, gaining a deeper understanding of these aspects can help you recognize and address such behavior more effectively.

Understanding Manipulation

Manipulation, in its most basic sense, is a covert way of influencing someone's perceptions, behavior, or actions for personal gain. It's a cunning strategy used by individuals who seek to control situations or people without revealing their true intentions. Often, manipulators have "hidden agendas" that they don't disclose, aiming to achieve their objectives while keeping others in the dark about their real motives. Understanding this, you'll be better equipped to recognize when it's happening and navigate situations in which manipulation might occur.

Think back to your own experiences. Have you ever found yourself doing something you didn't really want to do but couldn't pinpoint exactly why you agreed to it? Or have you ever left a conversation feeling as if you've been led into agreeing with something but aren't quite sure how it happened? This is often manipulation at work. And most likely you also recall a time when you wanted someone to do something and instead of asking them directly, you found a roundabout way to make it happen? Perhaps as a child, you knew how to frame your requests to your parents to get that extra hour of TV or that candy bar at the checkout line. Or maybe in a relationship, you subtly swayed your partner to choose the restaurant or movie you preferred without explicitly stating your preference. These are also forms of manipulation, more benign and often socially accepted. Still, they serve to illustrate the underlying concept: influencing someone's behavior or decision subtly without them fully realizing it. Understanding manipulation from both angles, as the influencer and the influenced, can provide a well-rounded perspective on how these dynamics manifest in our day-to-day interactions, including in the workplace.

The Psychology of Power

Understanding power dynamics is crucial when we talk about manipulation, particularly within the context of a workplace. Power, in essence, is the ability or capacity to influence others' behavior or outcomes, often coupled with control over resources. This control can be over tangible resources such as time, money, and promotions or over intangible ones such as information, opportunities, and decision-making processes.

Let's consider a real-life example. Picture a team leader, Anna, who consistently delegates the most sought-after projects to the same subset of employees, consequently leaving the rest feeling sidelined and disheartened. This act of selective distribution is a manifest exercise of power, wielding a significant influence on team morale and interpersonal dynamics. Anna's dominion over such resources (here, assignments) empowers her to shape her team members' experiences and prospects within their careers.

At first glance, some might interpret Anna's behavior as favoritism, bestowing opportunities on those she personally prefers. This perception is valid, as favoritism can erode trust and cohesiveness within a team, leading to resentment and a decrease in overall morale. However, it's also crucial to consider an alternative perspective: perhaps Anna continuously assigns specific tasks to those individuals because she genuinely believes they are the most qualified for these roles. This approach, rooted in a desire to maximize team efficiency and success, nonetheless requires a delicate balance. Without transparent communication and understanding of her decision-making process, Anna risks creating an environment where her actions are misconstrued, perpetuating feelings of exclusion and undermining team unity.

Thus, this example underscores the complexity of power dynamics in leadership. It highlights the importance of mindful decision-making and open communication to mitigate potential misunderstandings and foster an inclusive, motivated team environment.

Power isn't inherently harmful or destructive; it becomes a problem when misused or abused, mainly when it results in manipulation or coercive control. It's also important to remember that power dynamics aren't static; they can shift based on various factors, such as changes in roles, responsibilities, relationships, or even workplace culture. Therefore, understanding the fluid nature of power dynamics can be a valuable asset in identifying, navigating, and mitigating manipulative behavior in the workplace.

Understanding Influence and Persuasion

Influence and persuasion are closely intertwined with the concepts of manipulation and power. They represent the tactics employed by individuals to shape others' thoughts, attitudes, and behaviors according to their own agenda. While these tactics can be used positively, such as motivating a team to meet a deadline, they can also be used to manipulate others for personal gain.

Consider an example: Your colleague, Brian, has a knack for convincing people to see things from his perspective. He often uses compelling arguments and presents data in a way that supports his point of view. Most of the time, his persuasive skills are appreciated, but you've noticed occasions when Brian selectively presented information to persuade others towards a decision that primarily benefits him. The line between healthy persuasion and manipulation becomes blurred when the influence leads to unfair benefits for one party at the expense of others. Awareness of this subtlety is essential, especially in workplace scenarios where influential skills can be misused.

Pay close attention to the dynamics of influence and persuasion, and you will unlock the door to recognizing and resisting manipulation. You'll find that not only can you safeguard your own interests, but you'll also enhance your ability to communicate clearly and assertively, ensuring that your voice is heard and respected.

Grasping Power Imbalances

Power imbalances are frequently at the heart of manipulative situations, particularly within the workplace. Those with higher positions, more significant influence, or more resources often have the power to affect others' experiences, decisions, and overall wellbeing.

Understanding these dynamics can help you assert yourself effectively in situations where you feel disadvantaged by the power differential.

Consider a scenario: You are part of a project team, and Amanda, the project manager, is responsible for assigning tasks and approving days off. With her position comes the power to control your workload and time-off requests. Most of the time, Amanda is fair, but occasionally, she leverages her power to favor certain team members, giving them easier tasks or approving their vacation requests quickly. You feel frustrated and manipulated due to this uneven distribution of power.

The situation with Amanda highlights how power imbalances can lead to manipulative dynamics, causing stress and discomfort to those at the receiving end. It's crucial to remember that the power itself isn't the problem. The issue arises when the power is misused to control or influence others unfairly, just as Amanda did in our example.

The "Us vs. Them" Mentality in Leadership Dynamics

You probably have found yourself in situations where workplace dynamics shift subtly, creating an invisible divide between team colleagues and blurring the lines between allies and adversaries, even without an apparent reason at the surface. The "Us vs. Them" mentality is not exclusive to interactions between different teams or departments; it can also arise within the same group, fueled by leadership styles that foster division rather than unity. Such a mentality can transform a previously cohesive team into factions, with members increasingly viewing each other through a lens of competition and suspicion.

Such an environment diminishes collaboration and productivity and erodes the sense of belonging and mutual respect that underpins effective teamwork. Leaders who inadvertently or deliberately cultivate this divisive atmosphere may do so under the guise of driving performance or establishing clear accountability. However, the long-term consequences often include lowered morale, increased turnover, and a tarnished organizational culture. Recognizing and addressing the roots of this "Us vs. Them" dynamic is essential for leaders who wish to rebuild trust and foster a workplace where collaboration thrives over competition.

A compelling illustration of this phenomenon was shared with us by Tom, a former hospital manager, who experienced first-hand the competitive dynamics that can emerge under toxic leadership.

Tom observed a distinct division within his department, primarily driven by the contrasting leadership approaches between himself and his superior. While his superior tried to maintain a facade of kindness, akin to how a kindergarten teacher might speak to her students, her strict and manipulative behavior ultimately alienated her team. In contrast, Tom's more respected and effective leadership style led to higher performance and loyalty among his direct reports. However, this disparity bred a competitive "Us vs. Them" mentality within the same department, highlighting how toxic leadership can erode team cohesion from within.

Tom's decision to step down and return to his original position reflects the challenging nature of leadership roles in toxic environments. It underscores the importance of understanding the impact of leadership styles on team dynamics and the potential for internal competition to undermine organizational goals.

Tom's personal account serves as a valuable reminder that leadership is not solely about directing others; it's about fostering an environment of collaboration, trust, and respect. Recognizing and addressing the roots of divisiveness, including the "Us vs. Them" mentality, is crucial for building a cohesive and effective team.

Understanding Social Influence and Conformity

Social influence and conformity play substantial roles in shaping behaviors and attitudes in any group setting, including the workplace. In fact, their effects can often be seen in situations where manipulation takes place. Being aware of these dynamics will help you to maintain independent thinking and decision-making, essential skills in navigating manipulative situations in the workplace.

- **Social Influence** refers to the way in which individuals change their behavior to meet the demands or standards of their social environment. It can manifest in various forms like compliance, where individuals adjust their behavior based on explicit requests, or obedience, where people follow directives from an authority figure.

  An everyday example of social influence can be seen in office dress codes. Even without explicit rules, you might observe that most employees in a company dress in a certain way, prompting you to adjust your wardrobe to fit in. This is a form of non-coercive influence and is generally harmless.

- **Conformity**, a type of social influence, is the act of matching attitudes, beliefs, and behaviors to group norms. It's a powerful force that can affect our decisions and perceptions significantly. A classical study by Solomon Asch demonstrated that people were willing to disregard their own perceptions and agree with a group's incorrect judgment to fit in.

  In a workplace setting, imagine a team meeting where everyone appears to agree with a new policy that you privately disagree with. Instead of voicing your concerns, you might find yourself agreeing with the group to avoid conflict or exclusion. This is conformity in action. However, when used manipulatively, a leader might exploit the power of conformity to coerce team members into agreement, stifling dissent and potentially leading to harmful decisions or a toxic workplace culture.

The Role of Coercion in Manipulation

Coercion is a potent element in manipulation, serving as a more forceful, overt tool in the arsenal of those seeking to control others.

Coercion involves the use of force, threats, or intimidation to compel someone to act against their will or interests.

The crucial aspect of coercion is that it leaves the coerced individual feeling as though they have no choice but to comply. It creates a power imbalance where one person holds the threat of negative consequences over another. In a sense, coercion is the opposite of persuasion, which attempts to change someone's mind through reasoning or appealing to their self-interest.

Let's consider a real-life example: Imagine a team leader, Alex, who insists that everyone on his team stay late to finish a project, even though it's not a critical deadline. When one of his team members, Lisa, explains that she can't stay because she needs to pick up her child from daycare, Alex threatens to give her a poor performance review or suggests she might not be "committed" enough to the team. In this scenario, Alex uses coercion — the threat of negative consequences — to make Lisa comply.

Sometimes, coercion can be subtle and not so overt. For example, **Claudia** recalls an experience with a former boss, Judith. Whenever an employee tried to leave the office at 7:30 PM, Judith would remark, "Oh, you're leaving already?" This seemingly innocent comment had a coercive undertone, making employees feel obligated to stay longer, often outlasting their colleagues. This is a form of subtle coercion that manipulates employees into acting against their interests without the use of explicit threats.

While there might be situations where tough decisions have to be made and sacrifices are required, it's crucial to differentiate between legitimate leadership and coercive manipulation. A healthy work environment fosters open communication, considers individual needs, and promotes a balance between personal life and work responsibilities.

Influence of Personality Traits

Personality traits can significantly influence an individual's propensity to manipulate others. While it's crucial to remember that no single trait "causes" manipulative behavior, some traits are more commonly associated with such behavior. We'll delve deeper into the specific personality traits of manipulators and their implications in a later discussion, offering a more nuanced understanding of how these characteristics manifest in manipulative behaviors.

On the flip side, however, certain personality traits might also make one more susceptible to manipulation. For example, people with high levels of agreeableness and conscientiousness may be more inclined to meet others' demands and expectations, making them potential targets for manipulative individuals.

Consider, for example, a team member named Alex. Alex is known for being exceptionally agreeable and conscientious. He always wants to do the right thing and rarely says "no" when asked for help. A manipulative coworker, seeing these traits in Alex, might exploit them to offload their tasks onto him. They know that Alex is likely to agree due to his personality traits.

However, it's crucial to understand that possessing these personality traits doesn't automatically designate you as a manipulation target. Instead, it suggests a potential vulnerability that can be managed and safeguarded when acknowledged. If Alex's story strikes a chord with you or reminds you of someone you know, you'll be pleased to learn that later in this book, we'll delve deeper into understanding why saying "no" can be so challenging, how self-worth plays a role, and what proactive steps you can take. But for now, let's go beyond mere behavior patterns to uncover what fuels them.

At the heart of our actions and reactions lies a deeply rooted belief system. Through the lens of cognitive-behavioral psychology, our convictions about ourselves, others, and our environment profoundly influence our behavior. These core beliefs can be uplifting, such as "I am competent" or detrimental, like "I am unworthy." When individuals harbor negative core beliefs, like feeling they're "not good enough," it can manifest in various behavioral tendencies. They might incessantly seek validation, shirk from challenges, fearing failure, or become susceptible to manipulation due to undervaluing their worth and placing undue importance on others' opinions.

Consider the earlier example of Alex. While his agreeable and conscientious traits make him vulnerable to manipulation, if Alex also holds a core belief that he must always please others to be valued, this belief would further amplify his susceptibility. He might take on extra tasks because of his natural tendency to help and a deep-seated need for validation stemming from his core beliefs.

This underscores the importance of introspection and self-awareness in understanding manipulative dynamics. Recognizing and challenging negative core beliefs can be a critical step in not just understanding one's vulnerabilities but also in building resilience against manipulation.

> "Behavior is the result of a thought. Always."
>
> *- Claudia*

With this understanding, we recognize that our actions and reactions are not random but are deeply influenced by our core beliefs and thought patterns. It's crucial to delve deeper into these foundational thoughts as they guide our responses to the world around us, including manipulative behaviors in the workplace.

While our personality traits and core beliefs may influence our behavior, they don't rigidly dictate it. At any point in our lives, we have the capacity for growth, change, and the development of new behaviors and coping strategies. By understanding our personality traits and core beliefs, we can better understand our tendencies and vulnerabilities, making us better prepared to deal with manipulative behavior when we encounter it.

Given the profound influence that core beliefs have on our behavior and vulnerability to manipulation, we've dedicated an entire chapter to delve into this topic further. In Chapter 6, "Understanding and Changing Core Beliefs", we will deeply explore these foundational thoughts, guiding you in identifying your core beliefs, understanding their origins, and offering actionable strategies to reshape negative or self-limiting beliefs.

Cognitive Biases and Manipulation

Our cognitive biases, or the systematic errors in our thinking, can also influence our susceptibility to manipulation. These biases often operate unconsciously, skewing our perception of reality and shaping our decisions and actions in ways that may not serve our best interests. Understanding these biases can help you recognize when your perception might be skewed, enabling you to make more objective judgments and decisions. This awareness can be crucial in identifying how manipulative individuals may exploit these biases to influence your behavior, ultimately helping you maintain a healthier and more balanced workplace dynamic.

Consider the **"confirmation bias"**, for example. This is our tendency to seek out and favor information that confirms our existing beliefs while disregarding information that contradicts them. A manipulative individual may exploit this bias by presenting information that aligns with your existing views, leading you to agree with their propositions without critically evaluating their validity.

Similarly, the **"halo effect"** is another cognitive bias that can be manipulated. This bias causes us to allow our overall impression of a person to influence our evaluation of their specific traits. For instance, if we admire our boss's creativity, we might overlook or downplay their manipulative behavior, attributing it to their 'quirky' or 'demanding' nature.

Here's a typical workplace example: Let's say you have a colleague, Lisa, who is known for her charismatic and friendly personality. People tend to like her, and she's good at her job. However, she often delegates some of her tasks to others subtly. When her colleagues realize what's happening, they might dismiss it, attributing it to Lisa just being 'busy' or 'in need of assistance.' That's the halo effect in action.

Another bias that plays a role in manipulation is the **"insight bias"**. This is the tendency to believe that one's understanding of a situation is better or more profound than it actually is, leading to overconfidence in one's judgments. Manipulators can prey on this bias, making you feel that you have unique insight or understanding, thereby sidestepping critical examination.

Favoring those who belong to our group – the so-called **"ingroup bias"** – can also be exploited. We naturally tend to trust and prefer people who are like us or share our affiliations. Manipulators can exploit this by highlighting shared similarities or allegiances, making us more likely to comply with their requests or overlook their questionable actions.

For example, a toxic leader, let's call her Doris, might gather her team for meetings where she praises their work, contrasting it with subtle jabs at other departments. "Our team is the best; others just coast along," she might say, even if not that explicitly. Encouraging reliance solely within the team, she frequently implies mistrust of other departments. This "Us vs. Them" mentality bolsters unity in her group but at the cost of company cohesion. Her tactics foster division and suspicion, undermining collaboration and the broader objectives of the organization.

Lastly, the **"authority bias"** underscores our inclination to trust or value the opinions of perceived authorities, even when they may be wrong. A manipulator who presents themselves as an expert or has a high-status title can exploit this bias, making their deceitful intents or proposals appear more credible.

The Importance of Recognizing and Addressing Manipulative Behavior

Have you ever felt like a situation at work was "off," but you couldn't quite put your finger on why? It could be due to a subtle form of manipulation that can often fly under the radar.

Recognizing and addressing manipulative behavior is crucial, not just for maintaining a healthy work environment but also for protecting your own mental and emotional well-being. It helps preserve the integrity of professional relationships, ensure workplace equity, and even contribute to the overall success of your organization. Let's take a closer look at these aspects and underline their significance through real-world examples, providing a more comprehensive understanding of why tackling manipulation is so vital.

Protecting Personal Well-Being

Manipulation in the workplace isn't just a professional issue – it's a personal one, too. Exposure to manipulative behaviors can take a significant toll on your physical and emotional health, often leading to increased stress, heightened anxiety, and creeping self-doubt.

Consider a scenario where you're working under a manager who frequently uses guilt-tripping as a tool to get work done. Over time, you may start feeling excessively worried about not meeting their expectations or letting your team down. This persistent worry can manifest as stress-related ailments such as headaches, stomach issues, sleep disturbances, and fatigue. Prolonged exposure to such stress might lead to more severe conditions like high blood pressure, weakened immune response, and even anxiety disorders. These physical and emotional reactions disrupt your peace of mind and can erode your confidence.

In the context of addressing workplace stress and its health implications, Claudia and I can **highly recommend** the book "**The Myth of Normal: Trauma, Illness, and Healing in a Toxic Culture**" by Gabor Maté. This insightful book explores the profound impact of societal pressures and stress on our health, challenging the conventional definitions of 'normal' and highlighting the necessity of understanding health in its full socio-political and emotional context. It offers a compassionate guide towards holistic healing, emphasizing the importance of authenticity and interpersonal connections.

However, recognizing these manipulative tactics is the first step towards safeguarding your personal well-being. By understanding what's happening, you can create boundaries, seek support, and practice self-care strategies to manage the impact of these behaviors. Remember, your health and well-being are paramount, and recognizing manipulation can be your first line of defense against the potential harm it can cause.

Maintaining Professional Relationships

Manipulation, while damaging to individuals, can also create profound ripples in the professional relationships within an organization. Trust, a cornerstone of effective teamwork and collaboration, can be eroded by manipulative behaviors. When individuals feel they cannot trust their colleagues or superiors due to deceptive practices, the result is often strained relationships and a decrease in open communication.

For instance, let's look at a situation where a co-worker regularly takes credit for your ideas. They twist the facts subtly, making it seem like they've contributed significantly to the project when, in reality, they're capitalizing on your efforts. Over time, this erodes your trust in them, making collaboration difficult. You might start withholding your ideas, leading to less productive brainstorming sessions and, ultimately, stifling the team's creativity and efficiency.

Furthermore, manipulation can cause misunderstandings and foster unhealthy competition, leading to a work environment where cooperation takes a backseat to self-protection. Such an atmosphere can hinder the organization's overall productivity and growth.

However, with the right strategies, you can work towards maintaining healthy professional relationships even in the face of manipulation. This includes recognizing the signs of manipulation, fostering open communication, and standing up against unfair practices. By promoting a culture of honesty, empathy, and mutual respect, you can help ensure a work environment that values and nurtures healthy professional relationships.

Ensuring a "Fair" and Just Workplace

Obviously, the term "fair" in the workplace context can be subjective and open to various interpretations. However, we believe the term still remains essential as it encapsulates the ideals of equitable practices and the desire for a harmonious working environment with balanced responsibilities and opportunities.

Workplace dynamics often swing due to the manipulative tactics of certain individuals. This can manifest not only as an imbalanced distribution of tasks, where some employees may find themselves burdened. In contrast, others ride the wave of others' hard work, but also as unequal access to promotions, bonuses, or growth opportunities. Such disparities and favoritism not only sow seeds of resentment among the team but can also lead to a decline in overall productivity, morale, and trust within the organization.

Imagine a scenario where a senior team member constantly passes off their responsibilities to newer team members, framing it as a "learning opportunity." On the surface, it may seem like a generous act of mentorship. However, as patterns emerge, it becomes evident that it's a tactic to dodge responsibilities. Such behaviors lead to overworked employees who feel undervalued and unrecognized.

Therefore, the onus falls on both management and you as an employee to ensure that manipulative behaviors are identified and addressed. Communication is key: you should feel empowered to voice your concerns, and management should be receptive to feedback. Moreover, clear policies should be in place to discourage manipulative practices and encourage transparency, accountability, and fair play.

Whistleblower hotlines have emerged as one of the tools designed to report and address manipulative behaviors in organizations. They offer anonymity and a platform for employees to communicate their concerns without fear; well, at least in theory, they should. In reality, we've all heard these stories from "insiders" who claim that one might be better off not relying on the anonymity of such systems or that sometimes the management of an organization might instruct hotline providers to ignore reports of specific individuals or about particular issues.

Speaking from her personal experience, **Claudia** witnessed the challenges posed by whistleblowing hotlines within a pharmaceutical industry organization. Employees often received conflicting guidance on utilizing these hotlines. While some managers endorsed them as crucial communication channels, encouraging with phrases like, "go for it, that's important," others dissuaded their use, suggesting a more direct approach through personal dialogues to resolve concerns. This inconsistency undeniably created confusion and hesitation among employees regarding the best way to address their issues. Claudia's advice is to always approach such tools with caution, stay informed and prioritize one's well-being and security.

Finally, organizations should invest in training sessions that foster a culture of transparency, respect, and mutual growth. By making efforts in this direction, businesses are not just enhancing their workplace environment but are also paving the way for improved teamwork, greater employee satisfaction, and, ultimately, enhanced overall performance.

To wrap it up, while the notion of "fairness" might be intangible and vary from one individual to another, striving for a workplace that minimizes manipulation and promotes balanced opportunities is both an ethical and pragmatic pursuit.

Supporting Organizational Success

Unchecked manipulation in the workplace not only has immediate, individual-level consequences, but it also profoundly affects the larger success of the organization. It can stifle creativity, discourage innovation, and, most critically, affect employee retention. Generation Z, entering the workforce with a keen sense of justice, inclusivity, and a demand for transparent work environments, is even less tolerant of manipulative practices. These younger professionals, typically born from the mid-to-late 1990s to the early 2010s, seek workplaces where their values align with organizational culture. Talented individuals, especially from this generation, are less likely to stay in an environment where manipulation is prevalent, and their departure can lead to a significant loss of knowledge and expertise for the organization.

Imagine an organization where a boss consistently takes credit for the team's ideas and achievements. Over time, this manipulative behavior will likely demotivate the team, making them less inclined to innovate or put in extra effort. This can have a serious negative impact on the organization's ability to stay competitive, adapt to market changes, and ultimately achieve its goals.

A positive work culture characterized by trust, open communication, and mutual respect doesn't just materialize from a catchy slogan on an elevator poster. It requires consistent and genuine effort. On the other hand, when cultivated, such an environment is more likely to retain talent and foster innovation. By recognizing and addressing manipulative behavior, you can help build such a culture and directly contribute to the overall success of your organization.

Remember, organizational success goes beyond mere metrics like hitting targets or increasing profit margins. It encompasses creating a workplace that deeply respects and values its members, champions fair practices, and acknowledges genuine effort.

As we progress in this book, you'll find that standing up against manipulation is not just about dealing with challenging bosses or colleagues. It's about staying true to oneself, remaining authentic, and ensuring that you can look in the mirror every morning with integrity and pride. More and more, the tides are shifting in the business world. In the future, it will be the companies with healthy corporate cultures that thrive and succeed. Gone are the days when job-seekers lined up for opportunities; now, talented professionals pick and choose, ready to leave if they find the environment toxic. The market has transformed; businesses can no longer afford to treat employees with disregard or neglect. This being said, upholding and promoting a culture of fairness and respect isn't just an ethical imperative; it's a driving force for overall organizational success.

What You Should Know Before Reaching Out to HR

1. Understanding HR's Primary Role

Let's start with a reality check about HR's role in the corporate world. You might think of Human Resources as the go-to place for support and resolution in the workplace – a kind of workplace guardian angel, right? Well, it's a bit more complicated than that.

Here's the scoop: HR primarily exists to protect the company's interests. Now, don't get me wrong, many HR professionals are genuinely committed to employee well-being, but at the end of the day, their main job is to safeguard the organization. This means that their decisions, actions, and advice are often influenced by what's best for the company, sometimes even at the expense of individual employee concerns. And at times, it's not even about the broader company interests but rather about what the top manager overseeing HR desires, even when it may not benefit the company. Even a top manager may lack competence or pursue personal interests. Thus, many HR leaders may prioritize satisfying that manager over what is best for the company or employee well-being.

Imagine you're playing a game of chess. HR is like a strategic player, constantly thinking several moves ahead. Their goal? To maintain balance, avoid legal pitfalls, and keep the company's reputation shiny and bright. When you approach them with a complaint or concern, they're not just listening to you; they're also thinking about potential legal risks, financial implications, and how it could impact the company's image.

This doesn't mean HR is the "bad guy." Far from it. They can be fantastic allies and provide valuable support. But, and here's the critical bit, their support has its limits, defined largely by the company's interests. Understanding this dual role of HR is crucial. It helps you set realistic expectations and plan your approach strategically if you ever need to knock on their door.

So, before you make a beeline to HR, take a moment to think about the bigger picture. How might your issue intersect with the company's interests? Could there be more at play than just your individual concern? This insight doesn't mean you should avoid HR altogether, but it does mean going in with your eyes wide open and understanding the chessboard you're stepping onto.

2. Potential for Retaliation

Now, let's talk about a slightly uncomfortable topic, but it's one we can't afford to sweep under the rug – the risk of retaliation. It's like walking into a forest; you need to be aware of the wildlife around you. In the workplace, "retaliation" is one of those wild creatures you might encounter, especially after you've raised a concern with HR.

Retaliation in the workplace isn't always as dramatic as in the movies. We're not necessarily discussing getting fired on the spot or having your desk ceremoniously dumped outside. It's often more subtle, sometimes so slight that you might wonder if you're just imagining it. One day, you're on the fast track, getting all the exciting projects, and the next, you find yourself sidelined, no longer invited to key meetings, or suddenly receiving unusually harsh feedback.

Here's the kicker – retaliation isn't just about hurting your feelings; it can have real consequences on your career trajectory. It might manifest as being passed over for promotions, not getting the support you need, or finding that your work environment has become inexplicably hostile. This can be tricky to navigate because it's not always easy to prove, and it's often cloaked in layers of corporate speak.

But here's what you need to remember: retaliation, in any form, is not okay. It's like a toxic weed in the workplace garden; it needs to be recognized and dealt with. However, the burden of proof often falls on you, the employee. This is why documenting everything becomes essential – from emails and meeting notes to any changes in how you're treated.

Understanding this potential risk is crucial; it's not meant to scare you off from standing up for yourself but to prepare you for the terrain you might have to navigate. Forewarned is forearmed, as they say. So, if you're considering approaching HR about an issue, think it through. Weigh the potential risks against the possible benefits and have a game plan. It's all about playing it smart and safe in the corporate wilderness.

3. Documentation and its Implications

Let's delve into an aspect of workplace dynamics that is often overlooked yet crucial – documentation. Consider it akin to leaving a breadcrumb trail in the professional landscape. When you bring a complaint or concern to HR, this trail transforms into a formal record. It's important to remember that written records tend to persist, sometimes beyond our initial intentions.

Documentation in HR is like a double-edged sword. On one hand, it's there to create an official record of your concerns, which sounds great, right? But on the flip side, this record becomes part of your permanent file. It's like posting something on social media; once it's out there, it's hard to take back.

So, what does this mean for you? Well, it's all about being mindful of the long game. When your complaint is documented, it could impact how you're viewed within the company. Let's say you're up for a promotion or a transfer, and someone decides to leaf through your file. Sure, they'll see your accomplishments, but they'll also see that complaint you lodged two years ago. It might not be fair, but it's often the reality of how things work.

This isn't to say you should never file a complaint – far from it. It's more about understanding the weight of documentation. It's like capturing a moment in time, and you want to ensure that picture is as clear and accurate as possible. Be factual, objective, and transparent about the issue. Avoid emotional language or exaggerations, as these can weaken your case and potentially backfire.

Remember, the goal of documentation is to protect both you and the company. It's your shield and sword in the corporate arena, so wield it wisely. Before you head off to HR, take a moment to consider the implications and how it might play out in the future. It's all about playing chess, not checkers.

4. Varied Effectiveness of HR Interventions

Approaching HR interventions can sometimes feel like navigating through a box of chocolates – unpredictable and varied in effectiveness. This analogy, reminiscent of Forrest Gump's famous line, highlights the uncertainty that often accompanies HR processes: "you never know what you're gonna get."

When you bring a concern to HR, the outcome can be a bit of a wild card. Sometimes, it's like hitting the jackpot – your issue is resolved smoothly, and everything works out better than you hoped. Other times, it's like expecting a gourmet truffle and ending up with the one chocolate nobody wants.

The effectiveness of HR in addressing your concerns largely depends on a few factors. First, there's the company culture. In some organizations, HR is empowered to make significant changes and take employee concerns seriously. In others, HR might be more of a paper-pushing entity, following procedures without rocking the boat too much.

Then, there are the HR professionals themselves. Some are like workplace superheroes, armed with empathy, fairness, and problem-solving skills. Others might be more by the book, cautious, and less willing to challenge the status quo. It's not just about their attitude but also their capacity – overloaded HR departments might not have the bandwidth to give your issue the attention it deserves.

This variability means that your experience with HR can differ drastically from your colleague's. Each case is a unique puzzle, and the pieces don't always fit how you expect. So, before you approach HR, it helps to do a bit of recon. Get a feel for how they've handled similar issues in the past. Talk to trusted colleagues (discreetly, of course) to gather insights. This intel can give you a clearer picture of what to expect.

Remember: Approaching HR is not a step to be taken lightly. It's crucial to understand that while HR can be a valuable ally, their primary allegiance is to the company. This can sometimes lead to outcomes that aren't in your favor, especially in complex situations involving legal and ethical considerations.

Be aware of the potential for subtle retaliation and the long-term implications of having your concerns documented. These realities don't mean you should avoid HR altogether but rather approach with a strategy, understanding the landscape, and being prepared for various outcomes.

It's all about being informed and cautious, not fearful. With this knowledge, you're better equipped to navigate the nuances of workplace dynamics and make decisions that protect your interests and career.

5. Legal and Ethical Complexities

Before concluding this chapter, it's important to briefly touch upon a vital aspect: the legal and ethical complexities in the workplace. These aspects can be subtle yet significant in influencing how HR deals with your situation. Gaining an understanding of employment laws and the intricate ethical dilemmas is crucial, as they deeply impact these scenarios.

However, given the breadth and complexity of these topics, we've decided to expand on legal and ethical considerations in a dedicated free ebook available on our website, **toxicleadership.info**. By scanning the QR code at the beginning of the book, readers can sign up to access this bonus content. This resource will serve as a comprehensive guide, offering insights and advice to help you confidently understand and navigate the complexities of legal and ethical issues in the workplace.

So, for now, remember: legal and ethical considerations are a big part of the HR equation. Keep this in mind as you prepare to approach HR.

Key Takeaways

- Manipulation involves covertly influencing someone's behavior for personal gain, which can occur in both personal and professional contexts.

- Power dynamics play a significant role in workplace manipulation, with individuals exploiting their control over resources, decisions, and information.

- Social norms and expectations can make individuals more susceptible to manipulation, highlighting the importance of awareness and resilience.

- Coercion is a manipulation tactic that uses threats or pressure to influence behavior, emphasizing the need for individuals to recognize and resist such approaches.

- Understanding persuasion techniques helps differentiate between ethical persuasion and manipulative influence, which is crucial for maintaining integrity in professional interactions.

- Personality traits can predispose individuals to use manipulation, underscoring the value of recognizing these traits in the workplace.

- Cognitive biases such as confirmation bias and the halo effect can make individuals more vulnerable to manipulation by distorting perception.

- HR's primary role is to protect the company's interests, not the well-being of employees; before reaching out to HR, document everything and prepare for potential outcomes to navigate the process effectively.

Manipu
lation
Master
class

3

Understanding Manipulative Behavior and Tactics

The Psychology of Manipulative Bosses

Manipulative bosses often have underlying psychological factors that drive their behavior. In this section, we will explore the psychological traits and motivations that usually contribute to manipulative behavior in the workplace, including narcissism, desire for control, power dynamics, and other factors. In understanding these factors, you'll be better equipped to identify and respond to manipulative behavior, thus empowering yourselves and promoting a healthier work environment.

Narcissism

Narcissistic individuals have an inflated sense of self-importance, a strong need for admiration, and a lack of empathy for others. When combined with a position of power, these traits can foster manipulative behavior that can be detrimental to a work environment. Narcissistic bosses may exploit and manipulate their employees to maintain their self-image, fulfill their desires, and control perceptions of them.

In the workplace, a narcissistic boss's behavior may manifest in various ways, including:

- Taking credit for their employees' work, accomplishments, or ideas

- Belittling or criticizing employees in front of others to enhance their own image

- Expecting special treatment or privileges that they believe they are entitled to

- Frequently talking about themselves and their achievements, often exaggerating their accomplishments

- Regularly using the "I" form instead of the inclusive "we," especially when discussing successes

- Becoming defensive or angry when faced with criticism or disagreement

- Reacting with envy or resentment towards others' successes or accomplishments

- Showing little concern for their employees' well-being, feelings, or needs

To illustrate this, consider the character Gordon Gekko from the movie "Wall Street." Gekko, a ruthless and ambitious corporate raider, uses his charm, charisma, and manipulative skills to achieve his goals at any cost. He believes in the mantra "Greed is good" and has little regard for the lives and well-being of others, including his employees.

A specific scene that demonstrates Gekko's narcissistic and manipulative nature is when he convinces young stockbroker Bud Fox to engage in insider trading to benefit Gekko's investments. Gekko exploits Bud's ambition and desire for success, offering him a taste of the high life, knowing full well the illegal and unethical nature of their actions. This manipulation leads Bud down a path of moral compromise, resulting in severe consequences for him and those around him.

However, not all narcissistic bosses are as extreme as Gekko. Narcissism exists on a spectrum, and some may exhibit more subtle manipulative tendencies, using charm and charisma to influence others. Regardless of the extent, understanding these characteristics is vital in recognizing and protecting yourself from such manipulative behavior.

In later chapters, we will provide specific strategies for dealing with narcissistic bosses. For now, it's essential to understand that recognizing these behaviors is the first step in maintaining a healthy work environment.

Meet Our Expert: Dr. Alina Kastner

In case you want to dive deeper into the world of narcissism, both in personal and professional relationships, we highly recommend the work of our dear colleague and friend, Dr. Alina Kastner, MSc.

Alina is a powerhouse in her field, seamlessly blending her roles as a Systemic Family Psychotherapist, Work Psychologist, and coach. She's grabbed headlines in the New York Post and Newsweek with her sharp insights on spotting a narcissist on a first date.

For an in-depth look at the science behind narcissism, check out Alina's article published in the Journal of Experimental Psychopathology. Co-authored with her colleagues, this article draws fascinating links between narcissistic behavior and cocaine addiction. The full article is cited and linked in the references at the end of this book.

For a regular dose of her wisdom (and some seriously good advice), follow Alina on TikTok. Her videos are not only informative but also engaging, making complex psychological concepts accessible to everyone. Whether you're dealing with a narcissist or just curious about the topic, Alina has something to offer.

Desire for Control

In some instances, manipulative bosses are driven by a powerful desire for control, a theme discussed in Chapter 2. This drive can lead such individuals to employ various tactics designed to influence their employees' thoughts, feelings, and actions. Bosses with a high need for control may use manipulation as a tool to maintain their authority, keep their status unchallenged, or compensate for feelings of inadequacy or insecurity.

Controlling bosses' behavior can manifest in several ways:

- Frequent monitoring of employees' activities or demanding constant updates about work progress

- Making decisions unilaterally, without considering employees' input or opinions

- Discouraging open communication, criticism, or disagreement to uphold their authority

- Resorting to threats, intimidation, or punishment as a means to control employees' actions

- Setting unrealistic expectations or goals and demanding unquestioned compliance

- Dismissing or ignoring employees' concerns or ideas, asserting that they "know best."

- Creating a dependency by withholding critical information or resources

- Micromanaging every detail shows a lack of trust in employees' capabilities to complete tasks without constant oversight.

- They refuse to admit their mistakes and lack the capacity for self-reflection, presenting themselves as infallible by exerting control over how others perceived them.

For a relatable illustration of a controlling boss, let's revisit the character Michael Scott from the television series "The Office". Michael, the often-clueless regional manager of the Dunder Mifflin Paper Company, exudes a strong need for control and approval. His misguided and impulsive decisions often result in awkward and uncomfortable situations for his team.

One instance showcasing Michael's controlling behavior is when he insists on leading a group presentation despite his employees' apparent disinterest. His compulsion for validation and control sees him dominating the conversation, ignoring his employees' input, and forcing participation in his flawed attempt to motivate them. This behavior not only undermines team productivity and morale but also Michael's credibility as a leader.

Recognizing such behavior patterns in your workplace can equip you with the knowledge needed to develop effective strategies for controlling bosses like Michael Scott.

Desire for Power

The desire for power, distinct from the neutral phenomenon of power dynamics, can contribute to manipulative behavior in bosses. Individuals with a strong desire for power may feel entitled to exploit or control their employees to achieve their ambitions. This personal inclination, coupled with their authority, can drive bosses to employ manipulative tactics to assert their dominance and reach their objectives.

Signs that a boss's desire for power is driving manipulative behavior can include:

- Taking credit for employees' work or ideas without proper recognition

- Making decisions that primarily benefit the boss at the cost of employees or the organization

- Using authority to gain favor or special treatment

- Withholding critical information or resources to maintain control

- Exploiting employees' vulnerabilities for personal gain

- Promoting competition or rivalry among employees to retain control

- Creating an environment of fear or uncertainty, ensuring employees' dependency

An apt example of a boss who skillfully navigates power dynamics is Frank Underwood from the television series "House of Cards," played by Kevin Spacey. Underwood, a cunning and ruthless politician, manipulates his colleagues and subordinates to consolidate his power, illustrating a quintessential Machiavellian mindset.

One scene that showcases Underwood's manipulation of power dynamics is when he persuades a young reporter, Zoe Barnes, to collaborate with him by offering her exclusive information. Their conversation unfolds as:

Underwood: "You have something I want. I have something you want."

Zoe: "What do I have that you want?"

Underwood: "You have talent, ambition, and a willingness to go beyond what's expected of you."

Underwood offers exclusive political intel to advance Zoe's career in exchange for her loyalty and discretion. This alliance serves Underwood's goals as he uses Zoe to spread narratives that further his political ambitions while maintaining control over her.

Insecurity

Insecurity can contribute to manipulative behavior in the workplace. Bosses who feel insecure about their abilities or position may resort to manipulation to maintain control and protect their status. They may feel threatened by the success or competence of their employees and use manipulative tactics to undermine or control them.

Examples of insecure boss behavior may include:

- Constantly seeking validation or praise from employees
- Taking credit for others' achievements to boost their image
- Overreacting to criticism or reacting defensively
- Sabotaging the work or success of others to maintain a sense of superiority
- Refusing to delegate tasks for fear of losing control
- Micromanaging employees to maintain a sense of control
- Excessively comparing themselves to others or making unfavorable comparisons

Two characters that exhibit insecure boss behavior are Andy Bernard from "The Office" and Principal Skinner from "The Simpsons."

Andy Bernard, played by Ed Helms, is the Regional Manager at Dunder Mifflin Scranton. He often struggles with insecurities, leading him to seek validation from his employees and superiors. In one episode, Andy becomes obsessed with winning the office's approval by hosting an office talent show. His need for validation is so strong that he ends up performing a cringe-worthy rendition of "Take a Chance on Me" by ABBA in front of his employees. This scene highlights his need for attention and approval, which often leads to awkward and manipulative behavior.

Principal Skinner, voiced by Harry Shearer, is the principal of Springfield Elementary School in "The Simpsons." He often exhibits insecurity in his position, leading to manipulative behavior in his interactions with teachers and students. In one episode, Skinner becomes paranoid that his job is at risk after receiving a letter from the Superintendent. He begins to micromanage the teachers and students in an attempt to maintain control over the school, ultimately causing chaos and discontent among the staff and students.

Fear of Failure

Fear of failure can also contribute to manipulative behavior in bosses. They may be unwilling to accept responsibility for their mistakes or shortcomings, instead choosing to manipulate employees into taking the blame or covering up their failures. This fear of failure can make it difficult for bosses to admit when they are wrong or accept constructive criticism, further reinforcing their manipulative behavior.

Examples of boss behavior driven by fear of failure may include:

- Avoiding difficult conversations or decisions to prevent potential failure

- Blaming employees for their own mistakes or failures

- Manipulating situations to make themselves look better or more competent

- Refusing to admit mistakes or accept responsibility for their actions

- Discrediting or undermining others to protect their own reputation

- Focusing on maintaining an image of success rather than addressing problems

Walter White, portrayed by Bryan Cranston in the television series "Breaking Bad," is an example of a character who exhibits manipulative behavior driven by a fear of failure. As a high school chemistry teacher turned methamphetamine manufacturer, Walter White's transformation into the manipulative Heisenberg persona is fueled by his desperation to provide for his family after being diagnosed with terminal lung cancer.

In one scene, when his partner Jesse Pinkman, played by Aaron Paul, confronts Walter about the quality of their methamphetamine product, Walter manipulates the situation to shift the blame onto Jesse. Instead of acknowledging the possibility of a mistake or a problem with their production process, Walter insists that Jesse's incompetence is the cause of the issue. This interaction highlights Walter's unwillingness to accept responsibility for his actions and his tendency to manipulate others in order to maintain an image of success.

From the volatile meth labs of the fictional Albuquerque to the polished boardrooms of real-world pharmaceuticals, fear of failure and its resulting manipulations can manifest anywhere. In a real-life example from the pharmaceutical industry, **Claudia** once witnessed the power of a 360-degree feedback survey and the manipulative behavior it can elicit from those fearing failure.

Claudia's then-boss, Lena, had summoned the entire team into a meeting room shortly before the survey was to be administered. She set a clear expectation: "I assume you will rate me well because at the end of the year, you would all want a favorable evaluation from me." Such a statement was an overt attempt to manipulate the feedback process, implying a quid pro quo – good reviews in exchange for job security or advancement.

However, the results didn't pan out as Lena had hoped. Despite her not-so-subtle hint, her feedback was predominantly negative. Initially, she seemed momentarily cooperative, likely following the principle of "be nice to them." Soon after, however, she was visibly upset and struggled to cope with the candid feedback. Lena had perhaps assumed that her team would falsify their responses in her favor. But the majority opted for honesty, and she wasn't prepared for it.

This incident underscored the significant implications of the 360-feedback in that company. Contrary to merely being an avenue for feedback, it was instrumental in deciding promotions or even terminations. The weight of these outcomes only heightened Lena's desperation to manipulate the process and her subsequent inability to handle genuine feedback.

Understanding the role that fear of failure can play in manipulative boss behavior, as demonstrated by Walter White or Lena, can help you identify these patterns in your own workplace and develop strategies to address and respond to them effectively.

Perfectionism

Who doesn't know a boss who sets unattainably high standards for themselves and their employees? Perfectionism can be another factor that leads to manipulative behavior. Bosses with perfectionist tendencies may have unrealistic expectations of their employees and may use manipulation to push them to meet those expectations. They may also be overly critical and use negative reinforcement or other tactics to control their employees' performance.

Examples of boss behavior driven by perfectionism may include:

- Setting unattainable goals or expectations for employees

- Constantly critiquing or finding fault with employees' work

- Micromanaging or excessively controlling employees' tasks and responsibilities

- Focusing on minor details rather than the overall success of a project

- Using manipulative tactics, such as guilt or fear, to push employees to work harder or longer hours

Steve Jobs, the late co-founder of Apple Inc., was known for his perfectionist tendencies, which sometimes led him to engage in manipulative behavior with employees. Jobs was famous for pushing his team members to their limits, demanding the highest quality work, and setting nearly impossible deadlines. While his perfectionism contributed to Apple's groundbreaking innovations, it also led him to be overly critical and controlling, which could create a challenging work environment for his employees.

Meryl Streep's portrayal of Margaret Thatcher in the movie "The Iron Lady" also demonstrates a boss driven by perfectionism. Thatcher, the former British Prime Minister, is depicted as a strong-willed and determined leader who demands excellence from her cabinet members. Throughout the movie, Thatcher is seen challenging and criticizing her colleagues, pushing them to deliver flawless results. Her uncompromising expectations and focus on perfection create tension and unease in her working relationships.

Recognizing the role that perfectionism can play in manipulative boss behavior, as demonstrated by Steve Jobs and Meryl Streep's portrayal of Margaret Thatcher, can help you identify these patterns in your workplace and develop strategies to address and respond to them effectively.

Machiavellianism – Power Before Morality

Who hasn't heard of a boss who always seems to have a hidden agenda and manipulates others for personal gain? Machiavellianism refers to a manipulative and strategic approach to interpersonal relationships that places power and personal gain above moral and ethical considerations. Bosses who exhibit Machiavellian traits may be more likely to use manipulation as a means to achieve their goals, even at the expense of others. These individuals may be adept at reading and exploiting others' emotions and vulnerabilities, making them exceptionally skilled at using manipulative tactics in the workplace.

Examples of Machiavellian boss behavior may include:

- Using deceit or misrepresentation to further their goals
- Exploiting others' weaknesses or vulnerabilities for personal gain
- Manipulating others' emotions to elicit specific reactions or behaviors
- Pursuing their goals with disregard for ethical considerations and the well-being of others
- Engaging in strategic alliances or relationships solely to further their interests, with little concern for moral values

Littlefinger, or Petyr Baelish, from the "Game of Thrones" series, is an excellent example of a Machiavellian character. As a cunning political player, Littlefinger manipulates those around him to achieve his goals, often using their emotions and desires against them. He is known for his ability to read people, understand their motives, and exploit their weaknesses for his advantage.

One scene that showcases Littlefinger's Machiavellian nature is his conversation with Sansa Stark in the garden. Littlefinger uses his knowledge of Sansa's feelings for him to manipulate her emotions and gain her trust. He persuades her to believe he is acting in her best interest while concealing his true intentions.

Littlefinger: "Sometimes, when I try to understand a person's motives, I play a little game. I assume the worst. What's the worst reason you have for turning me against my sister? That's what you do, isn't it? That's what you've always done. Turn family against family, turn sister against sister. That's what you did to our mother and Aunt Lysa and that's what you tried to do to us."

Sansa: "I'm not playing your games, Littlefinger."

Littlefinger: "I never asked you to. But if you won't, at least learn to play the game."

This scene demonstrates how Littlefinger uses his Machiavellian traits to manipulate Sansa, showcasing his cunning and manipulative nature. By understanding characters like Littlefinger, you can better recognize Machiavellian behavior in the workplace and develop strategies to protect yourself and others from these tactics.

Lack of Empathy

Empathy refers to the ability to emotionally understand what other people are experiencing and respond with care and consideration, and it plays a critical role in effective leadership. It's what enables leaders to forge strong connections with their team members and respond to their needs with care and consideration. However, bosses who lack this crucial trait often view their employees merely as a means to an end, ignoring their workforce's emotional nuances and well-being. This absence of empathy, while harmful in its own right, can also signal the presence of other personality traits or disorders, such as narcissism. Narcissists, for instance, are often so preoccupied with their desires and concerns that they overlook or dismiss the feelings and needs of those around them.

Signs of a lack of empathy in a boss can include:

- Dismissal or invalidation of employees' feelings or experiences
- Little to no recognition of employees' hard work or achievements
- Unwillingness to provide support or assistance to struggling employees
- Favoritism or unfair treatment of certain employees
- Disregard for employees' personal lives or well-being
- Predatory behavior or exploitation of employees' vulnerabilities

A famous character who represents a boss with a lack of empathy is again Miranda Priestly from "The Devil Wears Prada." The high-powered editor-in-chief of a top fashion magazine consistently demands the impossible from her staff, dismisses their struggles, and gives no recognition for their hard work. Her lack of empathy is displayed when she nonchalantly hands over a task to her new assistant, Andrea Sachs, without considering if it's a reasonable request, expecting Andrea to fulfill her wishes without questioning.

In one particularly telling scene, Miranda publicly berates Andrea for not understanding her preferences and demands. This behavior creates an environment of fear and stress, discouraging open communication and teamwork among the staff. Miranda's lack of empathy has a direct negative impact on her employees, fostering a toxic workplace culture that results in high turnover and low morale.

Case Study 1: The Contrast in Empathy

During a challenging period of my career, **I, Markus**, encountered a stark contrast in behavior from two individuals in my workplace, which served as a clear illustration of the difference between superficial niceness and genuine empathy. This experience unfolded while I was on long-term sick leave, recovering from the toxic behavior of my then-boss, Ethan, which had significantly impacted my health and necessitated a period of rehabilitation.

The first interaction came from Ethan himself. Late one evening, at 8:23 PM, I received a message on my private WhatsApp from him. The message read:

"Dear Markus, I would like to call you in the coming days. When would be a good time for you? Best wishes, Ethan."

While seemingly polite, this message lacked any acknowledgment of my current health situation. Ethan did not inquire about my willingness or readiness to engage in a conversation; he presumed availability and did not clarify the purpose of the proposed call. This approach felt invasive and disregarded the personal and professional boundaries, as well as the sensitivity of my situation.

In contrast, the second message I received was from Devon, the Head of HR. This message was sent to my private email, a channel I had provided for essential communications during my leave. It arrived at a more appropriate time, 4:20 PM, and carried a markedly different tone:

"Dear Markus, I hope you're doing reasonably well under the circumstances. Do you have time for a personal conversation between us? I would like to discuss your department's current situation with you and ask whether you want to stay in this department after all... Best regards, Devon."

Devon's message was considerate and professional. He acknowledged the difficulties I was facing, made it clear that the choice to engage in a conversation was mine, and transparently stated the purpose of the potential discussion. This approach respected my autonomy and the challenges I was navigating, demonstrating genuine empathy and professionalism.

These two messages, received within days of each other, highlighted the profound difference between superficially nice gestures and truly empathetic behavior. Ethan's message, devoid of empathy and consideration, contrasted sharply with Devon's thoughtful and respectful approach. This experience underscored the importance of empathy in leadership and HR practices, revealing how critical it is to approach employees with genuine understanding and respect, especially in times of vulnerability.

While I was soon engaged in a fruitful phone call with Devon, you might be curious about my reaction – or perhaps, in hindsight, how I should have reacted – to Ethan's WhatsApp message. We'll delve into that discussion later. In the meantime, feel free to ponder your own potential reactions. How would you have responded, or how do you wish you had reacted?

Case Study 2: "Just Sleeping"

During the COVID-19 pandemic, **Claudia** was employed in the pharmaceutical industry. When her father fell gravely ill with COVID-19 and was placed in a coma, Claudia sought to spend more time by his side and approached her supervisor, Carol, with a request to reduce her working hours. Carol's response was devoid of empathy. She bluntly told Claudia that she didn't understand the request, as her father was "just sleeping now anyways." Carol said it's either full hours or nothing.

As this utter lack of empathy conflicted deeply with Claudia's values, she chose to leave the company. Although initially uncertain about leaving perceived security, this incident catalyzed Claudia's decision to transition into self-employment. Driven by her strong values, this move ultimately led to a more fulfilling path.

Image Management: A Facade of Leadership

Manipulative bosses often employ image management as a strategic facade, prioritizing the perception of effectiveness and control over genuine leadership qualities and team well-being. While superficially maintaining the leader's status, this approach can have detrimental effects on organizational culture, employee morale, and trust.

The Perils of Prioritizing Appearance over Substance

At the heart of manipulative leadership lies the overemphasis on image management — the practice of carefully creating one's appearance, behaviors, and interactions to project a desirable image to others, often at the expense of authenticity and ethical leadership. This manipulation tactic not only misleads stakeholders about the leader's true capabilities and the organization's health but also sets a dangerous precedent for valuing appearance over actual performance and integrity.

Case Study: The Cost of Image Management in a Baltimore Hospital

One of our readers, Ryan, a former hospital employee in Baltimore, witnessed firsthand the consequences of a leadership overly fixated on image management. Ryan's supervisor consistently emphasized that "appearance or image was everything," a philosophy that translated into a work environment where employees were either unduly reprimanded for minor issues or disproportionately praised for insignificant accomplishments. This approach led to a pervasive atmosphere of resentment, as staff members resorted to doing the bare minimum to avoid negative attention. Moreover, focusing on image over substance fostered a culture of finger-pointing and blame-shifting, further eroding the team's cohesion and morale.

The consequences of this image-centric culture were deeply felt by Ryan, particularly after he stepped down from his supervisory role. The erosion of trust between him and his boss resulted in a cautious approach to his work, often finding himself avoiding his supervisor to escape the stress and scrutiny associated with the image-obsessed environment. This case poignantly illustrates the long-term detriment that an overemphasis on image can inflict on workplace trust, employee engagement, and overall productivity.

Ryan's experience serves as a cautionary tale for organizations and leaders alike, highlighting the critical importance of fostering a culture where genuine achievements and transparent communication are valued above the superficial management of appearances.

Attachment Theory in Workplace Dynamics

Attachment Theory – What's That?

When psychologists talk about "Attachment Theory," what they mean is a framework that helps us understand how our early relationships with caregivers shape our behavior in future interpersonal connections, including those in the workplace. Initially developed to understand the bond between infants and their primary caregivers, this theory has significant implications for adult relationships, providing insights into various interaction styles that emerge in professional environments.

Attachment Theory posits that the nature of our early attachments significantly influences our behavior in later relationships. This theory, pioneered by John Bowlby and later expanded by Mary Ainsworth, has evolved to become a cornerstone in understanding relational dynamics among adults. This Theory is more than an academic concept; it's a key tool for deciphering the intricate dynamics of professional relationships. It helps explain the behavior patterns of different individuals in the workplace, from a supervisor's micromanagement to a team member's hesitance in decision-making.

The Four Attachment Styles:

1. **Secure Attachment**: Characterized by a sense of safety and comfort in relationships. Individuals with this style tend to have a balanced approach to relationships, feeling secure and connected without being overly dependent or anxious.

Imagine a team leader, Alex, who is known for his balanced approach. He trusts his team, delegates tasks efficiently, and is open to feedback. When problems arise, Alex remains calm and solution-focused, providing support without micromanaging. His team feels valued and empowered, leading to a productive and harmonious work environment.

2. **Anxious-Preoccupied Attachment**: Marked by a heightened sense of insecurity and anxiety about being abandoned. People with this style often seek high levels of intimacy and approval, fearing rejection.

As a project manager, Sarah often seeks constant reassurance from her superiors and peers about her performance. She worries excessively about meeting expectations and can become distressed if she feels she's not getting enough feedback or approval. This sometimes leads to her taking on more work than she can handle, fearing that saying no might disappoint others.

3. **Dismissive-Avoidant Attachment**: Defined by a desire for emotional independence, often distancing oneself from forming deep connections. Those with this style might prioritize self-reliance and usually appear aloof or uninterested in close relationships.

John, a senior analyst, prefers to work independently and often seems aloof or disengaged in team meetings. He is skilled but rarely seeks or offers help, maintaining a strong boundary between his professional and personal life. While he delivers on his tasks, his reluctance to engage in deeper team collaboration can sometimes create a sense of distance from his colleagues.

4. **Fearful-Avoidant Attachment** (also known as Disorganized): Involves a mix of anxiety and avoidance. Individuals with this style might desire close relationships but fear getting too close, often resulting in mixed signals and erratic behavior.

Linda, a marketing executive, shows a mix of desire for close collaboration and a fear of getting too involved in team dynamics. She might enthusiastically lead a team brainstorming session one day but then become withdrawn and hesitant to make decisions the next. Her fluctuating involvement and mixed signals often leave her team confused about her commitment and leadership style.

It's important to note that attachment styles, though shaped by early experiences, are not set in stone. Individuals, including those in leadership positions, can evolve towards a more secure attachment style through self-awareness, personal development, and sometimes professional guidance. This aspect of Attachment Theory offers a hopeful perspective for both personal and professional growth. For instance, a manager who recognizes their tendency toward an anxious-preoccupied attachment style can actively work on building trust and reducing their need for constant reassurance. Similarly, an employee who identifies with a dismissive-avoidant style can learn strategies to engage more openly with colleagues. The journey towards a more secure attachment style can lead to improved interpersonal relationships, enhanced leadership skills, and a more positive workplace environment, benefiting both the individual and the organization.

As we delve deeper into these attachment styles and their manifestations in the workplace, we will not only explore their influence on the dynamics of leadership and teamwork but also offer practical strategies for interacting with and responding to different attachment styles. This understanding is crucial for navigating the interpersonal challenges we frequently encounter in professional settings. The forthcoming sections will provide actionable insights and tools to help you effectively engage with colleagues and superiors of various attachment backgrounds, enhancing both personal and team effectiveness in your work environment.

Attachment Styles and Manipulative Bosses

In the realm of professional leadership, the attachment styles of bosses can significantly influence their management approach and, in some cases, their tendency towards manipulative behaviors. Understanding these styles is not only crucial to comprehending their actions but also essential for developing strategies to work with or manage them effectively.

1. Secure Attachment in Bosses

Bosses with a secure attachment style tend to exhibit a balanced leadership approach. They are confident in their role, comfortable with delegating tasks, and supportive of their team's autonomy. Their management style promotes a positive and productive work environment, encouraging open communication and mutual respect. These leaders typically do not resort to manipulative tactics, as they trust their team and are secure in their abilities.

2. Anxious-Preoccupied Attachment in Bosses

Bosses with an anxious-preoccupied attachment may display a high need for control and reassurance. This can manifest as micromanagement or a constant need for affirmation from their team and superiors. In their quest for validation, they may resort to manipulative tactics like guilt-tripping employees to ensure loyalty or over-commitment. Their anxiety about workplace relationships and performance might lead to a tense and high-pressure work environment.

3. Dismissive-Avoidant Attachment in Bosses

Leaders with a dismissive-avoidant attachment style often maintain an emotional distance from their team. They may appear unapproachable or indifferent to their employees' needs or concerns. In extreme cases, such bosses might use manipulation as a tool to maintain their autonomy, using tactics like withholding information or being overly critical without offering constructive feedback. This detachment can create a disconnected and disengaged team dynamic.

4.   Fearful-Avoidant (Disorganized) Attachment in Bosses

Bosses with a fearful-avoidant attachment style exhibit inconsistent and erratic behavior. Their leadership might swing between being overly involved and completely disengaged. This unpredictability can be a form of manipulation, as employees are left uncertain about expectations and the boss's reactions. These leaders might unintentionally manipulate through mixed messages and inconsistent standards, leading to confusion and instability within the team.

Link Between Attachment Styles and Manipulative Behaviors

While not all bosses with insecure attachment styles resort to manipulation, those who do might find these tactics as a way to compensate for their internal insecurities. Anxious-preoccupied leaders might manipulate to maintain a sense of control and validation, while dismissive-avoidant bosses might do so to create distance or assert independence. Understanding these underlying motivations is crucial for employees navigating these complex dynamics and for organizations aiming to foster healthier leadership practices.

Attachment Styles and Employees' Susceptibility to Manipulation

In the complex world of workplace dynamics, an employee's attachment style can significantly influence their interactions with colleagues and bosses, especially in situations involving manipulation. Just as leaders' attachment styles shape their approach to management, employees' styles can affect how they perceive and respond to manipulative behavior.

Impact of Attachment Styles on Response to Manipulation

Secure Attachment: Employees with a secure attachment style often have a strong sense of self and are less likely to be swayed by manipulative tactics. They are typically confident in their judgment, can set healthy boundaries, and are less prone to being exploited by guilt or fear. For example, when faced with a micromanaging boss, a securely attached employee might address the issue directly or seek HR support instead of internalizing the stress or feeling inadequate.

Anxious-Preoccupied Attachment: These employees might find themselves more vulnerable to manipulation, particularly tactics that play on their fears of rejection or underperformance. They may overextend themselves or fail to speak up against unreasonable demands, as their need for approval makes them susceptible to tactics like guilt-tripping or emotional blackmail.

Dismissive-Avoidant Attachment: Such individuals might resist manipulation through detachment, but their reluctance to engage deeply with others could leave them isolated. Their tendency to withdraw might mean missed opportunities for support or collaboration in countering manipulative behaviors in the workplace.

Fearful-Avoidant (Disorganized) Attachment: Employees with this style can have unpredictable responses to manipulation. Their mixed desire for connection and fear of getting too close might make them erratic in confronting or succumbing to manipulative tactics. They may oscillate between challenging manipulative behaviors and becoming inadvertently complicit in them.

Strategies to Recognize and Navigate Attachment Patterns

By acknowledging and understanding your attachment styles, you can become more adept at navigating manipulative tactics in the workplace, leading to healthier professional relationships and a more empowering work environment. Here are some strategies you can use:

☑ **Self-Reflection**: Regularly assess your reactions to workplace situations. Do you find yourself overly anxious about approval, or do you tend to distance yourself emotionally? Recognizing these patterns can help you understand your attachment style.

☑ **Seeking Feedback**: Sometimes, it's helpful to get an external perspective. Trusted colleagues or mentors can offer insights into your workplace interactions and how your attachment style might influence them.

☑ **Professional Development**: Workshops or training sessions on emotional intelligence and interpersonal skills can provide tools to understand and adapt your attachment style professionally.

☑ **Counseling or Coaching**: For deeper personal patterns, consider counseling or coaching. These professionals can help you explore your attachment style more thoroughly and develop strategies to build a more secure attachment approach in your professional life.

Attachment Styles & Team Dynamics

Understanding the diverse attachment styles present in a workplace can be transformative in how team dynamics and communication unfold. Each style brings its unique influence, affecting everything from daily interactions to resolving conflicts. Let's have a closer look:

- **Secure Attachment**: Those with a secure attachment style often act as stabilizers within a team. Their comfort with open communication and ability to handle feedback constructively contribute to a positive and collaborative atmosphere. They are typically the mediators who facilitate understanding and bridge gaps between different team members.

- **Anxious-Preoccupied Attachment**: Employees with this style may seek constant reassurance and approval, leading to frequent check-ins or reliance on others for decision-making. While their commitment to team approval can be beneficial, it might also result in dependency, potentially slowing down the team's progress and decision-making capabilities.

- **Dismissive-Avoidant Attachment**: Such individuals might contribute to a sense of detachment within the team. Their preference for working independently and reluctance to engage in emotional discussions can lead to a lack of cohesion and missed opportunities for deeper team bonding and collaboration.

- **Fearful-Avoidant (Disorganized) Attachment**: Their unpredictability can introduce an element of inconsistency in team dynamics. While their diversity of perspectives can be a strength, it can also lead to confusion and misalignment within the team, especially under stress.

Awareness of different attachment styles can be a powerful tool in enhancing interpersonal understanding and managing conflicts. Here are some ways to leverage this awareness:

- ☑ **Tailored Communication:** Adjust your communication style to better connect with team members of different attachment styles. For instance, provide more reassurance and clarity for anxious-preoccupied colleagues while respecting the need for space and independence of dismissive-avoidant individuals.

- ☑ **Conflict Resolution Strategies:** Understanding attachment styles can inform how you approach conflict resolution. Securely attached individuals can be invaluable in mediating conflicts, as they tend to be more balanced and empathetic in their approach.

- ☑ **Professional Development Sessions:** Organizing team sessions on attachment styles can improve mutual understanding. These sessions can help team members recognize their own styles and learn how to interact more effectively with different types of people.

- ☑ **Encourage Self-Awareness:** Promote a culture of self-awareness where team members are encouraged to understand their attachment styles and how these might impact their workplace interactions. This understanding can lead to more empathetic and effective teamwork.

At a Glance

The table below provides you with a brief overview of how the four primary attachment styles — Secure, Anxious-Preoccupied, Dismissive-Avoidant, and Fearful-Avoidant — play out in workplace dynamics. Encapsulating the behaviors of bosses, employees, and team interactions is a practical tool that will help you foster self-awareness and improve interpersonal relations in a professional context.

Attachment Style	In Bosses	In Employees	In Team Dynamics
Secure	Flexible, open to feedback, fosters growth	Reliable, consistent, open communication	Cohesive, collaborative, high trust
Anxious-Preoccupied	Needs constant validation, micromanages	Seeks approval, may be clingy or overly dependent	Tension, lack of autonomy, possible conflicts
Dismissive-Avoidant	Aloof, unapproachable, lacks empathy	Independent to the point of isolation, avoid seeking help	Siloed, competitive, lacks cohesion
Fearful-Avoidant	Unpredictable, may alternate between engagement and withdrawal	Hesitant to trust, inconsistent performance	Unstable, fluctuating trust levels, unpredictable

Strategies for Leaders and HR Professionals

Even though our primary focus throughout this book is on empowering employees who suffer under toxic bosses, we still want to pivot our focus towards leaders and HR professionals. What role does understanding attachment styles play in their day-to-day management and strategic planning? How can this knowledge be effectively leveraged to nurture a healthy, productive, and inclusive work environment? For those at the helm of team management and organizational development, recognizing and addressing the diverse attachment styles present in the workplace is a critical skill. This understanding not only streamlines team management but also guides the creation of tailored development programs, meeting the unique needs of each employee.

In order to recognize and adequately address different attachment styles, leaders and HR professionals should...

- **...develop a keen sense of observation** to identify the attachment styles of team members. This could be done through regular interactions, performance reviews, and feedback sessions. Leaders should consider how employees react to stress, feedback, and team dynamics.

- **...adapt their management style** to suit different attachment needs. For instance, provide more structured guidance and reassurance to anxious-preoccupied employees while offering autonomy and space to dismissive-avoidant individuals.

- **...facilitate open communication** by creating an environment where employees feel comfortable discussing their work styles and needs. HR professionals should encourage team leaders to have open dialogues with their team members about the best ways to support them.

- **...be equipped with the skills to recognize and manage conflicts** arising from clashing attachment styles. Training in empathetic listening and mediation would be particularly beneficial.

In order to effectively implement training and development initiatives that accommodate different attachment styles, leaders and HR professionals should...

- **...conduct workshops** to educate employees about different attachment styles and how these influence workplace behavior. Such workshops can empower employees to better understand themselves and their colleagues, fostering empathy and collaboration across the team.

- **...include modules on emotional intelligence and attachment theory** in leadership development programs. These programs can train leaders to recognize their attachment styles and understand the impact these styles have on their leadership approach.

- **...implement mentorship programs** where employees have the opportunity to learn from leaders or colleagues who exhibit secure attachment traits. Additionally, offer coaching for individuals interested in developing a more secure attachment style.

- **...provide support through well-being initiatives** that recognize attachment issues can be linked to deeper emotional patterns. The CEO should act as a role model, fostering an environment where discussing well-being is free from taboo. When senior leadership sets a positive example, these initiatives are more likely to succeed. Wellness programs, counseling services, or employee assistance programs can address these underlying concerns effectively.

- **...incorporate one-on-one transformational coaching into leadership development programs** in order to develop leaders who are both qualified and capable of fostering a positive work environment. Providing personalized coaching for leaders can address individual challenges and enhance their ability to lead effectively. Training the entire staff won't be effective if leadership remains unqualified or toxic.

- **...regularly solicit feedback on these initiatives** and remain open to making adjustments based on that feedback. Continuously assess the impact of these programs on workplace dynamics and employee satisfaction to ensure their effectiveness.

Claudia's Expertise in Transformational Coaching

Claudia, through her company SPARK, is having great success with personalized coaching programs for developing effective and empathetic leaders. Her approach focuses on each leader's unique needs, enhancing emotional intelligence, communication skills, and team dynamics. This has led to increased resilience and a positive atmosphere in many organizations.

In her 1:1 and group programs, she is working on both conscious and unconscious levels.

Common Manipulation Tactics

After discussing the psychological traits that can foster manipulative behavior in bosses, we now want to delve into the specific tactics manipulative bosses might employ. By understanding these tactics, you can better recognize and respond to manipulative behavior when it occurs.

Before we do so, please note that these tactics can sometimes overlap, as they all involve similar dynamics of power, control, and manipulation. However, each tactic can manifest in various ways, and understanding their distinct nuances can help identify and respond to them more effectively. Also, remember that these tactics do not operate in isolation but are often employed together, further reinforcing the manipulator's control.

Gaslighting

Gaslighting is a form of psychological manipulation that involves making someone doubt their own memory, perception, or sanity. The term originated from the 1944 movie "Gaslight," in which a husband manipulates his wife into believing she is going insane. He does this by deliberately changing small elements in their environment, like dimming the gaslights in their home, and then insisting that she is imagining the changes. The ultimate goal of gaslighting is to make the victim question their reality and become more reliant on the manipulator.

Here are a few more examples of gaslighting from the movie:

- The husband, Gregory, hides his wife Paula's belongings and then accuses her of being forgetful when she cannot find them. This causes Paula to doubt her memory and question her sanity.

- Gregory constantly undermines Paula's confidence by dismissing her concerns, telling her that she is being overly sensitive or imagining things, which further exacerbates her feelings of self-doubt.

- Gregory isolates Paula from her friends and family, making her more dependent on him and increasing his control over her. He convinces her that she is too unwell to go out or see anyone, further reinforcing her belief that she is losing her mind.

In the workplace, gaslighting can take on several forms, here are some examples:

- **Denying Previous Conversations or Agreements**: A supervisor might insist that a certain conversation never happened, or that the terms of an agreement were different, leading the employee to question their memory or doubt their understanding.

- **Discrediting the Employee's Knowledge or Abilities**: An employee might be told repeatedly that they are not competent enough for certain tasks or that their successful results were just flukes, which can erode their confidence in their skills.

- **Manipulating Information or Situations**: For example, a manager may alter data or misrepresent a scenario to make an employee look irresponsible or unprepared, thus casting doubt on their competence and reliability.

- **Trivializing Feelings or Reactions**: When employees express concerns or dissatisfaction, their feelings might be dismissed as overreactions, or they are accused of being too sensitive, which can make them question their own emotions and reactions.

- **Withholding or Hiding Information**: By strategically withholding information necessary for an employee's tasks or professional advancement, a manipulator can cause significant self-doubt in the employee's decision-making and capabilities.

In her experience within the Fast Moving Consumer Goods industry, **Claudia** encountered a subtle yet impactful instance of gaslighting. This occurred when her supervisor, Paul, under the guise of oversight, deliberately discarded her vacation request into the trash, only to claim later that he never received it and that she went on vacation without his approval. The shock came when Claudia found her request, crumpled and discarded, in the trash bin. Reflecting on this incident ten years later, Paul apologized, admitting that he was overwhelmed at the time and used such tactics to divert attention from his shortcomings.

This incident vividly demonstrates the insidious nature of gaslighting. It's a manipulative tactic that extends beyond personal relationships and into the professional realm. Claudia's experience is a testament to how gaslighting can take form in seemingly minor actions but leave a lasting psychological impact. It highlights the crucial need for awareness and vigilance to recognize and confront gaslighting in any setting.

Exploiting Guilt and Fear

Manipulative bosses can harness employees' feelings of guilt or fear as leverage to assert control and influence their actions. This manipulation can be quite insidious, as it often capitalizes on an individual's natural desire to do well or fit into a team.

- ☺ **Guilt** is a potent tool in a manipulator's arsenal. For instance, a boss may repeatedly reference an employee's past mistake, maintaining a constant undercurrent of guilt. This tactic can be leveraged to push employees into accepting more workload, compromising on their rights, or consenting to unfavorable conditions under the premise of making amends. This manipulative tactic can hinder an employee's ability to stand up for themselves, promoting a culture of anxiety and self-doubt.

- ☺ **Fear** is another tactic that can be manipulated to control behavior. A boss might create an environment of fear by resorting to aggressive behavior, making veiled or explicit threats about job security, or publicly humiliating employees. This climate of fear can stifle open communication, discourage risk-taking, and make employees more prone to manipulation.

Again, the character Miranda Priestly from the film "The Devil Wears Prada" embodies these tactics. Priestly, a high-profile fashion magazine editor, uses her authority and influence to instill fear in her employees. One scene illustrates this when Priestly reprimands her new assistant, played by Anne Hathaway, for failing to meet her high and often unreasonable expectations. She publicly humiliates her assistant and uses her guilt and fear to maintain firm control over her and the rest of the staff.

Undermining Confidence and Self-Esteem

Manipulative bosses often employ tactics aimed at undermining their employees' confidence and self-esteem, making them more pliable and open to manipulation. This tactic typically involves belittling employees, consistently criticizing their work, or making them feel incapable or incompetent. A boss using these tactics can create an environment where employees are constantly second-guessing themselves, eroding their self-confidence and making them more reliant on the boss's approval and guidance. This dynamic consolidates the boss's power and opens the door to further manipulation and control.

This manipulative tactic may include:

- **Constant Criticism**: Continuously pointing out mistakes, often in public, can damage an employee's self-confidence. A boss may exaggerate or magnify errors while downplaying the employee's achievements, creating an imbalance that favors the boss's authority.

- **Negating Accomplishments**: A boss may belittle or dismiss an employee's accomplishments. By doing so, the boss undermines the employees' confidence in their abilities, which in turn increases the employees' reliance on the boss's validation.

- **Creating Self-Doubt**: A manipulative boss may question an employee's decisions or ideas, instilling self-doubt. This method can make the employee more likely to seek the boss's approval, making them easier to control.

The character Sheldon Cooper from the television series "The Big Bang Theory," despite not being a boss, exemplifies this tactic. Sheldon, played by Jim Parsons, frequently belittles his friends and colleagues, often undermining their self-confidence. For example, he consistently criticizes and questions his roommate Leonard's scientific abilities and ideas, creating self-doubt and reliance on Sheldon's approval.

Neurolinguistic Programming (NLP)

NLP is a psychological approach that involves analyzing strategies used by successful individuals and applying them to reach a personal goal. It relates thoughts, language, and patterns of behavior learned through experience to specific outcomes. NLP is not inherently hostile or malicious. In fact, NLP techniques have been successfully applied in various therapeutic contexts, including Rapid Transformational Therapy (RTT®), to promote positive behavioral change and healing. When used ethically, NLP can be a powerful tool for personal growth and transformation. However, like many psychological approaches, NLP can be misused and manipulative bosses might employ NLP techniques to subtly influence their employees' thoughts, behaviors, and emotions.

NLP-based manipulative tactics can involve:

- **Mirroring**: This technique involves mimicking the body language, speech patterns, or attitudes of the person you're interacting with to establish a sense of rapport and familiarity. A manipulative boss might subtly mirror an employee's gestures, posture, or verbal style to build trust and facilitate influence.

- **Pacing and Leading**: This tactic involves matching the rhythm, tone, and content of an employee's communication (pacing) and subtly changing one's behavior to guide the employee's behavior (leading). Over time, the employee begins to unconsciously follow the boss's lead.

- **Embedded Commands**: This technique involves embedding commands within a larger sentence or paragraph. These commands might not be overtly noticeable but can influence an employee's thought process or behavior. For example, a boss might say, "While you're working on the report, you might find it helpful to incorporate the latest sales data," subtly directing the employee to include specific information.

- **Use of Metaphors**: Metaphors can be used to convey complex ideas or instructions in a way that bypasses conscious objections. A manipulative boss can implant ideas or suggestions in an employee's mind by telling a story or using an analogy. For example, a manipulative boss might say, "We need all hands on deck, like a crew in a storm," suggesting that everyone must work overtime without directly ordering it. By telling a story or using an analogy, the boss can implant the idea of urgency and collective effort in an employee's mind, subtly coercing them into working longer hours without an explicit directive.

- **Anchoring**: This involves creating a connection between an emotional state and a specific trigger, such as a gesture, word, or tone of voice. A manipulative boss might use anchoring by associating positive emotions with compliance or negative emotions with dissent. For instance, they might express approval or praise (triggering positive emotions) when an employee agrees with their ideas, thereby anchoring submission to positive reinforcement.

An example of a character who employs NLP tactics is Dr. Hannibal Lecter, portrayed by Anthony Hopkins in "The Silence of the Lambs." Dr. Lecter uses his advanced understanding of human psychology, including NLP, to manipulate others, though his usage is far from ethical or typical of a workplace setting.

One instance in the film that showcases Dr. Lecter's use of NLP techniques occurs during his interactions with FBI trainee Clarice Starling. He often mirrors Clarice's language and body language, building a rapport and subtly influencing her perceptions and responses. A notable scene involves Lecter subtly leading Clarice through a traumatic childhood memory. He paces his language and tone with hers, creating a connection, then gently guides her deeper into the memory.

When **I, Markus**, sat down for my appraisal talk with Ethan, my boss at the time, he used a compelling metaphor to describe my career trajectory. He likened it to approaching a ramp, one that would supposedly lead to a significant upward path in my career. The message was clear: keep up the speed, maintain the effort, and this ramp will catapult you to greater heights. Yet, as the conversation unfolded, it became apparent that the ramp was an illusion; there was no concrete plan or strategy behind his words.

While Ethan's initial feedback was somewhat positive, the formal rating ultimately turned out to be dishearteningly negative, which sharply contrasted with the promising future he had depicted. It was as if he dangled a carrot in front of me, motivating me without any substance to back it up. The more we spoke, the more I realized that this vision of an accelerated career path was a facade. It was a tactic to keep me driving forward, yet the destination, that promising ramp, wasn't really there — it was just a mirage.

This experience was a stark reminder that without a solid plan or genuine support, motivational words can be manipulative, encouraging hard work that might not lead anywhere. It taught me the importance of seeking clarity and tangible goals in career discussions rather than getting swept away by persuasive but empty rhetoric.

Emotional Blackmail

At its core, emotional blackmail is a form of psychological manipulation. It occurs when someone, whether friend, family member, romantic partner, or coworker, uses your emotions against you. They exploit your vulnerabilities to achieve their objectives. This kind of manipulation is particularly effective because emotion beats logic, always: even the most rational individuals can find themselves swayed or manipulated when their emotions are skillfully leveraged.

- Emotional blackmailers often employ tactics such as guilt-tripping, threats, ultimatums, or playing the victim. These methods make you feel obligated to comply with their demands.

- They might, for example, invoke potential negative consequences for noncompliance, such as a poor performance review or delayed promotion, playing on fears and insecurities.

- A manipulative boss might also exploit an employee's empathy and goodwill. They could use personal crises or emotional displays as leverage, eliciting sympathy or obligation. This tactic can pressure employees to work harder, stay later, or extend themselves beyond their official duties, overriding logical boundaries of professional conduct.

A vivid example of emotional blackmail in popular media is – once again – found in the character Miranda Priestly, who frequently uses emotional blackmail to manipulate her assistant, Andrea. For instance, when Miranda tasks Andrea with an impossible-to-fulfill assignment — acquiring an unpublished Harry Potter manuscript for her kids — she implies that failure could cost Andrea her job. Here, fear and obligation become tools of manipulation, showcasing how emotions can overpower logical assessments of the situation.

When **I, Markus,** was facing a challenging period due to my son's serious health diagnosis, I found myself under immense familial pressure. This situation demanded frequent therapies, doctor visits, and constant care due to his developmental delays, which inevitably affected my performance at work. Recognizing the need to balance my professional life with these pressing family responsibilities, I approached my new boss, Ethan, with a request to work part-time. Given our company's reputation as "family-friendly," I believed this would be a straightforward request.

However, Ethan's response was unexpectedly conditional. He required me to seek the approval of every department head I worked with as a legal consultant before he would consider my request. This requirement was met with surprise from the department heads, as they found it unusual but were nonetheless supportive of my situation.

Once my part-time status was approved, Ethan began to subtly use this 'favor' as a means of emotional blackmail. He frequently reminded me of the company's support during my family crisis, often making statements like "We are investing in you now, and someday you will pay us back."

This sentiment reached a crescendo during my annual performance review. In a disconcerting move, Ethan projected a photo of my family on the screen (yes, he did, and we'll come back to that later!). He began the meeting by highlighting how the company was aiding my family life, implying a debt of gratitude I owed to the company and him.

This experience was a clear example of emotional blackmail in the workplace, where personal circumstances were leveraged to create a sense of indebtedness and control.

Teaser: The subsequent meeting I insisted on having with my boss after this performance review finally went south turned out to be yet another episode of attempting to break an employee using manipulative techniques. Moreover, it will reveal how even a skilled manipulator can be caught off guard. Stay tuned; we'll get to it later.

Triangulation

Triangulation is a manipulative technique involving the use of a third party to exert influence or control. In the workplace, manipulative bosses might employ triangulation by relaying information or criticism indirectly through another employee, thereby avoiding confrontation. This tactic can foster tension and mistrust among team members, facilitating the boss's ability to maintain control.

Additional examples of triangulation in the workplace include:

- **Assigning Blame through Third Parties:** A boss might blame a third party for unpopular decisions or failures, distancing themselves from responsibility and any negative repercussions, thus manipulating team perceptions and sentiments.

- **Playing Employees Against Each Other:** A boss could tell one employee something in confidence about another, in hopes that it will be shared and cause rifts or competition, effectively weakening alliances among staff.

- **Spreading Gossip or Rumors:** By disseminating misleading or harmful information about individuals or groups within the organization, a manipulative boss can create divisions and rivalries that enhance their own power and control.

A noteworthy example of a character utilizing triangulation is Petyr Baelish, or "Littlefinger," from the television series "Game of Thrones." Littlefinger is notorious for manipulating relationships and events to his advantage. One instance of his use of triangulation is when he uses Lysa Arryn to poison her husband and then blames the Lannisters, inciting a conflict that ignites the series' main events. Littlefinger's manipulations foster mistrust and tension among the key players, allowing him to maintain control and advance his ambitions.

Playing the Victim

Playing the victim, also known as victim-playing or self-victimization, is a manipulation tactic wherein an individual portrays themselves as a victim of circumstances or someone else's behavior in order to gain sympathy, empathy, or concession from others. In the workplace context, a manipulative boss might use this tactic to evade responsibility or manipulate employees into doing more work, taking the blame for errors, or tolerating unacceptable behavior.

- For instance, a boss might blame personal problems, such as a difficult divorce or health issues, for their poor behavior or performance at work. By eliciting sympathy, they can manipulate employees to pick up the slack or overlook inappropriate actions. This tactic can be particularly insidious because it manipulates the target's natural empathy and desire to help.

- Also, a boss might claim they are under extreme stress and need their employees to work longer hours, even if the workload does not warrant it. By positioning themselves as victims, the boss can manipulate employees' emotions and coerce them into meeting unreasonable demands.

One famous portrayal of a character who often resorts to playing the victim is Cersei Lannister from the television series "Game of Thrones." Despite her position of power, Cersei frequently uses her hardships and past traumas as tools for manipulation. For instance, she often references her love for her children and the lengths she must go to protect them, eliciting sympathy and justifying her ruthless actions.

In one scene, Cersei has an intense conversation with her brother, Tyrion, in which she says, "I am a lioness. I will not cringe for them." By projecting herself as a protective mother fighting against adversity, she effectively plays the victim card to manipulate those around her.

Divide and Conquer

The divide-and-conquer tactic is a strategy that military strategists and politicians have used for centuries. It involves creating divisions among individuals or groups, making them easier to control. In the context of workplace manipulation, bosses might use this approach to foster competition or discord among team members, preventing them from uniting against unfair treatment or practices.

Examples of divide-and-conquer behavior in the workplace may include:

- Encouraging competition or rivalry among team members

- Highlighting the differences between employees to sow discord

- Giving preferential treatment to certain employees to create resentment

- Withholding information from specific individuals to create an imbalance of power

- Deliberately miscommunicating or twisting information to confuse or mislead employees

Consider the character of Lord Voldemort from J.K. Rowling's Harry Potter series as an illustration of a figure using the divide and conquer approach. Though not a traditional boss in a corporate sense, Voldemort cleverly manipulates and turns his followers, the Death Eaters, against one another. This keeps them from uniting and potentially rebelling against him.

In one particular scene from "Harry Potter and the Goblet of Fire," Voldemort tells his Death Eaters, "I expect more than mere cooperation. I expect a vow of loyalty." He fosters fear and discord among his followers, often punishing them severely for failures while showing favoritism to others, ensuring they remain divided and under his control.

Micromanagement and Control

Micromanagement can serve as a devious tactic employed by manipulative bosses. In essence, it refers to an excessive involvement in an employee's work, extending to a level that feels overly intrusive and controlling. Manipulative bosses may resort to micromanagement not only as a tool to assert their authority but also as a mechanism to exert continuous control over their team members.

⊛ Imagine a scenario where every minor detail of your work is under constant scrutiny, making you feel as though you are incapable of completing tasks independently. This can induce a sense of dependency and insecurity, as you might start second-guessing your abilities and looking up to the boss for every little guidance. Such a situation is ideal for a manipulative boss, as it makes it much easier for them to steer your actions according to their whims.

Take the case of the character Mr. Burns from "The Simpsons," a typical micromanager. His obsessive control over every aspect of the nuclear power plant and his employees' lives underlines the potential of micromanagement as a manipulative tactic. He uses his position to instill fear and uncertainty among his employees, thereby maintaining a stronghold on their actions.

When I, Markus, was assigned to create a detailed report for a scientific project requiring financial support from our company, I encountered a clear example of micromanagement myself. While it initially seemed like a routine task, it quickly turned into a lesson in control and manipulation.

After completing a thorough evaluation, I presented the report to my boss, Ethan, expecting a discussion on the content. However, to my surprise, Ethan was more interested in interrogating the exact steps of my process rather than the conclusions of the report itself. As an experienced lawyer, this level of scrutiny was new to me. I was used to having my legal expertise trusted and respected. Ethan's approach made me feel as though I was back at the beginning of my career, inexperienced and unsure. This was not only uncomfortable but also quite demoralizing.

At the end of the day, my report remained largely unchanged, but my emotions and morale certainly suffered. This was a clear case of micromanagement used not just to oversee work but to control and manipulate, trying to undermine my confidence and professional self-esteem.

Playing on Emotions

Playing on emotions involves manipulating someone's feelings to achieve a desired outcome. Recognizing when a boss is playing on your emotions can be challenging. However, once you are able to differentiate genuine emotion from calculated manipulation, it will enable you to maintain your autonomy. Making decisions based on rational thinking helps safeguard against emotional manipulation.

The tactic can manifest in several ways, including:

- **Excessive Praise:** A boss might excessively praise an employee's work to encourage them to take on additional responsibilities beyond their current role.

- **Emotional Manipulation for Loyalty:** Manipulating an employee's emotions to gain their loyalty and trust, potentially for ulterior motives. For instance, a manager might share selectively personal achievements or challenges to create a bond that compels the employee to commit more deeply to company goals.

- **Exploiting Empathy:** A boss may exploit an employee's empathy or compassion by sharing personal sob stories or struggles, which guilts the employee into overworking or accommodating unreasonable demands.

When you're wondering whether the behavior of your boss is genuine or an attempt at emotional manipulation, ask yourself these questions:

- **Does this behavior align with my boss's usual conduct?** Is the behavior consistent with how your boss typically acts, or does it only appear in situations where he/she stands to gain something?

- **Is this behavior common in my workplace or industry?** Compare the behavior to standard practices in your professional environment. Does it seem out of place or in line with typical managerial actions?

- **How does this behavior affect my decision-making?** Does it make you feel pressured to act in ways you wouldn't normally consider reasonable or in your best interest?

- **Is there a fair exchange?** Look at the balance of what's being asked and what's being offered in return. Does the interaction feel mutually beneficial, or does it seem one-sided?

- **What does my gut tell me?** Listen to your instincts. If something consistently feels manipulative or makes you uncomfortable, it might need further scrutiny.

Returning to popular media, take the example of the movie character Miranda Priestly, known for her manipulative behavior. In one instance, Priestly wins the sympathy of her assistant, Andrea, by sharing her troubles, only to leverage this sympathy to compel Andrea to fulfill demanding tasks.

A subtle form of manipulation in the workplace encountered by **Claudia** involves bosses nominating employees as "advocates" for specific tasks or projects. This experience, drawn from her years in the pharmaceutical industry and insights as a practicing psychotherapist, highlights a nuanced strategy. Bosses present this nomination as an honor, suggesting a high level of trust and confidence in the employee. They often use flattering terms like "pioneer" or "early bird" to evoke a sense of pride and empowerment.

However, from Claudia's observations, this is often a façade. In reality, these employees are often unknowingly placed as front-line buffers. They are positioned to absorb any potential criticism or backlash, shielding the boss from any negative consequences. This tactic is a clear example of playing on an employee's emotions — using their desire for recognition and trust to manipulate them into a potentially compromising position. It demonstrates how manipulative bosses can exploit the emotional vulnerabilities of employees, masking their true intentions under the guise of opportunity and empowerment, thereby leaving the employees exposed to being scapegoated.

Exploiting Power Dynamics

We have talked about Power dynamics before as they play a pivotal role in any organization. Individuals who hold positions of authority wield a certain level of influence over their subordinates. Unfortunately, manipulative bosses often misuse this authority to manipulate situations to their benefit and maintain control over their employees.

Examples of exploiting power dynamics in the workplace may include:

- Exerting undue influence or pressure on employees to comply with unreasonable demands

- Favoritism or exclusion, whereby certain employees are given preferential treatment, creating an imbalance of power

- Withholding resources, rewards, or information as a means of maintaining control

- Using the authority to intimidate, belittle, or undermine employees

- Encouraging a culture of fear or uncertainty to keep employees in a constant state of apprehension

So, be on alert when you spot a boss in your organization who consistently leverages their authority to exert undue influence, shows favoritism, withholds crucial resources, or creates an environment of fear and uncertainty.

The Role of Workplace Culture in Fostering Manipulative Behavior

The Impact of Company Values and Culture

The ethos and culture of an organization critically shape the behavior of its workforce, from top executives down to entry-level employees. When an enterprise cultivates a nurturing work environment — valuing teamwork, collaboration, and mutual respect — it significantly curbs the possibility of manipulative behavior taking root.

For instance, consider a corporation that espouses transparency and open communication. In such an ecosystem, employees can express their worries and address complications without fear, thereby reducing the space in which manipulative superiors can maneuver.

Conversely, a toxic work atmosphere can encourage rivalry, mistrust, and unhealthy competition, providing fertile ground for manipulative superiors to thrive. In these scenarios, employees may feel forced to adopt manipulative tactics themselves as a means of professional survival or advancement. If an organizational culture rewards aggressive conduct and ruthless competition, it might incentivize staff members to sabotage their colleagues or resort to manipulative tactics to climb the corporate ladder.

The Influence of Lenient Management Styles

Management styles significantly shape the behaviors deemed acceptable within a workplace. A lenient stance towards manipulative behaviors can often inadvertently endorse such conduct.

When higher management fails to address manipulative behaviors or seemingly rewards them, it sends a potent message: such actions are acceptable. Consequently, a permissive environment may develop, where superiors feel at liberty to utilize manipulation as a means to their ends without fearing significant repercussions.

Such lenient management styles can normalize manipulative behaviors, integrating them into the organization's culture. This normalization can impede employees' ability to voice concerns or challenge manipulative tactics, perpetuating a cycle of manipulation and control.

How Toxic Work Environments Enable Manipulative Behavior

Toxic work environments are characterized by high levels of stress, burnout, and interpersonal conflict. They often result from poor management practices, lack of clear communication, and a disregard for employee well-being. In such environments, manipulative bosses can exploit the chaos and uncertainty to assert control over employees. They may use manipulation tactics to maintain their authority, undermine the confidence of their employees, and shift the blame for their failures.

Imagine a company where communication is poor, and employees are constantly pressured to meet unrealistic deadlines or goals. A manipulative boss might take advantage of the situation by pitting employees against each other, creating a sense of urgency, and blaming employees for failures. This kind of toxic environment can make employees feel isolated and afraid to speak up, allowing manipulative behavior to continue unchecked.

Take for instance the high-pressure environment in "The Devil Wears Prada," where the ruthless editor-in-chief rules the fashion magazine with an iron fist. Remember that iconic scene where Miranda casually tosses her coat and bag onto her assistant's desk, expecting her to attend to every whim? This movie perfectly captures the essence of a toxic work environment where manipulation, fear, and unreasonable demands are the norm.

Or do you remember when Homer Simpson had to deal with his manipulative boss, Mr. Burns? In the episode "Last Exit to Springfield" (Season 4, Episode 17), Mr. Burns tries to cut the dental plan for his employees to save money. When the employees decide to strike and Homer becomes the union leader, Mr. Burns employs various manipulative tactics to break the strike and undermine Homer's authority. For instance, Mr. Burns invites Homer to his office and attempts to bribe him with a luxurious private office and other perks in exchange for convincing the employees to give up the dental plan. This scene showcases a manipulative boss using bribery and exploiting an employee's weakness to achieve his goals. It also demonstrates how a toxic work environment, created by a boss prioritizing profits over employee welfare, can enable manipulative behavior.

In a striking parallel to these modern workplace dynamics, the documentary "**The Happy Worker – Or How Work Was Sabotaged**" reveals how tactics from the "Simple Sabotage Field Manual," originally designed by the Office of Strategic Services during World War II for undermining enemy operations, eerily resonate in today's corporate settings. This manual advised ordinary citizens in occupied territories on how to employ nonviolent methods to disrupt organizational efficiency, including tactics like encouraging unnecessary bureaucracy, promoting managerial interference, and fostering inefficient employee behaviors.

The documentary draws a thought-provoking comparison between these wartime sabotage strategies and the manipulative practices observed in toxic workplaces today. It suggests that, although not purposeful sabotage as in wartime, these behaviors can have a similar effect: diminishing workplace efficiency, breeding a toxic atmosphere, and contributing to employee burnout and dissatisfaction. Including this perspective in our discussion about toxic work environments provides a historical lens to understand how seemingly innocuous practices can evolve into manipulative behaviors that profoundly impact organizational health and employee well-being.

We highly recommend you watch John Webster's insightful documentary, "The Happy Worker – Or How Work Was Sabotaged." This film humorously yet incisively uncovers the systemic issues in today's corporate world, revealing how they contribute to creating toxic work environments. It's a crucial exploration for you to understand the complex dynamics that affect both organizational health and employee well-being.

- **Production Year:** 2022
- **Director:** John Webster
- **Country:** Finland
- **Duration:** 78 minutes
- **Available on:** ARTE and other streaming platforms

The Role of Leadership in Shaping Workplace Culture

Leaders play a critical role in shaping the workplace culture and setting the tone for employee behavior. When leaders model ethical behavior, prioritize employee well-being, and encourage open communication, they foster a positive work culture that minimizes manipulative behavior.

Think about a leader who actively listens to employee concerns, addresses issues fairly and transparently, and encourages collaboration and support among team members. They create an environment where manipulative behavior is less likely to occur. Employees in such a culture will feel more confident in addressing any instances of manipulation they encounter, knowing that their concerns will be taken seriously and addressed appropriately.

However, when leaders engage in manipulative tactics or turn a blind eye to such behavior, they contribute to a toxic work environment that allows manipulative bosses to thrive. Suppose a high-level executive is known for using manipulative tactics to achieve their goals and faces no repercussions. In that case, this sends a message to other leaders within the organization that such behavior is acceptable, leading to a culture where manipulation becomes the norm.

It is essential for leaders to actively promote a culture of trust, accountability, and respect to prevent manipulative behavior in the workplace.

High-Stress and High-Stakes Work Environments

High-stress and high-stakes work environments can inadvertently foster manipulative behavior. In situations where there is constant pressure to meet unrealistic deadlines or goals, outperform sales targets, or navigate complex decision-making processes, bosses might resort to manipulation as a means of maintaining control and ensuring desired outcomes.

Such a tense atmosphere can lead to the normalization of manipulative tactics. They may be seen as essential tools for success, rendering them a generally accepted part of conducting business. This normalization can blur the lines between appropriate and manipulative behavior, making it more difficult for employees to identify and confront such practices.

Consider, for example, the world of investment banking or high-level consultancy. These fields are notoriously known for their high-stress environment with grueling hours and intense competition. Managers in these situations might resort to tactics like setting up "win-lose" scenarios, where employees are forced to compete against each other for favorable assignments, or by using fear tactics, such as threatening job loss if certain ambitious targets aren't met.

Alternatively, consider high-stakes industries such as technology start-ups, where there's immense pressure to innovate and outperform competitors. A boss might manipulate by constantly shifting goalposts, imposing unreasonable expectations, and creating a sense of urgency that leads to employees overworking and making sacrifices in their personal lives.

If you understand the role workplace culture plays in enabling manipulative behavior, you can empower yourself. You'll become more aware of the factors contributing to such behavior and can take proactive steps to address it in your work environment. In the sections to come, we'll guide you on how to detect and tackle manipulative behavior in your workplace.

Lack of Accountability Structures

One factor that can contribute to the presence and persistence of manipulative behavior in the workplace is the lack of appropriate accountability structures. When there are no clear expectations for behavior, no mechanisms (such as whistleblower hotlines) to report or address misconduct, and no consequences for harmful actions, it's easier for manipulative bosses to operate with impunity.

Without proper accountability, manipulative bosses are less likely to face repercussions for their actions. In some cases, they may even be rewarded for results obtained through manipulative tactics, further reinforcing their behavior. This situation harms the immediate victims of manipulation and contributes to a toxic work culture overall.

In a well-structured workplace, systems would be in place to report and address manipulative behaviors. This might include a confidential reporting mechanism, a fair investigation process, and a straightforward disciplinary procedure for misconduct. Supervisors would be trained on handling reports of manipulation, and employees would be educated on their rights and responsibilities.

In line with the discussion on the importance of accountability structures, **Claudia**, as previously noted, has observed a critical shortfall in many organizations. While whistleblower hotlines and similar mechanisms are sometimes established with the intent of addressing misconduct, her experience has shown that they can often be (intentionally) toothless and not lead to any significant consequences for reported manipulative behaviors. This lack of effective enforcement not only undermines the purpose of such accountability mechanisms but also perpetuates a culture where manipulative tactics are tacitly condoned. Employees, aware of the ineffectiveness of these hotlines, may feel even more discouraged from reporting, knowing that their concerns are unlikely to result in meaningful action. This creates a scenario where, despite the presence of formal structures, manipulation continues unchallenged, further eroding trust and respect within the workplace.

An example of a lack of accountability structure leading to manipulative behavior can be seen in the character of Frank Underwood from the TV series "House of Cards." As an influential political figure, Underwood often employs manipulative tactics to gain control and power. However, he is rarely held responsible for his actions due to a lack of accountability structures. Instead, his behavior is frequently overlooked, ignored, or even rewarded, leading to a toxic environment where manipulation is normalized and unchecked.

In summary, a lack of accountability structures can allow manipulative behavior to thrive in the workplace. Implementing effective accountability mechanisms is a key step towards deterring such behavior and fostering a healthier, more respectful work culture.

Fostering a Healthy Work Culture to Prevent Manipulation

As key drivers of organizational culture and policy, those in HR, management, and ownership positions hold a significant role in shaping an environment that discourages manipulative behavior. Fostering a healthy, ethical, and respectful work culture should be at the heart of your approach. Here's how you can lead this change:

- **Establishing clear values and expectations:** As a figurehead, your communication about the company's values and expectations concerning ethical behavior and mutual respect should be explicit and transparent. Furthermore, you must ensure these principles are upheld consistently throughout all organizational levels.

- **Providing training and resources:** Lead the charge in offering essential training and resources that will equip your employees with the knowledge and skills to recognize and handle manipulative behavior. By facilitating an open dialogue about workplace dynamics, you provide much-needed support for those grappling with manipulative superiors or colleagues.

- **Encouraging open communication:** As leaders, endorse a culture where employees can openly express their concerns without fear of retaliation. This proactive stance can help identify and mitigate manipulative behavior before it escalates into a larger issue.

- **Holding leaders accountable:** Accountability must be integral to your organization's leadership ethos. By swiftly and fairly addressing instances of manipulative behavior, you convey an unequivocal message that such actions have no place within your company.

- **Promoting teamwork and collaboration:** Champion an environment where teamwork and collaboration are the norm. Encouraging employees to support one another towards shared objectives decreases the opportunities for manipulative behavior, leading to a more supportive and positive workplace.

By initiating and promoting a manipulation-free work culture, you, as leaders, play a crucial role in minimizing manipulative behaviors. The outcome? A more supportive, positive, and productive environment for your entire workforce.

Case Studies of Manipulative Bosses and Toxic Work Cultures

Case Study 1: The Micromanaging Boss

Let's explore the case of Helen, who works in a marketing agency. The agency is a well-established firm with an impressive portfolio of clients. Helen's boss, Jessica, is the Head of the Marketing Department.

Jessica, in her mid-forties, has worked her way up the ranks and is recognized for her remarkable expertise in the field. However, her management style presents a significant challenge for the team – she is a micromanager.

Jessica insists on reviewing all work personally and controls even the minutest details of every project. When a team member creates a draft for a client proposal, Jessica doesn't just provide feedback; she rewrites it entirely. She requires her team to cc her on all emails and wants to approve routine correspondence before it is sent.

This level of control extends to work schedules as well. Jessica likes to know where everyone is and what they are doing at all times. She insists on daily updates and frequent check-in meetings that often feel more like interrogations than collaborative discussions. She believes that this intense involvement ensures the highest quality of work.

However, this micromanagement has profound effects on the team's morale and productivity. Helen and her colleagues constantly feel under scrutiny, which creates an environment of anxiety and stress. Their creativity is stifled because they fear Jessica's criticism if they deviate from her preferred way of doing things.

Moreover, the team members are losing confidence in their abilities. They're reluctant to make decisions independently because they anticipate Jessica will change them. This has led to decreased productivity, as employees spend more time reporting their actions than actually working.

Despite their frustration, the team feels powerless. Jessica's control is so pervasive that they can't see a way to change the situation. It's clear that unless Jessica changes her management style or the upper management intervenes, the work environment will remain oppressive, and employee turnover could increase.

Through this case study, we can see the damaging effects of micromanagement. It's a cautionary tale about the importance of balanced leadership and the dangers of excessive control in a managerial role.

Case Study 2: The Emotional Blackmailer

In this case study, we examine the experiences of Alex, a junior software engineer at a fast-growing tech startup. Alex's boss, Brian, is the Chief Technology Officer (CTO) of the company.

Brian is a charismatic leader, revered for his technical prowess and sharp strategic mind. However, there's another side to his leadership style that's not as commendable – Brian is an emotional blackmailer.

Whenever the team faces tight project deadlines, or an urgent software bug to fix, Brian is known to exert emotional pressure on the team. He often tells them how disappointed he would be if the work is not completed in time, emphasizing how much he has personally invested in the team and how their failure could jeopardize the company's reputation.

Moreover, Brian is adept at exploiting personal dynamics. If a team member has to leave work early for personal reasons or requests vacation time, Brian reminds them of how hard he works and how he rarely takes time off, subtly suggesting that they should do the same.

Even performance reviews are not immune to Brian's emotional blackmail. He's known to remind employees of the times they've let him down right before discussing their performance, instilling a sense of guilt and making them more likely to accept less-than-deserved ratings or to take on extra work without protest.

Alex and his colleagues feel constantly guilt-tripped and manipulated, which has created an environment of stress and fear. Despite their love for their work, the emotional strain leads to burnout, job dissatisfaction, and decreased productivity. Yet, the power imbalance and Brian's charismatic persona make it difficult for the team to voice their concerns or seek change.

This case study highlights the harmful impacts of emotional blackmail in the workplace. It underscores the importance of emotional intelligence in leadership and demonstrates how manipulation can erode trust and productivity within a team.

Case Study 3: The Gaslighting Boss

This case study revolves around Sarah, a creative designer at a leading advertising firm, and her boss, Emily, the creative director. Emily is an experienced professional known for her groundbreaking work in the industry. However, her impressive track record is overshadowed by her manipulative management style, characterized by gaslighting.

Sarah often finds herself confused after meetings with Emily. They'll discuss a project's direction, Sarah will start working on it, and then Emily will abruptly change her feedback or deny previous discussions. Sarah once worked over a weekend to meet Emily's sudden change in project specifications, only for Emily to question why Sarah was not following the original plan.

This pattern repeats frequently, with Emily altering her instructions or denying statements she has previously made. This gaslighting behavior has left Sarah questioning her understanding and memory, which has subsequently shaken her confidence.

Sarah's experience isn't unique within the team. Emily's gaslighting also extends to other members, causing widespread uncertainty and confusion. Employees are now spending significant time double-checking and triple-checking their work, hesitant to rely on their judgment. This has resulted in a slow-paced, stressful environment where creativity and innovation are stifled.

Gaslighting, as exemplified in this case, can inflict substantial psychological damage. It undermines the confidence and morale of employees and creates an environment of fear and second-guessing. In the long term, this toxic atmosphere can lead to high employee turnover and deteriorated team performance.

This case study underscores the significance of trust and clear communication in leadership roles. It highlights the need for leaders to encourage confidence and autonomy in their teams rather than employing manipulative tactics such as gaslighting.

Case Study 4: The Toxic Work Culture

Our next case study takes us into a state-owned company steeped in government connections and political ties. Despite the prestige associated with this enterprise, it harbors a deep-seated toxic work culture.

Most employees here boast impressive qualifications, many of them having advanced university degrees and even a few with habilitations. However, these credentials often don't reap the benefits they should due to the company's hiring and promotion practices, which heavily favor connections over qualifications. It's a common scenario where employees land their roles not due to their academic achievements or expertise but because of their political affiliations or personal networks.

Promotion opportunities in this company are few and far between, creating an intensely competitive environment. The stakes are high, given the significant salary increases associated with climbing the career ladder. But those who ascend are typically not the ones with the most merit but those who are adept at "playing the game" – ingratiating themselves with the right people.

This promotion practice has an incredibly demoralizing effect on the highly qualified and competent employees who see their hard work and dedication overlooked. The sense of constant competition and the realization that it's not their capability or commitment but their connections that will determine their advancement breeds disillusionment and frustration.

Moreover, this situation can lead to a host of psychological issues, such as decreased self-esteem, anxiety, and even burnout. After all, continuously striving for recognition and advancement, only to be bypassed for reasons unrelated to merit, can take a severe toll on one's mental health. It's not surprising, then, that this toxic culture stifles innovation and decreases overall productivity.

This case underscores the critical importance of merit-based hiring and promotion practices in cultivating a healthy work culture. It serves as a stark warning – while political and personal connections might yield short-term gains, they can't replace the long-term value of qualifications, experience, and dedication, nor can they cultivate a psychologically healthy and productive work environment.

Case Study 5: The Deflecting and Scapegoating Boss

In this case study, we explore the manipulative tactics of Carol, a division head in a large pharmaceutical company. Her behavior aligns with several manipulation tactics outlined earlier in this book.

The Art of Ambiguity

Carol frequently employs vague language to deflect responsibility. She often says, "You know, it's all political," without ever clarifying her meaning. While not a textbook example of Gaslighting, such ambiguity can make employees question their understanding of workplace dynamics. This tactic allows Carol to avoid accountability and fosters confusion and self-doubt among her team members.

The Scapegoat Strategy

When a project executed under Carol's guidance faces disapproval from upper management, she doesn't hesitate to throw her team under the bus. Rather than defending them, she portrays them as incompetent, effectively **Undermining Confidence and Self-Esteem**. This not only demoralizes her team but also protects her image at their expense. By blaming her team in front of management, she also employs the **Divide and Conquer** strategy, ensuring she remains the central figure in the office dynamics.

Emotional Manipulation

Carol often plays on her team's emotions, particularly guilt and fear, making them more susceptible to her manipulative behavior. This aligns with the tactic of **Playing on Emotions**, where emotional triggers are used to exert control.

By understanding Carol's tactics, you equip yourself to recognize and counter similar manipulative behaviors in your workplace. We will revisit this case study later to discuss effective strategies for responding to such tactics.

Case Study 6: The Overbearing Supervisor

Sticking with the pharma industry, let's dive into another real-world scenario. This time, we're looking at Angelika, another former boss of Claudia who really took micromanagement to the next level. Angelika, driven by a fear of missing details, had adopted a highly rigid system for handling communication. She insisted on having every email printed and organized into binders, which then became the centerpieces of her notoriously lengthy team meetings. These

Jour Fixe sessions, often lasting up to four hours, involved a detailed review of each email with relevant team members. While intended for thoroughness, this approach proved to be a time-consuming and inefficient practice that detracted from actual productive work.

Angelika's need for control was further exemplified by her daily routine of arriving at the office with a trolley full of these email binders. This practice not only symbolized her micromanagement style but also highlighted her inability to delegate and trust her team. Even during her sick days, Angelika's system persisted, requiring an assistant to print and deliver the emails to her home.

This behavior, rooted in Angelika's anxiety and her fear of losing control, had significant repercussions. It led to decreased productivity as the team spent more time reviewing emails than focusing on core tasks. Employee morale suffered greatly under the weight of these exhaustive and unproductive meetings, leading to frustration and potential burnout. Additionally, the overemphasis on minor details stifled creativity and strategic thinking, hampering the team's ability to innovate and adapt.

Angelika's case serves as a stark reminder of the detrimental effects of excessive micromanagement in the workplace. It underscores the need for a balanced approach to leadership, emphasizing the importance of trusting and empowering team members. Such a shift from overbearing supervision to a more trusting and autonomous work environment can significantly enhance team morale, foster creativity, and improve overall productivity.

Case Study 7: The Master of Power Dynamics

Judith, a mid-level manager in the Fast Moving Consumer Goods industry, exemplifies her mastery over power dynamics with subtle yet impactful comments like, "What, you're leaving already?" at 7 PM. Such seemingly innocuous remarks are loaded with implications, instilling in her employees a sense of obligation and fear of not meeting her unstated expectations, thereby exploiting the power dynamics prevalent within the workplace. This manipulation method is not just about overworking her team but setting a tone where her approval becomes essential for their sense of job security and worth.

Judith's approach to leveraging her position is emblematic of a broader pattern of behavior exhibited by managers like her, who understand how to manipulate power dynamics within the workplace. For instance, in team meetings, a boss might single out an employee for praise due to their willingness to work late, subtly setting expectations for the rest of the team. This behavior, while seemingly promoting dedication, actually serves to instill a sense of competition among team members, undermining collaboration and fostering an environment where employees feel pressured to sacrifice personal time to meet these unstated standards of commitment.

Moreover, during performance reviews, such bosses may emphasize the importance of "team spirit" and "going the extra mile" as benchmarks for assessing an employee's value to the team. This insinuates that those who do not regularly stay late or volunteer for extra work are not fully contributing to the team's success. This tactic cleverly disguises manipulative intentions as a call for teamwork and dedication, reinforcing the manager's control by implying that professional worth and team loyalty are measured by the willingness to prioritize work over personal well-being.

Case Study 8: The Toxic Remote Work Culture

Sherry, a dedicated nurse educator, transitioned to online teaching to better balance her professional aspirations with family needs. Initially, this shift was supported by a flexible work arrangement and a supportive administration, allowing Sherry to thrive and deliver exceptional work.

However, the landscape dramatically shifted due to significant administrative turnover, which introduced new leadership that was less familiar and supportive of the nuances of remote work. This change ushered in a toxic work culture that not only challenged Sherry's work-life harmony but also began eroding the once positive and empowering remote work environment. The new leadership's approach, marked by a lack of trust and a tendency towards micromanagement, contrasted starkly with the previous administration's values. As Sherry's remote colleagues resigned or were not rehired due to more stringent remote work agreements, she found herself advocating for the rights of remote employees, fighting against the growing mistrust and micromanagement that had started to permeate her work life.

This case highlights the critical aspect of remote work under toxic leadership: the dependency on trust and clear communication. The inability of the new leadership to trust and effectively communicate with their team created an environment where remote workers, in particular, felt isolated, undervalued, and over-scrutinized. Sherry's experience underscores the negative impact such leadership has on morale, productivity, and employee retention.

Furthermore, Sherry's advocacy points to the importance of empowering remote employees and the role of constructive leadership in fostering a healthy remote work culture. It demonstrates that leadership preparedness, empathy, and effective communication are key to maintaining a positive and productive remote work environment.

As organizations continue to navigate the complexities of remote work, Sherry's story serves as a reminder of the pivotal role leadership plays in either cultivating a supportive and inclusive culture or contributing to a toxic workplace environment.

The Pandemic Effect: Exacerbating Workplace Manipulation

At the turn of the 2020s, the world was thrust into an unprecedented era. Beyond the clear and immediate health implications, the COVID-19 pandemic began to reshape the very fabric of society. The rhythm of daily life, the pulse of bustling cities, and the dynamics of workplace interactions all underwent rapid transformations.

Offices once filled with chatter and the rhythm of daily work shifted to the virtual hum of online meetings and notifications. As businesses scurried to adapt to these unforeseen challenges, a new landscape of professional interactions was formed. Within this landscape, while many found resilience and innovation, several underlying issues began to surface more prominently.

Amidst the turmoil of the pandemic, various psychological issues began to surface with greater intensity. Individuals grappled with feelings of isolation, heightened anxiety, depression, and a pervasive sense of uncertainty. These challenges, coupled with the adjustments required by new working paradigms, intensified the strains on mental well-being. One particularly pronounced issue in this evolving landscape was the magnification of manipulative behavior within the workplace. The blend of stress, uncertainty, and unfamiliar working conditions created a fertile ground for toxic leaders to wield their influence, often in more overt and aggressive ways than before.

Heightened Emotions and Aggressive Pursuits

The stress of the pandemic heightened emotions, pushing many to their limits. On one hand, many felt anxiety over the health risks of the virus, the safety of their loved ones, and the looming economic challenges intensified the need for security and predictability in the workplace. This atmosphere of fear and uncertainty often led to shortened patience and heightened tensions.

Conversely, some, swayed by conspiracy theories, grew anxious over perceived threats to their freedoms. Their heightened skepticism made them potentially more challenging to manage or collaborate with.

These heightened emotions, regardless of their root cause, led to more direct and obvious manipulative behaviors in the workplace. Feeling the weight of their concerns, many, especially in leadership roles, dropped the pretense and pursued their goals more openly. This straightforward push for personal agendas, sometimes at the cost of others, was a notable shift from the more hidden tactics of workplace manipulation.

The Virtual Window: Blurring Personal and Professional Boundaries

Remote work and increased use of video conferencing merged our personal and professional worlds in unexpected ways. The "Blick ins Wohnzimmer," or the "look into the living room," is more than just a phrase. It represents an unintended invasion of privacy, where colleagues and managers gain a glimpse into spaces once kept personal.

This merging of spheres provided new avenues for manipulation:

Judgment and Scrutiny: Backgrounds on video calls inadvertently became a topic of judgment. From furniture quality to room tidiness, seemingly trivial details were open to observation and critique.

Intrusive Conversations: This newfound "window" into an employee's personal space sometimes led to unwarranted comments, perpetuating power imbalances and enabling manipulative dialogue under the cloak of casual conversation.

Specific Pandemic-Era Manipulative Tactics

In the unprecedented landscape of the pandemic, traditional workplace norms were upended, creating opportunities for manipulation. Recognizing and understanding these nuances is critical to completely grasp modern-day workplace manipulation. Here's a closer look at some pandemic-specific tactics:

Manipulation in the Guise of Empathy: While genuine concern was prevalent, some individuals used the guise of empathy to extract personal or sensitive information. Recognizing the line between authentic concern and prying can help discern genuine intentions.

Overstepping Virtual Boundaries: The blurred lines between personal and professional spheres allowed some to cross boundaries under the pretext of casual conversation or concern. Understanding these intrusive tactics can highlight the importance of maintaining privacy even in virtual settings.

Exploiting Pandemic-Related Fears: Manipulators utilized the dual anxieties – about health and freedom – to further their agendas, taking advantage of the pervasive mood of uncertainty.

Tech-Induced Work Expectations: The Double-Edged Sword

As the pandemic redefined the workspace through necessity, it also accelerated a trend that was already on the horizon: the digitization of work. While providing flexibility and continuity, this technological revolution ushered in a new set of challenges for employees and employers alike.

Always-On Culture and Boundary Erosion

The convenience of digital connectivity has led to an "always-on" work culture, where employees are more and more expected to be perpetually reachable and responsive. Smartphones, laptops, and cloud services have all made work portable, but at the cost of blurring the lines between "on" and "off" hours. The result is a significant increase in employees feeling the pressure to extend their workday well beyond traditional hours, often without overtime compensation or acknowledgement.

Technological Leverage for Manipulative Ends

Managers have found in technology both a tool for efficiency and a lever for control. By sending late-night emails or scheduling after-hours meetings, they implicitly set new norms for availability, often without formal policy changes. This subtle shift in expectations can be a form of manipulation, as it coerces employees into a cycle of constant engagement with work under the guise of flexibility or dedication.

Technology's Ambiguity in Performance Measurement

Moreover, technology's promise of better tracking and performance metrics can be a double-edged sword. Data analytics and monitoring software, meant to optimize productivity, can also become surveillance tools when misused. This can foster a culture of mistrust and pressure, where employees feel watched and evaluated on not just their outcomes but also their online presence and activity levels throughout the day.

Reconciling Pandemic Adaptations with Long-term Technological Shifts

As we gradually emerge from the shadow of the pandemic, the task now lies in reconciling the immediate adaptations we made under duress with the long-term implications of our accelerated leap into the digital era. The pandemic has not only spotlighted but intensified the demands of an always-connected work culture, and it is incumbent upon organizations to carefully evaluate these new norms. In drafting policies that respect and protect the delicate work-life balance in a post-pandemic world, there must be an emphasis on retaining the human element amidst the digital workflow. Only then can we ensure that the technological solutions born out of a time of crisis do not become permanent facilitators of workplace manipulation but instead serve as bridges to a more empathetic and efficient professional environment.

Key Takeaways

- The psychology of manipulative bosses reveals that traits such as narcissism, desire for control, and fear of failure are common, underscoring the need for awareness and strategic responses to their tactics.

- Understanding the psychological drivers behind manipulative bosses can aid employees in developing strategies to safeguard their well-being and maintain professional integrity in challenging environments.

- Attachment styles significantly influence workplace interactions, impacting leadership, team dynamics, and individual behavior.

- Recognizing and adapting to various attachment styles within a team fosters improved communication, collaboration, and a more harmonious work environment.

- Tailored communication strategies can enhance connections with team members of different attachment styles, leading to more effective teamwork and conflict resolution.

- Leaders and HR professionals can leverage their understanding of attachment styles for better team management and development, fostering a healthier, more productive, and more inclusive work culture.

- Awareness of one's attachment style and those of colleagues can be a powerful tool in enhancing interpersonal understanding and managing workplace conflicts effectively.

4

Detecting Manipulative Tactics

Identifying Signs of Manipulation

Manipulative behavior can be subtle and challenging to detect. In this section, we will discuss some common signs of manipulation to help you recognize when you or your colleagues may be experiencing it.

Spotting Inconsistent or Contradictory Behavior

Manipulative bosses may exhibit inconsistent or contradictory behavior, making it difficult for employees to understand their intentions or expectations. For example, a boss might praise an employee's work in front of the team but later criticize the same work privately. Another example could be a boss who sets deadlines and then changes them without explanation, causing confusion and frustration among employees. This inconsistency can create a sense of instability in the workplace, making employees more susceptible to manipulation as they seek clarity and reassurance from their boss.

Emotional Fluctuations or Outbursts

A manipulative boss might use emotional fluctuations or outbursts to control employees. One day, they may be cheerful and friendly, only to become irritable and unapproachable the next, without any apparent reason. They may also have sudden outbursts of anger or frustration, targeting employees with belittling comments or passive-aggressive remarks. For example, a manipulative boss might say, "I thought you were competent enough to handle this task, but I guess I was wrong." Such statements can undermine employees' confidence and create an atmosphere of fear and uncertainty. This unpredictability can keep you and your colleagues on edge, making you more likely to comply with the boss's demands to avoid potential conflict. Additionally, emotional outbursts can serve to intimidate employees, making them more susceptible to manipulation.

These examples should provide a better understanding of what manipulative behavior might look like in the workplace, helping you and your colleagues recognize and address it when it occurs.

Attempts to Control or Dominate Conversations

Manipulative bosses often seek to control or dominate conversations, steering them in a direction that serves their interests. You may notice that your boss interrupts employees, dismisses their opinions, or monopolizes discussions to assert their authority and maintain control over the conversation. For example, when discussing a project, a manipulative boss might say, "We don't have time to consider everyone's ideas; we'll do it my way." By dominating conversations, manipulative bosses can limit the exchange of ideas, stifle dissent, and manipulate the narrative to suit their purposes.

Withholding Information or Resources

A manipulative boss may withhold information or resources to maintain control over employees. Consider a scenario where the boss keeps critical details about a project secret, making it difficult for employees to make informed decisions or work efficiently. He might say, "I'll give you the details when you need them," to maintain control over the flow of information. Similarly, a boss might intentionally not forward important updates from upper management to the team, leaving them uninformed about changes or decisions that could impact their work.

Alternatively, a manipulative boss might withhold resources, such as staff, funding, or time, to create a sense of scarcity and increase employees' dependence on them. This tactic can make you and your colleagues more susceptible to manipulation, as you may feel compelled to comply with the boss's demands to gain access to the information or resources you need to succeed.

Frequent Use of Guilt, Fear, or Obligation

Manipulative bosses may frequently use guilt, fear, or obligation to influence employees' actions. They might remind you of past mistakes or failures to make you feel guilty, then use that guilt to pressure you into taking on additional responsibilities or agreeing to unfavorable terms. For example, a boss might say, "After all the mistakes you've made, you should be grateful I'm giving you another chance." They may also use fear, such as threats of job loss or public humiliation, to coerce you into compliance. Additionally, they might exploit your sense of obligation, making you feel as though you owe the boss something in return for their support or guidance.

When I, Markus, found myself entangled in the challenging dynamics of work and family life, I approached my then-boss, Ethan, for a part-time arrangement. Understanding my predicament, Ethan agreed to a part-time schedule, but not without strings attached. He stipulated that I needed to secure consent from the various heads of divisions I liaised with — a move that placed them in an awkward position to do anything but agree — and required me to report back to him in writing. Further, Ethan made it clear that the company is providing me with some extraordinary support during these challenging times and implying an expectation of reciprocation.

This left me grappling with a sense of indebtedness, complicating my request for reduced hours with an undercurrent of guilt and an obligation to one day "pay back" the company. Also, it was clear that Ethan was crafting a narrative where he could later claim miscommunication on my part or an underestimation of the situation by the division heads should the reduced workload lead to complications. The "evidence" of this, provided by my hand, would sit conveniently in his inbox.

Summary of Typical Behaviors

As a helpful reference, we put together for you a list of common manipulative tactics and their corresponding behaviors:

Manipulative Tactic	Typical Behaviors of a Manipulative Boss
Neurolinguistic Programming (NLP)	Using specific language patterns to influence employees
Gaslighting	Denying or distorting facts to make employees question their memory or perception
Emotional blackmail	Threatening negative consequences if employees don't comply with demands
Exploiting guilt and fear	Using guilt or fear to pressure employees into certain actions
Triangulation	Pitting employees against each other to maintain control
Playing the victim	Blaming employees or circumstances for their own failures
Divide and conquer	Creating factions among employees to weaken potential opposition
Exploiting power dynamics	Using their position of authority to control or manipulate employees

Playing on emotions	Appealing to employees' emotions to gain compliance
Micromanagement and control	Exerting excessive control over employees' work or personal lives
Undermining confidence and self-esteem	Criticizing, belittling, or devaluing employees to weaken their confidence and sense of self

Assessing the Work Environment – Is Your Workplace Toxic?

In the previous chapter, "Detecting Manipulative Tactics," we focused on identifying specific behaviors of a manipulative boss. However, examining the overall workplace environment is equally crucial, as a manipulative boss can create a toxic work culture that affects all employees, not just the direct targets.

It's often challenging to determine whether a toxic workplace environment leads to manipulative behavior or if manipulative behavior contributes to a toxic environment. Even though we might not be solving this chicken-egg problem here, it's still safe to say that both factors can be interconnected and potentially exacerbate each other. To break this cycle, it is essential to assess the workplace environment for signs of toxicity while also examining the behavior of bosses. By tackling the root causes of a toxic work environment and fostering a healthy workplace culture, you can help reduce manipulative behaviors and create a more positive work experience for all employees.

Communication and Transparency

Healthy workplaces encourage open and honest communication, both between employees and between employees and management. In a manipulative work environment, communication may be vague, ambiguous, or lacking altogether. There may be a lack of transparency, with important information being withheld or only shared with select individuals. Ask yourself:

- Do you feel like your boss communicates openly and honestly with you?

- Is information shared freely, or do you often feel like you're left in the dark?

- Have there been instances where you've discovered important information was withheld or concealed from you?

Inadequate communication or a lack of transparency can foster an environment where manipulation thrives. When employees are kept in the dark about their roles, responsibilities, or the organization's goals, it breeds uncertainty and dependency on those who seem to hold the answers. For instance, a boss giving vague project instructions can make employees overly reliant for clarity, opening doors to manipulation.

Similarly, a lack of transparency around decision-making processes can leave employees feeling disempowered and disconnected from the organization. When employees are excluded from important discussions, they may be more likely to comply with the boss's demands without question, believing they have no other choice.

Even per se well-intentioned communication efforts like polished Town Halls (meetings designed for open dialogue between company leadership and employees) can fall short if transparency is not actually a core priority. At least in the pharma industry, Claudia experienced more than once that in critical situations, employees were required to submit their questions in advance for these meetings, limiting the opportunity for spontaneous, genuine dialogue and contributing to a sense of controlled and filtered communication.

Unfortunately, this form of "fake transparency" (the appearance of open communication while restricting free exchange and controlling the narrative) seems to be getting increasingly popular as organizations increasingly prioritize image management over authentic engagement.

In an era where corporate reputation and public perception are highly valued, some companies may resort to these tactics under the guise of openness while carefully curating what is shared and discussed. This trend not only undermines the trust between employees and management but also stifles the genuine exchange of ideas that is essential for innovation and growth.

Trust and Respect

A positive work environment is built on trust and respect among colleagues, employees, and management. In a manipulative workplace, trust and respect may be lacking or even non-existent. Consider:

- Do you feel like your boss trusts you and respects your abilities?

- Are your colleagues supportive and respectful, or do they engage in undermining or competitive behaviors?

- Does your boss encourage collaboration and teamwork, or do they pit employees against each other?

The role of trust in the workplace extends beyond mere professional courtesy; it's the foundation upon which effective teamwork, open communication, and a culture of mutual support are built. Employees who feel trusted are more likely to take initiative, share innovative ideas, and commit to the organization's goals. Conversely, a lack of trust can lead to a culture of fear and suspicion, stifling creativity and engagement. A boss who micromanages or second-guesses every decision erodes trust and undermines employees' confidence in their abilities.

Respect, similarly, is pivotal for fostering a healthy work environment. It ensures that all employees feel valued and recognized for their contributions, regardless of their position or tenure. Respect in the workplace manifests in how conflicts are resolved, how feedback is given and received, and how accomplishments are celebrated. Employees may feel undervalued in environments where respect is absent, leading to low morale and high turnover. A workplace that encourages respect among its members promotes a sense of belonging and inclusivity, driving productivity and satisfaction.

Employee Autonomy and Empowerment

In a healthy workplace, employees are given autonomy and are empowered to make decisions and contribute to the organization's success. A manipulative work environment may feature micromanagement, excessive control, or a lack of opportunities for employees to grow and develop. Reflect on:

- Do you feel like you have the autonomy to make decisions and take ownership of your work?

- Are you provided with opportunities for growth and development, or do you feel stifled in your current role?

- Does your boss encourage your ideas and input, or do they dismiss or undermine your contributions?

When employees are trusted with autonomy, they feel a greater sense of ownership and commitment towards their work and the organization's objectives. This autonomy allows individuals to utilize their skills and creativity to solve problems and make meaningful contributions, enhancing job satisfaction and productivity. On the other hand, a workplace that resorts to micromanagement or excessive control not only dampens motivation but also restricts employees' ability to grow and excel in their roles. Reflect on whether you are given the latitude to guide your work and decisions and if you are encouraged to pursue opportunities that allow personal and professional growth.

Empowerment in the workplace goes hand in hand with autonomy but focuses more on giving employees the resources, confidence, and support they need to take initiative and make decisions. An empowering environment is one where employees feel valued and know that their contributions have an impact on the company's success. It's a place where ideas are welcomed and efforts are recognized, fostering a culture of continuous improvement and innovation. Conversely, feeling stifled or undervalued can lead to disengagement and a lack of investment in the company's goals. Consider whether your boss actively seeks your input and supports you in turning your ideas into action, signifying a genuine commitment to empowerment and personal development.

Employee Well-Being and Work-Life Balance

A supportive work environment prioritizes employee well-being and promotes a healthy work-life balance. In a manipulative workplace, employees may be subjected to excessive workloads, unrealistic expectations, or a disregard for personal boundaries. Evaluate:

- Are you able to maintain a healthy work-life balance, or do you feel constantly overwhelmed by work demands?

- Does your boss respect your personal time and boundaries, or do they expect you to be available around the clock?

- Are employee well-being and mental health genuinely prioritized and effectively supported in your workplace, or are such programs merely token gestures to tick boxes on corporate responsibility checklists?

Well-being in the workplace includes physical, emotional, and mental health, which are crucial for employees to perform at their best. When employees are subjected to excessive workloads, unrealistic expectations, or a disregard for personal boundaries, it can lead to burnout, stress, and decreased productivity. It's important to evaluate whether you can maintain a healthy balance between your professional and personal life or if work demands consistently encroach upon your time, leaving you feeling constantly overwhelmed.

Furthermore, management's respect for personal time and boundaries is a key indicator of a company's commitment to work-life balance. A boss who expects round-the-clock availability clearly conveys that the company values productivity over employee well-being. On the contrary, leaders who encourage time off, flexible working hours, and respect personal boundaries demonstrate a genuine concern for their team's health and happiness.

High Levels of Employee Turnover or Dissatisfaction

One sign of a toxic workplace environment that fosters manipulative behavior is high employee turnover or widespread dissatisfaction among staff. If you notice that many of your colleagues are leaving the company or expressing frustration with their work, this could be an indication that there are underlying issues contributing to a negative atmosphere. A recent trend that exemplifies this dissatisfaction is "quiet quitting," where employees, feeling disengaged and undervalued, do the bare minimum required by their job, withdrawing their enthusiasm and extra effort. This passive form of disengagement often stems from a lack of recognition, poor management, or a hostile work environment created by manipulative bosses. Employee surveys, exit interviews, or simply talking to your coworkers can provide valuable insights into the factors that may be driving turnover, dissatisfaction, or "quiet quitting." Of course, manipulative bosses may contribute to a toxic workplace environment by creating a hostile atmosphere, making it difficult for employees to thrive or feel valued.

A Culture of Fear, Secrecy, or Competition

In the movie "Glengarry Glen Ross," we witness a cutthroat real estate sales office where employees are constantly under pressure. The salesmen are pushed to their limits by a ruthless boss who not only encourages a culture of competition but also leverages fear and secrecy to manipulate his employees. He uses fear by threatening to fire the lowest-performing salesmen and instills secrecy by offering confidential information to only those who prove their loyalty.

It's crucial to understand why a workplace environment characterized by these elements can create a breeding ground for manipulative behavior. When fear is pervasive, employees may become more susceptible to manipulation as they desperately try to hold on to their jobs. They might agree to take on extra work, work longer hours, or even engage in unethical behavior to avoid potential negative consequences.

Similarly, a culture of secrecy can leave employees feeling isolated and unsupported, making them more vulnerable to manipulation. For example, a boss might withhold important information, making employees dependent on them for critical knowledge. This dependency can then be used to coerce employees into compliance with the boss's demands.

Lastly, excessive competition can pit employees against one another, weakening their ability to support and rely on each other. This "divide and conquer" strategy allows manipulative bosses to maintain control and manipulate individual employees more efficiently. By encouraging a culture of collaboration, open communication, and mutual support, you can help counteract these negative dynamics and reduce the likelihood of manipulative behavior in the workplace.

Favoritism or Unequal Treatment of Employees

Favoritism or unequal treatment of employees can contribute to a toxic work environment, making it easier for manipulative behavior to thrive. When a boss consistently shows preferential treatment to certain employees, it can create resentment, jealousy, and dissatisfaction among the rest of the team.

Take, for example, a situation where a boss shows favoritism towards an employee who consistently agrees with their opinions (we all know one of these brown nosers, right?). This employee might receive more praise and recognition than other team members despite their lack of expertise or contribution. When other employees, who may have valid and well-reasoned opinions, challenge the boss's views, they find themselves at odds with the boss while the "brown noser" remains in their good graces. Even if the dissenting employees' views are later confirmed to be correct, they might still be overlooked for promotions or other opportunities in favor of the yes-man. This, of course, will very likely cause even more dissatisfaction and even frustration in the team.

Interestingly, some bosses may claim to value critical employees who challenge their views, asserting that dissenting opinions provide opportunities for learning and growth. However, at the end of the day, they might still gravitate towards those who support their opinions and ideas without question. This discrepancy could be rooted in the boss's personality traits, insecurities, or even narcissistic tendencies, which may make them feel more comfortable surrounded by agreeable individuals. A boss who struggles with self-doubt, fears being wrong, or possesses narcissistic traits may subconsciously prefer the reassurance and validation provided by "yes-men," even if they outwardly express a preference for critical feedback. Narcissistic bosses, in particular, may have a heightened need for admiration and affirmation, leading them to favor employees who reinforce their sense of self-importance.

In another scenario, a boss might assign more desirable tasks or projects to their favorite employees, leaving others with less interesting or more burdensome work. This unequal distribution of responsibilities can result in feelings of inequity and frustration among employees who believe they are being treated unfairly.

In all these cases, a divided and demoralized workforce may emerge, with employees competing against each other for the boss's attention and approval rather than collaborating and supporting one another.

As a leader, it's essential to treat all employees fairly and consistently to create a healthy and supportive work environment. Be mindful of your interactions with your team members and ensure that you're providing equal opportunities for growth, recognition, and responsibility. By fostering a sense of fairness and inclusiveness, you can help prevent the conditions that allow manipulative behavior to take hold in the workplace.

As an employee, it's crucial to recognize the signs of favoritism and unequal treatment in the workplace. By being aware of these issues, you can take steps to address them and advocate for a fair and inclusive work environment. If you feel comfortable, consider discussing your concerns with your boss or a trusted colleague. Alternatively, you can bring the issue to the attention of human resources or a higher-level manager. By actively addressing favoritism and advocating for equal treatment, you can help create a healthier, more supportive work environment that discourages manipulative behavior.

Management Style and Decision-Making Processes

The management style and decision-making processes within an organization can significantly impact the workplace environment and employees' susceptibility to manipulation. A manipulative boss may employ authoritarian or coercive management styles, leading to a culture of fear and compliance. Reflect on the following aspects of management and decision-making:

- Is the management style in your workplace collaborative and inclusive, or does it rely on top-down directives and control?

- Are employees involved in decision-making processes and given opportunities to contribute their ideas and expertise?

- Are decisions made transparently, with clear communication about the rationale and goals behind them?

Management style and decision-making processes are key factors in determining the level of employee engagement, satisfaction, and even trust within an organization. A leadership approach that values collaboration and inclusivity can empower employees, fostering a sense of ownership and commitment towards their work and the company's goals. In contrast, a management style that is overly authoritarian or relies heavily on coercion can instill a culture of fear and compliance, stifling creativity and innovation. Are employees regarded as valuable contributors to the decision-making process, allowing for a diverse range of ideas and expertise to be heard?

Furthermore, the transparency with which decisions are made and communicated can significantly influence employees' trust in management and their understanding of their role within the broader organizational context. An environment where decisions are made openly and the rationale behind them is clearly explained can enhance employees' alignment with organizational goals and reduce the likelihood of manipulation.

Organizational Values and Priorities

A healthy workplace environment is often characterized by a strong set of organizational values and priorities that promote integrity, respect, and employee well-being. In contrast, a manipulative boss may prioritize their interests over those of the organization and its employees. To assess the values and priorities in your workplace, consider:

- Are the organization's values clearly defined and communicated to employees?

- Do the actions and behaviors of management align with these values, or are there discrepancies between what is said and what is done?

- Are employee well-being and development prioritized, or do the organization's goals seem to focus solely on profit and productivity at the expense of its employees?

The significance of organizational values and priorities cannot be overstated, as they are the foundation of a company's culture and influence both management and employee actions. Strong values that emphasize integrity, respect, and employee well-being contribute to a vibrant work environment, attracting and retaining top talent. It's essential for these values to be not only articulated but also demonstrated through management's actions, fostering a unified and positive workplace. Evaluating your workplace involves discerning if there's consistency between the organization's stated values and its actual practices, particularly regarding employee treatment. This reflection can illuminate whether the company genuinely commits to a supportive culture or prioritizes short-term objectives over the long-term welfare of its team.

Group Dynamics and Power Structures

Furthermore, understanding group dynamics and power structures within your workplace can provide valuable insights into the overall health of the work environment. A manipulative boss may attempt to control and manipulate these dynamics to maintain authority and influence. To assess the group dynamics and power structures in your workplace, consider the following:

- Are there cliques or factions within the organization that create divisions among employees?

- Do certain individuals hold a disproportionate amount of power or influence, leading to an imbalanced work environment?

- Are decisions made collectively and fairly, or do a few individuals control the decision-making process?

Trusting Your Instincts and Intuition

In addition to carefully examining the workplace environment and specific behaviors of bosses, it's crucial to trust your instincts and intuition when it comes to identifying manipulation. Our instincts often serve as an internal alarm system, alerting us to potential issues or dangers that might not be immediately obvious.

However, in a society that increasingly values logical and analytical thinking, trusting these instincts can be challenging. Amplified by the information age and technological advancements, this trend emphasizes data-driven decision-making and empirical evidence, often overshadowing intuitive understanding. The prevalence of digital technology, presenting information in a structured, logical format, may further encourage reliance on external data rather than internal cues. As a result, intuitive skills might become underutilized, with individuals seeking external validation over internal insights.

Recognizing this shift is even more vital to understand the importance of nurturing and trusting your intuitive skills, especially as a defense against manipulative behaviors in the workplace.

Understanding Your Instincts and Intuition

Instincts and intuition are often used interchangeably, but they are slightly different concepts. Instincts are innate, automatic responses to situations that we have inherited through evolution. Intuition, on the other hand, is a form of unconscious reasoning based on our experiences and knowledge, enabling us to make quick decisions without conscious thought.

Both instincts and intuition can provide valuable insights when it comes to detecting manipulation. Your instincts might warn you that something is "off" about a boss's behavior or the workplace environment, while your intuition might help you recognize patterns or connect the dots between seemingly unrelated events.

Recognizing the Signs

To trust your instincts and intuition, you must first learn to recognize the signs. This might involve paying attention to physical sensations, such as a knot in your stomach, a racing heart, or sweaty palms, which can indicate that something is amiss. It might also involve being mindful of your emotions, such as feeling uneasy, anxious, or uncomfortable around a particular boss or in specific situations.

Reflecting on Past Experiences

One way to hone your instincts and intuition is to reflect on your past experiences, especially those involving manipulation or toxic work environments. Consider situations where your instincts or intuition alerted you to a problem and analyze the factors contributing to these feelings. By understanding the patterns and cues that triggered your instincts or intuition in the past, you can become more attuned to these signals in the future.

Trusting Yourself

Trusting your instincts and intuition requires confidence in your judgment and the ability to stand by your decisions, even if they go against conventional wisdom or the opinions of others. Suppose your instincts or intuition are telling you that something is not right. In that case, it's essential to listen to that inner voice and take appropriate action, whether that means confronting a manipulative boss, seeking advice from a trusted colleague, or exploring other job opportunities.

Seeking Validation and Support

While trusting your instincts and intuition is important, it can also be helpful to seek validation and support from others who might have similar experiences or perspectives. Discuss your concerns with colleagues, friends, or family, and gather additional information to help you make informed decisions. Remember, trusting your instincts and intuition does not mean you should disregard external input; instead, use these valuable resources to gain a more comprehensive understanding of the situation.

In other words, stay curious and be the best detective you can be! Do not just rely on your gut feelings but also proactively seek clues and insights from your environment and the people around you. By actively investigating and validating your observations with others, you enhance your ability to accurately identify manipulative behavior.

By adopting this investigative mindset, along with trusting your instincts and seeking support, you can more effectively navigate and address the challenges of toxic work environments and manipulative bosses. This balanced approach enables you to make more informed decisions and take appropriate actions to protect yourself and improve your workplace.

Key Takeaways

- Healthy workplaces encourage open communication and transparency, while manipulative environments may feature vague, ambiguous, or lacking communication.

- Trust and respect are foundational in positive work environments; in manipulative settings, these elements may be absent or exploited.

- High employee turnover or widespread dissatisfaction can indicate a toxic workplace environment perpetuated by manipulative behavior.

- A culture of fear, secrecy, or excessive competition is indicative of a manipulative environment that discourages collaboration and open communication.

- Organizational values and priorities that do not align with promoting integrity, respect, and employee well-being can facilitate a manipulative work environment.

- Emotional fluctuations or outbursts, used by manipulative bosses to control employees, undermine confidence and create an atmosphere of fear and uncertainty.

- Manipulative bosses often seek to dominate conversations, limit the exchange of ideas, and manipulate narratives to maintain control and stifle dissent.

- Withholding information or resources is a tactic used by manipulative bosses to create dependence and compel compliance with their demands.

- Excessive workloads, unrealistic expectations, and disregard for personal boundaries indicate a lack of concern for employee well-being and work-life balance.

- Favoritism or unequal treatment by bosses creates divisions among employees, undermining team cohesion and fostering a competitive rather than collaborative atmosphere.

- Trusting your instincts and intuition when something feels off, supported by reflecting on past experiences and seeking validation, is crucial in identifying manipulative tactics.

Yes
No
Maybe

5

Confronting Your Boss – Or Better Not?

Dealing with a manipulative boss can be a daunting and emotionally draining experience. In some cases, directly confronting the boss might not be a feasible option due to power dynamics, fear of retaliation, or concerns about potential consequences on one's career. In this chapter, we will explore various strategies for addressing the issue, including directly confronting the manipulative boss and alternative approaches for those who might not feel comfortable taking that step. Understanding and considering the different methods available allows you to choose the most appropriate course of action based on your unique situation and concerns.

First Things First: Assess the Situation and Gather Evidence

Before potentially confronting a manipulative boss, it's crucial to thoroughly prepare yourself to ensure the conversation is productive and effective. Begin by assessing the situation to determine the extent of the manipulative behavior and its impact on your well-being and work performance. Reflect on specific incidents, patterns, and tactics used by your boss to manipulate or undermine you. In the Appendix you will find a checklist for manipulative behaviors in the workplace, which can help you identify specific tactics and actions you have observed in your boss.

Once you clearly understand the situation, gather evidence to support your concerns. This process will help you build a strong case and ensure that you can present your concerns in a clear, concise, and objective manner. Start by:

☑ Identifying specific incidents of manipulation or toxic behavior

☑ Documenting these incidents, including dates, times, and any witnesses

☑ Collecting any relevant emails, messages, or other forms of communication

☑ Reflecting on the impact of the manipulative behavior on your well-being and work performance

By taking the time to prepare and gather evidence, you will be better equipped to confront your boss with confidence and clarity, setting the stage for a more effective and constructive conversation.

Choosing the Right Time and Setting for the Conversation

Choosing the appropriate time and setting for your conversation with your boss is crucial for ensuring a productive and meaningful discussion. By carefully considering these factors, you can help to create an environment in which both parties are more open to listening and understanding each other's perspectives.

DO's:

☑ Pick a time when your boss is in a good mood or more relaxed, such as after a successful meeting or project completion.

☑ Schedule a private meeting in a neutral location, like a conference room or an informal seating area.

☑ Ensure you have enough time for the conversation without feeling rushed or pressured.

☑ Consider your boss's preferred communication style, such as in-person or via video conference, and adapt accordingly.

☑ Be mindful of cultural or organizational norms that might influence the ideal setting for the conversation.

DON'Ts:

☒ Avoid choosing a time when your boss is under significant stress, as they may be less receptive to your concerns.

☒ Don't confront your boss in public or in front of colleagues, as this could create a hostile environment and damage your professional relationship.

☒ Don't initiate the conversation during a hectic workday, as your boss may be preoccupied or unable to focus on the discussion.

☒ Refrain from discussing the issue in an overly casual setting, such as during lunch or a social gathering, as this could detract from the seriousness of the topic.

☒ Don't force the conversation if your boss seems resistant or unwilling to engage. It may be more effective to reschedule or try a different approach.

By carefully considering the timing and setting for your conversation, you can help to create a more conducive atmosphere for discussing your concerns and addressing the manipulative behaviors you have observed.

Approaching the Conversation with Assertiveness and Clarity

Before diving into the specifics of assertive and clear communication, it's crucial to understand the strategy of externalizing the problem – a technique often used in various therapeutic approaches, where an issue is seen as separate from the individuals involved. This means viewing the issue as separate from both you and your boss – as an external challenge to be collaboratively addressed rather than a personal flaw in either party. Imagine the problem as a "knot" that both of you are working together to untangle. By externalizing, you transform potential confrontations into opportunities for collaborative problem-solving.

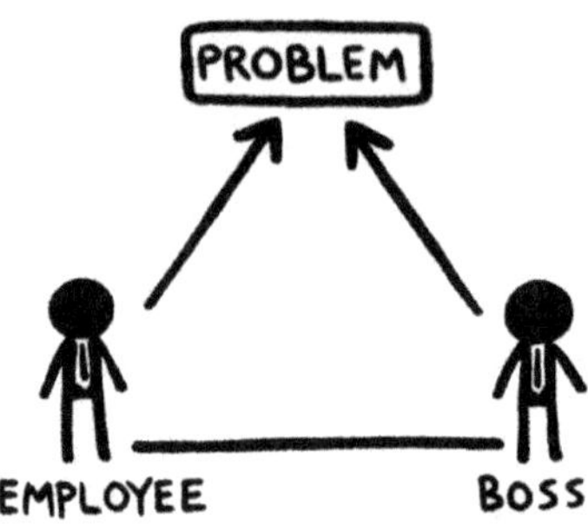

In practice, externalizing the problem involves a shift in language and perspective that transforms confrontational scenarios into collaborative problem-solving discussions. Here's how you can apply this strategy in real-life situations:

- **Reframe the Issue**: Start by reframing the issue as a mutual challenge rather than a personal fault. For example, instead of saying, "I'm upset because you never acknowledge my input," try, "I've noticed that we seem to have different communication styles. How can we improve this to ensure all voices are heard?"

- **Visualize the Problem as an Object**: Picture the problem as an object or entity outside of yourselves. For instance, if the issue concerns miscommunication, you might say, "It seems like this miscommunication gremlin is causing us both some trouble. Let's see how we can tackle it together."

- **Use Collaborative Language**: Employ language that emphasizes teamwork. Say, "We seem to have a challenge with meeting deadlines. What are your thoughts on how we can address this together?" instead of placing blame.

- **Invite Input for Solutions**: Actively encourage your boss to contribute ideas for solving the issue. You could say, "I believe we both want to improve the project's efficiency. What do you think would be an effective way for us to achieve this?"

- **Acknowledge Shared Goals**: Highlight common objectives. For example, "We're both aiming for the success of this project, so let's figure out a strategy that aligns with our shared goals."

By applying these strategies, you're not only addressing the issue at hand but also fostering a sense of partnership with your boss. This method of externalizing the problem can lead to more productive outcomes and a healthier workplace dynamic.

With this approach in mind, let's explore how to effectively confront your boss with assertiveness and clarity. Confronting a manipulative boss requires a direct yet respectful communication style. You want to express your concerns and feelings in a manner that is heard without appearing aggressive or accusatory.

Here are some tips to help you navigate the conversation assertively, clearly, and collaboratively:

- **Use "I" statements**: By framing your thoughts and feelings using "I" statements, you can express your concerns without putting your boss on the defensive. This helps to keep the focus on your perspective and feelings rather than making accusations.

Example of a <u>wise phrase</u> to use: "I feel uncomfortable when you dismiss my ideas without considering them."

Example of a <u>phrase to avoid</u>: "You always dismiss my ideas, and it's not fair."

- **Be Specific**: Clearly describe the situations or behaviors that concern you, and provide concrete examples. This helps to prevent any misunderstandings and ensures that your boss knows exactly what you are referring to.

Example of a <u>wise phrase</u> to use: "In last week's meeting, I noticed that my suggestion was not considered, and I'd like to understand why."

Example of a <u>phrase to avoid</u>: "You never listen to me."

- **Stay Focused on the Issue**: Keep the conversation centered on the specific issue at hand and avoid bringing up unrelated grievances or past issues. This helps to maintain a clear and productive dialogue.

Example of a <u>wise phrase</u> to use: "My concern is about how our team's workload is distributed, and I'd like to discuss possible solutions."

Example of a <u>phrase to avoid:</u> "You always do this, just like that time when..."

- **Remain Calm and Composed**: Even if the conversation becomes tense or emotional, maintain a calm and composed demeanor. This demonstrates your professionalism and helps to keep the discussion focused and productive.

Example of a <u>wise phrase</u> to use: "I understand that we may have different perspectives, but I'd like to find a solution that works for both of us."

Example of a <u>phrase to avoid</u>: "I can't believe you're doing this again!"

- **Offer Solutions or Suggestions**: Instead of only discussing the problems, try to offer potential solutions or suggestions to address the issue. This demonstrates your willingness to collaborate and find a mutually beneficial resolution.

An example of a <u>wise phrase</u> to use: "One possible solution could be to have regular check-ins to ensure that we're on the same page regarding tasks and expectations."

Example of a <u>phrase to avoid</u>: "You need to fix this, or I can't work like this anymore."

- **Paraphrase, Summarize, and Document**: At the end of your conversation, especially with toxic leaders, it is crucial to paraphrase and summarize the key points discussed. This not only ensures mutual understanding but also provides a clear record of what was agreed upon. Documenting these summaries can be invaluable, particularly if follow-up actions are needed or if there is a need to reference the conversation in the future.

Example of a <u>wise approach</u>: "To make sure I've understood correctly, we've agreed on implementing a weekly check-in meeting to discuss project progress and address any concerns. I'll document and share this plan with you to ensure we're aligned."

Example of an <u>approach to avoid</u>: Ending the conversation without any summary or leaving the understanding vague and undocumented.

By externalizing the problem and approaching the conversation with assertiveness, clarity, and a collaborative mindset, you can more effectively convey your concerns and work towards a positive resolution. Remember, the goal is to untangle the issue together, not to win a battle against each other.

Setting Boundaries and Standing Up for Yourself

When dealing with a manipulative boss, it's crucial to establish boundaries. By clearly defining your limits, you communicate what you will and will not tolerate in the workplace, ensuring that you protect your mental and emotional well-being. Here are some tips for setting boundaries and standing up for yourself:

- **Identify your Boundaries**: Reflect on the specific behaviors or situations that cause you discomfort or distress. Determine what your limits are and what you're unwilling to accept.

- **Communicate your Boundaries Clearly**: When discussing your concerns with your boss, be clear and assertive about your boundaries. Let them know what behaviors you find unacceptable and why.

Example of a <u>wise phrase</u> to use: "I am not comfortable with last-minute changes to my workload without prior discussion, as it affects my ability to manage my time effectively."

Example of a <u>phrase to avoid</u>: "You can't just dump work on me like that."

- **Be Consistent**: Consistency is key when enforcing your boundaries. Stand firm in your decisions and ensure that you're not wavering or sending mixed messages.

Example of a <u>wise phrase</u> to use: "As I mentioned before, I need at least 24 hours' notice for any changes to my schedule."

Example of a <u>phrase to avoid</u>: "I guess I can make an exception this time, but don't make it a habit."

- **Offer Alternatives**: If your boss continues to push your boundaries, propose alternative solutions that address their needs while still respecting your limits.

Example of a <u>wise phrase</u> to use: "I understand that this project is a priority, at the same time I'm already fully committed to other tasks. Can we discuss reallocating resources or adjusting deadlines?"

Example of a <u>phrase to avoid</u>: "There's no way I can do this. Figure something else out."

- **Be Prepared to Enforce Consequences**: If your boss repeatedly disregards your boundaries, be prepared to enforce consequences, such as escalating the issue to HR or considering alternative employment options.

An example of a <u>wise phrase</u> to use: "If this behavior continues, I will have no choice but to discuss the matter with HR to seek a resolution."

Example of a <u>phrase to avoid</u>: "If you don't stop, I'm going to quit."

- **Try Not to Take it Personally**: Remember that a toxic boss's behavior is a reflection of their issues or history and not a reflection of your worth or abilities. It's important to remind yourself that no one, including a toxic boss, is born that way; there are circumstances that have shaped their behavior. However, this is their story and has nothing to do with you.

Example of a <u>wise mindset</u> to adopt: "I understand that my boss's behavior is influenced by factors beyond my control and unrelated to my performance. Their actions are a reflection of their challenges, not my professional capabilities."

Example of a <u>mindset to avoid</u>: "My boss's treatment of me is because I'm not good enough or doing something wrong."

This approach of separating yourself from your boss's behavior helps maintain a healthy perspective and protect your self-esteem. It allows you to respond to situations more objectively and less emotionally, which is crucial in maintaining your well-being in a challenging work environment.

Remember, setting boundaries and standing up for yourself in the workplace, especially against a manipulative boss, is not just about asserting your rights; it's a fundamental step towards preserving your well-being and dignity. The journey to establish and maintain these boundaries may be challenging, but it is also empowering. It's about recognizing your value and the respect you deserve in a professional setting.

Each step you take to stand up for yourself not only strengthens your own position but also sets a precedent for a healthier, more respectful work environment. Your courage and resilience in facing these challenges not only benefit you but can also inspire and pave the way for others in similar situations. Embrace this journey with confidence and determination, knowing that you are advocating not just for yourself but for the betterment of your entire workplace.

Evaluating the Outcomes and Considering Next Steps

After your crucial conversation, it's time to take a step back and assess the fallout. Observe if there has been a shift in your boss's behavior. Are they more understanding? Do they employ fewer manipulative tactics? Have they shown a willingness to change their leadership style? If you observe positive alterations, that's a victory worth celebrating. But remember, change is a process, not an event. Continue to observe their behavior over time, keep the lines of communication open, and maintain your assertive stand.

But what if there's no change? Or worse, what if the situation deteriorates? It's essential to not feel defeated but consider this an opportunity to try different strategies. Reach out to your allies within the workplace, approach the human resources department, or tap into external resources such as employment lawyers or labor unions.

This step is about active vigilance, understanding that one conversation may not be enough to overturn years of ingrained behavior. It's about resilience, reminding yourself that if plan A didn't work, the alphabet has 25 more letters! Keep an open mind, stay focused on your goal of a healthier workplace, and trust in your capacity to navigate this journey successfully.

When to Escalate the Issue or Consider Alternative Employment Options

In some cases, confronting a manipulative boss may not lead to a resolution, and the situation may continue to negatively impact your well-being and career. Recognize when it's time to escalate the issue to higher levels of management, file a formal complaint, or consider alternative employment options. Prioritize your mental health and professional development, and remember that you have the right to work in a respectful and supportive environment.

Escalating the issue: If you've tried confronting your boss, seeking support, and implementing coping strategies, but the situation hasn't improved, it may be time to escalate the issue. This can involve:

- Filing a formal complaint with your HR department.

- Discussing the issue with a higher-level manager or executive.

- Seeking legal advice, particularly if your boss's behavior violates any laws or company policies.

When escalating the issue, be prepared to present a well-documented case, including specific examples of your boss's behavior, any evidence you've gathered, and a record of your attempts to address the situation.

Considering Alternative Employment Options: If the situation remains unresolved even after escalation or if the toxic environment is taking a significant toll on your mental and emotional well-being, it may be time to explore other job opportunities. This decision should be carefully considered, weighing the potential benefits of a new position against the costs of leaving your current role. Keep in mind that it's often easier to find a new job while you're still employed.

When considering alternative employment options, take the time to:

- Update your resume and LinkedIn profile.

- Network with professionals in your industry.

- Research potential employers to find a better fit in terms of workplace culture and values.

- Seek guidance from career coaches or mentors to help you identify new opportunities.

When Confronting Your Boss Might Not Be a Good Idea

As mentioned earlier, confronting your boss might not always be the best way to address the issue, particularly if it puts your job or professional reputation at risk. However, be aware that we are currently in a job seeker's market. Companies are desperately seeking good employees, and this shift in the market dynamics empowers you with more choices. As Claudia likes to tell her clients (and I can confirm that), "you don't have to do this shit if you don't want to!" Your skills and expertise are valuable, and there might be numerous organizations that would appreciate your contribution.

This being said – when should you not directly confront your boss? Direct confrontation may not be recommended if:

- You have limited evidence or documentation to support your claims.

- You're concerned about potential retaliation from your boss.

- The company culture discourages open discussions about conflicts.

- Your boss has significant power and influence within the organization, making it difficult to challenge them.

- You lack support from colleagues or higher management.

In such situations, it's essential to consider alternative strategies for addressing the problem while protecting your well-being and professional reputation. However, if you feel strongly about confronting your boss and have a solid Plan B in place, it could still be worth considering this approach. A viable Plan B could involve having a definite job offer from within or outside the company or a well-prepared strategy for coping with potential fallout from the confrontation. This can provide you with a safety net and the confidence to tackle the issue head-on. If you prefer to avoid direct confrontation, here are some alternative options:

Documenting and Reporting Incidents to HR or Higher Management

Instead of directly confronting your manipulative boss, consider documenting incidents and collecting evidence of their behavior. Maintain a detailed log of dates, times, and descriptions of interactions, along with any supporting materials such as emails or text messages. This documentation can serve as a valuable resource when reporting your concerns to HR or higher management.

Be mindful of your company's policies and procedures for addressing such issues. For example, some companies may have a designated reporting channel, like an ethics hotline or an online reporting system. In contrast, others may require you to submit a written complaint to a specific department or individual. In some cases, companies may have specific guidelines on the level of documentation required, such as requiring multiple instances of the same behavior or a clear pattern of misconduct. Ensure you follow the appropriate steps in reporting the incidents, as outlined by your company's policies.

It's important to be aware that your boss may have strong personal or professional relationships with individuals in HR or other divisions responsible for handling complaints. This could potentially influence the outcome of your complaint. If you suspect your boss's connections may hinder an objective investigation, consider seeking guidance from trusted colleagues or mentors on alternative channels for reporting your concerns or escalating the issue to a higher level in the organization.

Providing clear, well-documented evidence of your boss's manipulative behavior can help HR or higher management take appropriate action to address the situation.

Seeking Guidance and Support from Trusted Colleagues or Mentors

If confronting your boss directly isn't a viable option, seek guidance and support from trusted colleagues, mentors, or the works council if your company has one. These individuals or groups may have faced similar situations in the past and can offer valuable insights, advice, or encouragement. They may also be able to help you navigate your company's reporting and complaint processes, particularly if your boss has connections that could potentially influence the outcome.

When seeking guidance from colleagues, be mindful of their own relationships with your boss, as well as the potential risks to their professional standing. Choose to confide in individuals who you believe will be supportive and maintain confidentiality.

Mentors, either within or outside your organization, can be particularly helpful in providing objective advice, as they may have a broader perspective on the situation and be less influenced by internal politics. A mentor can help you evaluate your options, develop coping strategies, and, if necessary, connect you with resources or contacts that can further support you in addressing the issue with your boss.

In some companies, a works council or similar employee representative body may also be able to provide guidance or support. The works council can serve as a mediator between employees and management, ensuring that employees' rights and interests are protected. Engaging the works council can be a helpful avenue for addressing issues with a manipulative boss, especially if other internal channels prove ineffective or are influenced by your boss's connections.

Remember that seeking guidance and support from others can not only help you feel less isolated but also provide you with valuable insights and advice to help you effectively handle the challenges posed by a manipulative boss.

Building Alliances with Coworkers to Address the Issue Collectively

In some cases, you may not be the only one affected by your boss's manipulative behavior. Building alliances with coworkers who share your concerns can be a powerful strategy in addressing the issue collectively. By working together, you can provide each other with emotional support, share experiences, and develop a united front in dealing with the manipulative boss.

When forming alliances, keep the following considerations in mind:

Be cautious about sharing information with coworkers. Ensure that you trust them and that they have also experienced or witnessed the manipulative behavior. Sharing sensitive information with the wrong person could backfire and damage your professional reputation.

Focus on the facts and your shared experiences. Avoid engaging in gossip or personal attacks, as this can create a toxic work environment and undermine your credibility. Instead, concentrate on specific incidents, behaviors, and their impacts on your work and well-being.

Brainstorm and develop a collective strategy. This may include jointly documenting incidents, sharing information and resources, or deciding to address the issue with management or HR as a group. Be sure to consider each person's individual risks and concerns when developing your strategy.

Support each other emotionally. Dealing with a manipulative boss can be emotionally draining and isolating. By working together, you can provide each other with much-needed emotional support, validation, and encouragement.

Remember that there is strength in numbers, and collaborating with coworkers can help you more effectively address the challenges posed by a manipulative boss. By working together, you can also foster a sense of solidarity and support within your workplace, which can help mitigate the negative impacts of your boss's behavior.

Utilizing Internal Channels for Anonymous Reporting or Feedback

If confronting your boss directly isn't a viable option or you're concerned about potential backlash, you can consider using internal channels for anonymous reporting or feedback. Many organizations have established systems in place to address employee concerns while protecting their anonymity.

Before using these channels, consider the following:

- Research your company's specific policies and procedures regarding anonymous reporting. Ensure you understand the process and any potential limitations of using these channels.

- When submitting your report or feedback, focus on the facts and provide specific examples of the manipulative behavior you have observed. This will help the recipient understand the severity of the issue and take appropriate action.

- Consider any potential risks associated with using anonymous channels. While these systems are designed to protect your identity, there is always a possibility that your identity may be inadvertently disclosed or guessed by others. Weigh the risks and benefits before proceeding.

- Be prepared for potential changes in your workplace dynamics after submitting an anonymous report. Although your identity is protected, there may still be a shift in the atmosphere as management addresses the issue.

- Keep in mind that while anonymous reporting can be a helpful tool, it may not always lead to immediate or significant changes. In some cases, it may be necessary to explore additional strategies for dealing with a manipulative boss.

Utilizing internal channels for anonymous reporting or feedback can be an effective way to raise concerns about a manipulative boss without putting your job or professional reputation at risk. By carefully considering your options and following the appropriate procedures, you can contribute to a more positive work environment and protect your well-being.

Exploring Options for Job Transfer or Seeking Alternative Employment

Sometimes, despite your best efforts, the situation with a manipulative boss might not improve. In such cases, it's essential to consider other options for maintaining your well-being and career growth. One option is to explore possibilities for a job transfer within your organization. A transfer to a different department or team can provide you with a fresh start, a more supportive work environment, and opportunities for professional growth.

To explore this option, you can:

- **Identify other departments** or teams within your organization where your skills and expertise would be valuable.

- **Network with colleagues** from these departments and express your interest in potential opportunities.

- **Research internal job postings** and stay informed about vacancies.

- **Approach your HR department** to discuss the possibility of a transfer and inquire about the necessary procedures.

Alternatively, if a job transfer is not feasible or the workplace culture is toxic, you may want to consider seeking alternative employment opportunities. This can be a difficult decision, but it's essential to prioritize your mental and emotional well-being in the long run. When searching for a new job, take time to research potential employers, assess the workplace culture, and gather information about management styles to ensure that you find a healthier and more supportive work environment.

Remember that taking action to protect your well-being and career growth is a sign of strength and self-respect, not weakness.

> "If we have a choice, it doesn't feel so heavy and unfree."
>
> - *Claudia*

In the quest for maintaining well-being and career growth amidst challenges with a manipulative boss, it's crucial to remember that having options can significantly lighten the burden of feeling trapped or constrained. Claudia reflects, "if we have a choice, it doesn't feel so heavy and unfree," highlighting the psychological relief and empowerment that comes from knowing there are alternatives. This sense of autonomy not only benefits the individual but also impacts the broader organizational dynamic. As Claudia observes, "Companies too feel when employees have other options and are not dependent on the company," suggesting that an employee's leverage and sense of independence can subtly influence the workplace environment and the company's approach to employee relations.

Exploring the possibility of a job transfer within your organization or seeking alternative employment outside it are two avenues to consider when faced with an unimproving situation. A transfer can offer a new beginning in a more positive setting, while the decision to leave for a new opportunity should be guided by thorough research into prospective employers' cultures and management styles. Above all, taking steps to safeguard your mental and emotional well-being is a profound act of self-respect and strength.

Key Takeaways

- Before confronting a manipulative boss, assess the extent of the manipulative behavior and its impact on you, and gather evidence to support your concerns.

- Choose the right time and setting: Schedule a private and neutral meeting at a time when your boss is more likely to be receptive.

- Approach the conversation with assertiveness, employing "I" statements and specific examples to clearly articulate your concerns without accusation.

- Transform confrontational scenarios into collaborative problem-solving discussions by externalizing the issue, separating it from personal attributes.

- Clearly define and communicate your limits to your boss, indicating behaviors you find unacceptable.

- Paraphrase and summarize key points discussed after your conversation, ensuring mutual understanding and a record for future reference.

- Assess changes post-conversation, and if no improvement is observed, consider escalating the issue or exploring alternative employment.

- In situations where confrontation might risk your job or reputation, alternative strategies such as documenting and reporting incidents, seeking guidance, or building alliances may be advisable.

- If the situation does not improve, explore internal job transfers or seek new employment opportunities to maintain your well-being and career growth.

- Remember, having choices about how to deal with a manipulative boss — whether to confront, transfer, or leave — can provide psychological relief and a sense of autonomy.

Incompetent
Loser
Not Good Enough
I am enough
I am capable
I am worthy

6

Understanding and Changing Core Beliefs

In our journey to navigate and overcome workplace manipulation, we must delve into the realm of core beliefs. These deeply held convictions, often formed in early life, shape our perception of the world, influence our reactions to various situations, and significantly impact our professional interactions. They are the lenses through which we view not only ourselves but also our relationships with others, including manipulative bosses or colleagues.

In this chapter, we unpack the concept of core beliefs, exploring how they can both make us vulnerable to manipulation and serve as a stronghold against it. Understanding your core beliefs is like uncovering the blueprint that guides your reactions and decisions, especially under pressure. By bringing these beliefs to light, we empower ourselves to reshape them, transforming potential weaknesses into strengths.

We will guide you through techniques to identify beliefs that make you susceptible to manipulation and provide strategies to challenge and reshape these beliefs. The journey of altering your core beliefs is not just about resistance to manipulation; it's about constructing a resilient, empowered self capable of thriving in complex work environments.

> "You won't believe it when you see it. You will see it when you believe it. What we see and believe, we become."
>
> *- Marisa Peer*

Changing core beliefs isn't about altering who you are but rather about evolving into the best version of yourself. It's about replacing narratives that no longer serve you with ones that champion your growth and well-being.

What are Core Beliefs?

Core beliefs are the very essence of how we see ourselves, other people, the world, and the future. These beliefs are deeply rooted perceptions that we've developed over time, often from our early life experiences. They are the fundamental principles that dictate our thoughts, emotions, and behaviors in various aspects of life, including our professional environment.

At their core, these beliefs are our brain's way of making sense of and navigating through our experiences. They help in simplifying the complexity of the world around us. However, they are often overgeneralized, absolute, and seen as unchangeable truths about our reality.

These beliefs can be positive, such as "I am capable and competent," or negative, like "I am not good enough." They often fall into several categories, including beliefs about oneself (self-esteem), beliefs about others (trust and relationships), and beliefs about the world (a sense of safety or fairness).

In the workplace, these core beliefs manifest in how we perceive our roles, values, and relationships with colleagues and superiors. For example, if someone has a core belief that they are incompetent, they may consistently undervalue their contributions and feel more susceptible to manipulation or negative feedback. By bringing these beliefs to light, you can start to question their validity and reshape them to better serve your personal and professional growth.

Before we move on, let's explore more specific examples of common limiting beliefs and how they might manifest in the workplace:

"I'm not worthy of success."

This belief might lead individuals to shy away from challenging projects or leadership roles, thinking they're not deserving. It could also result in self-sabotaging behaviors, like procrastination or not advocating for oneself in discussions about pay raises or promotions. This makes them prime targets for manipulation as they may not resist or speak out against unfair treatment.

"Work isn't meant to be enjoyable."

Individuals holding this belief may endure toxic situations without seeking change, accepting negative environments as the norm. This passivity can encourage manipulative leaders who rely on employees' acceptance of poor conditions to maintain control. Challenging this belief can empower employees to seek or create a more positive work culture.

"I must be perfect to be valued."

Perfectionism can lead to overworking, anxiety about making mistakes, and difficulty delegating tasks for fear they won't be done "correctly." This makes one susceptible to manipulation, as individuals may take on unreasonable workloads or agree to unrealistic deadlines in an attempt to prove their worth.

"I shouldn't express my opinions because they're not important."

This core belief might prevent individuals from contributing valuable ideas or feedback during meetings. It can also lead to a lack of boundary-setting, allowing others to overload them with tasks. By not voicing concerns, they become easier targets for manipulators who exploit silence as acquiescence.

"Conflict should be avoided at all costs."

People who avoid conflict may tolerate inappropriate behavior, refrain from negotiating for better conditions or salaries, and accept additional tasks even when overloaded. Manipulators might take advantage of this avoidance to push their agendas without opposition.

How Core Beliefs Influence Reactions to Manipulation

Our core beliefs significantly influence how we react to manipulative behavior in the workplace. These deeply ingrained beliefs can either make us more vulnerable to manipulation or empower us to resist and respond effectively.

When we hold negative core beliefs, particularly about ourselves, we are more susceptible to manipulation. For example, if you have a core belief that you are unworthy or inadequate, you might be more likely to accept unfair treatment or manipulation, as it aligns with your internal narrative. Manipulators often exploit these insecurities, using tactics that reinforce these negative beliefs, making their victims feel dependent or fearful of asserting themselves.

On the other hand, positive core beliefs about oneself can serve as a protective barrier against manipulation. If you believe you are competent and deserving of respect, you are more likely to recognize and challenge manipulative behaviors. You'll be more inclined to question actions and intentions that don't align with this belief, making you less likely to be swayed by guilt, fear, or undue influence.

Moreover, core beliefs about others and the world also play a role. If your belief system includes a trust that others are fundamentally fair and kind, you might be caught off guard by manipulative behaviors, not recognizing them immediately due to this optimistic bias. Conversely, an overly suspicious view of others might lead to misinterpreting genuine actions as manipulative, damaging healthy work relationships.

Understanding the influence of core beliefs on our reactions to manipulation helps us to see why we respond the way we do and guides us in reshaping these beliefs to foster healthier responses and relationships. By cultivating more balanced and realistic core beliefs, we can improve our resilience against manipulation and contribute to a more positive workplace environment.

Techniques to Identify Harmful Core Beliefs

Identifying harmful core beliefs is critical in understanding how they influence our reactions to workplace manipulation. As we delve into the techniques for identifying these beliefs, it's important to recognize that this process can be both enlightening and immediate. You might find that simply learning about core beliefs leads to a moment of realization about your own. For instance, you may suddenly understand why criticism at work always makes you feel not just upset but fundamentally flawed, revealing a core belief of inadequacy. Or, you might recognize a persistent belief that you must always please others, stemming from a need for approval. Let's have a look at various methods that can help you uncover and assess these deep-seated beliefs, whether they're immediately apparent or require more introspection:

- **Self-Reflection and Journaling**: One of the most effective ways to identify your core beliefs is through self-reflection. Journaling about your experiences, maybe even particularly those involving manipulation, can help you uncover patterns in your thoughts and reactions. Pay attention to recurring themes or statements about yourself, others, or the world.

- **Identify Emotional Triggers**: Pay attention to situations that evoke strong emotional reactions. Often, these reactions are indicators of underlying core beliefs. For instance, if criticism at work consistently makes you feel disproportionately upset or inadequate, it could signify a core belief related to self-worth or competence.

- **Challenge Automatic Thoughts**: When you notice a particularly negative or self-defeating thought, pause and question it. Ask yourself what this thought says about your deeper beliefs. For example, if you often think, "I can't do anything right at work," it might reflect a core belief of incompetence or inadequacy.

- **Seek Feedback from Trusted Individuals**: Sometimes, it's hard to clearly see our core beliefs. Talking to trusted colleagues, mentors, or friends about how you react to certain situations can provide external perspectives. They might be able to point out beliefs or patterns you're unaware of.

- **Look for Patterns in Your History**: Reflect on your past experiences, especially those in your formative years. Our core beliefs often develop early in life. Patterns in how you reacted to authority figures, criticism, or challenges in the past can provide clues to your current core beliefs.

- **Professional Guidance**: Working with a therapist or counselor can be immensely helpful in identifying and understanding your core beliefs. These professionals are trained to help you uncover deeper patterns of thinking and provide strategies to address them.

By using these techniques, you can begin to uncover the core beliefs that shape your responses to manipulative behaviors in the workplace. This awareness is the first step towards changing these beliefs and developing healthier, more empowered responses to manipulation.

Steps to Challenge and Modify Core Beliefs

Challenging and modifying core beliefs is a transformative process that can significantly impact how you perceive and react to manipulative behavior in the workplace. It involves a conscious effort to identify, question, and ultimately reshape the beliefs that dictate your responses. Here's how you can embark on this journey of self-reflection and change:

- **Identify Harmful Beliefs**: Begin by pinpointing the core beliefs that are negatively impacting your behavior and mindset. Use techniques from the previous section to uncover these beliefs. For example, if you often feel powerless in the face of manipulation, you may hold a core belief that you are inherently weak or incapable.

- **Evaluate Their Validity**: Once identified, critically evaluate these beliefs. Ask yourself questions like, "Is there concrete evidence supporting this belief?" or "Could there be another way to view this situation?" This step is about challenging the factual basis of your beliefs and considering alternative perspectives.

- **Understand Their Origin**: Understanding where these beliefs come from can be enlightening. Were they formed in response to past experiences, societal messages, or family dynamics? This is where Rapid Transformational Therapy (RTT®) developed by Marisa Peer can play a crucial role. RTT® helps in quickly identifying the root causes of these beliefs, often formed in response to past experiences, societal messages, or family dynamics. Recognizing the origin with the help of RTT® can help contextualize the belief and reduce its power over you.

- **Reframe the Belief**: Reframing involves altering the narrative around a core belief. Turn a negative belief into a more positive, realistic one. For instance, if you believe you must always acquiesce to your boss's demands to be valued, reframe this to, "My value is not solely determined by compliance; my ideas and boundaries are equally important." Also, in this process of reframing, Rapid Transformational Therapy (RTT®) can be incredibly beneficial. RTT® can assist in deeper and more effective reframing by addressing the root causes of these beliefs.

> → If you find it challenging to identify or reframe beliefs on your own, consider reaching out to a certified RTT® therapist for guidance and support in this transformative journey.

- **Practice New Beliefs**: Integrating new beliefs into your daily life is essential for personal transformation, and it's important to remember that repetition is key to this process. Research suggests that it takes around 21 days to change one's core beliefs, provided the approach is consistent and focused. When you encounter situations that trigger old patterns of thinking, take a moment to pause and consciously remind yourself of the new beliefs you are working to establish. With deliberate practice and patience, these new beliefs will gradually become more ingrained, eventually guiding your responses and actions more naturally.

> "People do not decide their futures; they decide their habits and their habits decide their futures."
>
> - *F.M. Alexander*

- **Seek Support**: Sometimes, the process of modifying core beliefs can be challenging and may bring up emotional resistance. Don't hesitate to seek support from a therapist, coach, or support group, especially when dealing with deep-rooted or traumatic beliefs.

- **Monitor Progress and Adapt**: Personal growth is a dynamic process. Regularly assess how the changes in your beliefs are affecting your responses to manipulation. Be open to adapting your approach as you learn and grow.

By working through these steps, you can begin to shed limiting beliefs and adopt a mindset that empowers you to respond to manipulation in the workplace more effectively and healthily. Remember, changing core beliefs is a journey, not a one-time event, and it's okay to take it one step at a time.

More Examples

Here are a few more examples of how "practicing new beliefs" can manifest in everyday situations:

- **Affirmations for Self-Worth**: Suppose your old belief is "I must always achieve to be valued." A new belief could be, "My worth is inherent, not earned." Practice this by starting your day with affirmations like "I am valuable just as I am." Repeat this affirmation, especially before meetings or projects, reinforcing the belief that your value doesn't fluctuate with your performance.

- **Responding to Criticism Constructively**: If you previously believed "Criticism means I'm a failure," shift to "Criticism is an opportunity to grow." When receiving feedback, practice pausing to remind yourself of this belief, then respond by asking clarifying questions or expressing gratitude for the opportunity to improve. This practice helps reframe your perspective on criticism and reduces the fear of making mistakes.

- **Setting Healthy Boundaries**: If an old core belief is "Saying no makes me selfish or unlikeable," adopt a new belief such as "Setting boundaries is a sign of self-respect and respect for others." Practice this by consciously deciding to say no to additional requests when you're already overburdened. Prepare a couple of polite but firm ways to decline extra work or social obligations, reinforcing the idea that it's okay to prioritize your well-being and existing commitments.

My Journey with RTT®

Embarking on the path to recovery and eventually writing this book, a pivotal turning point was indeed my experience with Rapid Transformational Therapy (RTT®), facilitated by Claudia. This therapy addressed the trauma inflicted by a toxic workplace and went further to uncover and transform deeply ingrained belief patterns rooted in my childhood. These patterns, I discovered, significantly magnified the pain and challenges I faced under manipulative leadership.

RTT® enabled me to identify and resolve these longstanding beliefs, offering profound clarity and liberation from the narratives that constrained me. Through the principles and practices of RTT®, Claudia guided me through a transformative journey. This process not only healed the wounds of my recent past but also equipped me with newfound resilience and a deeper understanding of my psyche. This therapy proved essential, catalyzing not just a recovery from immediate trauma but fostering a profound, enduring change that has propelled me forward in my personal and professional life.

How Changing Core Beliefs Can Improve Your Workplace Resilience

Altering core beliefs not only transforms how you perceive and interact with your environment but also significantly bolsters your resilience in the workplace. Resilience, the ability to bounce back from challenges and stress, is crucial in managing and responding to toxic dynamics in general and manipulative behavior in particular. Here's how evolving your core beliefs can enhance this resilience:

- **Improved Self-Efficacy**: Changing limiting core beliefs to more empowering ones can dramatically increase your sense of self-efficacy. When you believe in your ability to influence your environment and outcomes, you are more likely to take proactive steps in dealing with workplace manipulation. This self-assurance helps you navigate challenging situations with confidence and assertiveness.

- **Reduced Emotional Reactivity**: Altering core beliefs that trigger negative emotional responses enables you to approach potentially manipulative situations with a more level head. You become less reactive and more thoughtful in your responses, allowing you to de-escalate situations and make decisions that are in your best interest.

- **Enhanced Problem-Solving Skills**: With a change in core beliefs, your perspective on challenges changes. Problems are no longer insurmountable obstacles but opportunities for growth and learning. This shift in mindset enhances your ability to think creatively and find effective solutions to workplace issues.

- **Increased Adaptability**: As you challenge and modify your core beliefs, you naturally become more adaptable to change. This flexibility is crucial in dynamic work environments where manipulative behaviors may arise unexpectedly. Adaptability allows you to adjust your strategies and maintain your composure, even in the face of adversity.

- **Strengthened Interpersonal Relationships**: By fostering beliefs that emphasize your worth and the value of healthy boundaries, your interpersonal relationships can improve. You're better equipped to establish and maintain positive connections with colleagues, and you're more likely to seek and offer support, creating a stronger support network.

- **Enhanced Emotional Intelligence**: Changing your core beliefs also impacts your emotional intelligence. You become more aware of your emotions and those of others, which is crucial in identifying and responding to manipulation. This heightened emotional intelligence facilitates better communication, empathy, and relationship-building skills, all of which are essential for a resilient response to challenging workplace dynamics.

- **Greater Job Satisfaction and Well-Being**: Your overall job satisfaction can improve as you align your core beliefs with a more positive and realistic perspective. You're less likely to internalize negative experiences or feel overwhelmed by manipulative tactics. This not only enhances your professional experience but also contributes to your overall mental and emotional well-being.

- **Empowerment to Advocate for Change**: With renewed beliefs, you're more empowered to advocate for positive changes in your workplace. This could mean pushing for better policies against manipulation, helping to foster a healthier work culture, or even mentoring others who face similar challenges.

Transforming your core beliefs equips you with the mental and emotional fortitude to not just survive but also thrive in challenging professional environments. This journey of reshaping your core beliefs is an ongoing process, with each step forward enhancing your ability to navigate the complexities of the workplace with strength and adaptability. Moreover, this transformation sets you up for sustained success and well-being, impacting not only your professional life but also your personal life. The benefits of such a profound inner change are truly far-reaching and holistic.

Key Takeaways

- Core beliefs, formed early in life, significantly shape our view of ourselves, others, and the world, influencing how we react in professional settings, including situations involving manipulation.

- Beliefs like "I'm not worthy of success" or "I must be perfect to be valued" can make individuals more susceptible to manipulation by undermining self-esteem and promoting overwork and compliance.

- Holding positive beliefs about oneself can act as a defense against manipulation, encouraging resistance to unfair treatment and fostering self-respect.

- Techniques such as self-reflection, journaling, and feedback from trusted individuals can help uncover core beliefs that predispose one to manipulation.

- Questioning the validity of negative core beliefs and reframing them into more positive and empowering beliefs are crucial for personal growth and resilience.

- There are a variety of therapies that can be effective in identifying, challenging, and modifying deep-rooted core beliefs, facilitating significant personal transformation.

- Consistent reinforcement of new, positive beliefs through practices like affirmations and constructive responses to criticism is essential for changing core beliefs.

- Changing core beliefs can improve self-efficacy, emotional intelligence, and problem-solving skills, leading to better handling of manipulative behaviors and toxic work environments.

- Aligning core beliefs with positivity and realism will enhance your overall job satisfaction and mental well-being, making you less likely to be affected by manipulation.

7

Personal Coping Strategies and Resilience-Building Techniques

Dealing with a manipulative boss can take a toll on your mental health, well-being, and overall job satisfaction. While addressing the issue with your boss or reporting it to the appropriate authorities is crucial, it's equally important to develop personal coping strategies and resilience-building techniques to protect yourself from the negative effects of manipulation. This chapter focuses on practical tools and approaches that can help you navigate the challenges of working with a manipulative boss and empower you to thrive in the workplace.

> "Only I can change my life. No one can do it for me."
>
> *- Carol Burnett*

Establish Boundaries

Setting clear boundaries is essential for maintaining a healthy work-life balance and protecting your well-being. Consider the following steps to establish and maintain boundaries with your manipulative boss:

- **Identify Your Limits**: First, recognize what you're comfortable with and what you're not. Make a list of your non-negotiables, such as working hours, workload, and personal values.

- **Communicate Your Boundaries**: Then, clearly express your limits to your boss in a professional and assertive manner. For example, if you're unable to work overtime on a regular basis, calmly explain your reasons and offer alternative solutions if possible.

- **Be Consistent**: Consistently reinforcing your boundaries is crucial to maintaining your credibility and making it clear that you won't tolerate manipulation. If your boss continues to push your limits, reiterate your boundaries and stand firm in your decision.

- **Learn to Say "No"**: Saying no can be challenging, especially when dealing with a manipulative boss. However, practicing assertiveness and learning to say no when necessary is essential for maintaining your boundaries and mental health.

- **Practice Self-Compassion**: Recognize that setting boundaries can be challenging, especially with a manipulative boss. Be kind to yourself and acknowledge your efforts to maintain your well-being.

> Melissa works as a marketing manager in a small company. Her boss, Sarah, frequently pressures her to work late and often calls her during weekends. Melissa realized that her work-life balance was suffering, so she decided to establish boundaries. She communicated her limits clearly to Sarah, explaining that she would not be available for work-related matters after 6 PM and during weekends. At first, Sarah continued to call, but Melissa remained consistent and assertive. Over time, Sarah respected Melissa's boundaries, and Melissa regained control over her personal time.

Remember that establishing boundaries is an ongoing process and may require adjustments over time. It's crucial to be self-aware and flexible in your approach while ensuring your well-being is prioritized.

Develop a Support Network

"I will take the ring to Mordor, though I do not know the way," Frodo says in the The Lord of the Rings: The Fellowship of the Ring. Gandalf, the wise wizard, responds, "I will help you bear this burden, Frodo Baggins, as long as it is yours to bear." Just like Frodo, who embarks on an arduous journey with a group of trusted friends, you, too, should lean on the strength of others to help you through your challenges.

As you continue reading this book and gain new insights into dealing with a manipulative boss, always remember that you don't have to face this challenge alone. In fact, it's crucial to understand that seeking support from others can make a significant difference in your ability to navigate this difficult situation.

One of the most effective ways to cope with a manipulative boss or toxic boss in general is to build a strong support network, both inside and outside your workplace. A solid support network can provide emotional and practical assistance, helping you navigate the complexities of your situation.

Identify Allies at Work: Look for colleagues who may be experiencing similar issues or are empathetic to your situation. These individuals can provide valuable insights, share their own experiences, and support you in addressing the problem collaboratively.

Seek Mentorship: A mentor, either within or outside your organization, can offer valuable guidance and advice on dealing with a manipulative boss. A mentor who has successfully navigated similar situations can share their wisdom and help you develop strategies to cope with or resolve the issue.

Maintain Strong Connections with Friends and Family: Your personal support network is vital during challenging times. Sharing your experiences with friends and family can help you gain perspective, relieve stress, and receive emotional support, strengthening your resilience.

Join a Professional Network or Support Group: Connecting with others who are dealing with manipulative bosses in various workplaces can provide additional insights, encouragement, and resources. You can find these groups online, through professional associations, or within your local community, helping you to learn from a diverse range of experiences and strategies.

Remember: you don't have to face this situation alone. By building a strong support network, you can better navigate the challenges posed by a manipulative boss and develop coping strategies to maintain your well-being and professional success.

Engage in Self-Care and Stress Management

Coping with a manipulative boss can be emotionally and mentally draining, as it may lead to feelings of anxiety, self-doubt, frustration, and helplessness. Over time, these negative emotions can accumulate and exacerbate stress levels, affecting both your mental and physical health. In extreme cases, prolonged stress can even contribute to burnout, characterized by chronic exhaustion, cynicism, and reduced productivity. Therefore, acknowledging the gravity of your situation and taking steps to safeguard your mental and physical health is imperative.

Given the crucial importance of self-care and stress management in dealing with workplace manipulation, we've dedicated an entire chapter to this topic. In Chapter 8, "Self-Care and Stress Management," you'll find an extensive exploration of strategies and practices vital for maintaining your well-being in challenging work environments. This chapter delves into various aspects of self-care, including physical, emotional, and spiritual practices, and provides a comprehensive toolkit for effective stress management. From physical self-care like exercise and sleep to emotional techniques such as mindfulness and even strategies for setting clear boundaries, Chapter 8 is a resource designed to empower you with holistic and personalized approaches to resilience and well-being in the face of manipulative behavior at work.

Cultivate a Growth Mindset

Carol Dweck, a renowned psychologist, has extensively studied the impact of mindsets on human motivation and success. In her book *Mindset: The New Psychology of Success* (2006), she identified two primary mindsets: growth and fixed. A growth mindset believes that intelligence and abilities can be developed and improved through dedication, hard work, and the right strategies. In contrast, a fixed mindset assumes that qualities like intelligence and personality are unchangeable traits.

Dweck's work highlights how our beliefs, conscious or subconscious, strongly influence our motivation, behavior, and achievements. People with a fixed mindset often focus on proving themselves and may avoid challenges, whereas those with a growth mindset embrace challenges as opportunities to learn and grow. The growth mindset fosters a passion for learning and improvement, which can lead to more success and resilience during challenging times.

To cultivate a growth mindset, it's important to focus on effort, embrace challenges, and learn from feedback. This mindset enables people to thrive during difficult situations and turn setbacks into future successes. It's also crucial to practice self-compassion and understand that failure is a part of the learning process.

A key aspect of developing a growth mindset is recognizing the power of the word "yet." This word can shift the focus from current limitations to future possibilities. When faced with a difficult problem, instead of thinking that you're not smart enough to solve it, consider that you just haven't solved it **yet**. This approach encourages persistence, resilience, and learning from mistakes.

To encourage a growth mindset in children, we're supposed to focus on praising their effort, strategies, and perseverance rather than their intelligence or talent. This approach builds resilience and a healthy attitude towards learning and improvement. By cultivating a growth mindset, individuals can better navigate challenges and setbacks, ultimately leading to greater success and fulfillment.

Here are some ways to cultivate a growth mindset:

- ☑ **Embrace Challenges**: View difficult situations, such as dealing with a manipulative boss, as opportunities to learn and grow. Seek out new challenges and push yourself beyond your comfort zone.

- ☑ **Learn from Feedback**: Be open to feedback and criticism, whether it comes from your boss or colleagues. Use this input to improve your skills, behavior, or approach to a particular issue.

- ☑ **Focus on Effort, not just Results**: Recognize that effort and persistence are key factors in achieving success. Celebrate your progress and the effort you put into overcoming obstacles, even if the results are imperfect.

- ☑ **Stay Curious and Open-Minded**: Approach your work and interactions with others with curiosity and a willingness to learn. This attitude will help you develop a deeper understanding of your situation and the people around you.

- ☑ **Practice Self-Compassion**: Be kind to yourself when things don't go as planned. Recognize that setbacks are a natural part of the learning process, and use them as opportunities to grow and improve.

> *"A ship in harbor is safe, but that is not what ships are built for."*
>
> *- John A. Shedd*

Cultivating a growth mindset, you will become more resilient, adaptive, and open to change, which will help you navigate the challenges of dealing with a manipulative boss more effectively.

Adopting the Observer Role

The modern workplace is a dynamic environment characterized by a myriad of interactions, challenges, and opportunities. Each day presents us with situations where we are required to react, decide, and communicate. Amidst this complex web, adopting the observer role can be a potent strategy to navigate workplace intricacies more effectively.

The observer role refers to the conscious effort to view situations from a detached, unbiased perspective. Imagine watching a movie where you're an audience member witnessing the events, emotions, and actions but not being directly entangled in them. Positioning oneself in this way makes it possible to see the broader context, free from the immediate emotional impulses that often cloud our judgment.

In this subchapter, we will delve into the significance of the observer role, highlighting its benefits in the workplace context. By understanding the practical techniques to assume this role and recognizing its potential challenges, readers will be equipped with a valuable tool to enhance their professional interactions and decision-making capabilities.

Benefits in the Workplace

The fast-paced nature of the contemporary workplace can often lead to quick, emotion-driven decisions. While emotional intelligence is undoubtedly vital, there are situations where an objective, detached perspective offers invaluable insights. Adopting the observer role can lead to several benefits in a professional setting:

Emotional Detachment for Clearer Decision-Making: Think of those times when high-pressure situations or unexpected conflicts arise. Emotions can cloud your judgment, right? By stepping into the observer role, you can distance yourself from these intense feelings, even if just for a moment. This allows you to base your decisions on facts and the bigger picture rather than just immediate reactions.

Enhanced Self-Awareness Preventing Impulsive Reactions: When you take a moment to observe your actions and reactions from a distance, patterns begin to emerge. Recognizing these patterns boosts your self-awareness. This newfound insight can be your shield, helping you pause, reflect, and choose responses that align with your best interests.

Building Resilience Against Manipulative Behaviors: Let's face it; office politics and manipulative tactics are realities many of us grapple with. By adopting the observer role, you can discern such tactics, understand the underlying intentions, and craft responses that sidestep the drama, keeping your integrity intact.

In essence, the observer role isn't about suppressing emotions but about gaining the ability to choose how and when to engage with them. It offers a vantage point from which individuals can navigate their professional journey with a mix of empathy and objectivity.

Practical Techniques

Adopting the observer role is not about simply deciding to be detached; it requires practice and consistent application of specific techniques. Here are some actionable methods that will help you cultivate this role in the workplace:

- ☑ **Recognizing Emotional Triggers**: Start by understanding what strikes a chord with you. Try listing situations, remarks, or behaviors that tend to evoke strong emotional reactions in you. Recognizing these triggers equips you to better anticipate and handle your responses when they're triggered.

- ☑ **Visualization Exercises for Mental Distancing**: When faced with a challenging situation, take a moment to close your eyes and visualize watching the scene from a balcony or as an audience member in a theater. This mental shift can help in distancing oneself from the immediate emotions, offering a broader perspective.

☑ **Journaling or Reflective Practices Post-Event**: After significant meetings, discussions, or events, take a few minutes to jot down your thoughts, emotions, and reactions. Over time, this practice not only offers insights into personal patterns but also helps in refining the observer role. It's like having a conversation with yourself from a detached perspective.

☑ **Mindful Breathing**: Whenever you find your emotions escalating or stress building, your breath can be your anchor. Engage in deep, mindful breathing to center yourself, making it smoother for you to shift into the observer frame of mind.

☑ **Setting Intentional Reminders**: Place reminders around your workspace or set periodic notifications on your phone with messages like "Take a step back" or "Observe, don't react." These cues can serve as a nudge to adopt the observer role, especially in heated moments.

While these techniques can be invaluable, they require regular practice and effort on your part. Yet, with time and dedication, they can seamlessly integrate into your routine, empowering you to gracefully handle the intricacies of your professional environment.

Balancing Engagement and Detachment

While the observer role offers numerous benefits, especially in emotionally charged or complex situations, it's still important you find a balance between detachment and genuine engagement. Here's how to maintain that equilibrium:

Understanding the Value of Both: Recognize that both engagement and detachment have their respective places in the workplace. Engaging authentically builds rapport, trust, and deeper connections with colleagues, while detachment can provide clarity, emotional neutrality, and objectivity in situations that require them.

Read the Room: Assess the dynamics of each situation. There are moments when it's more beneficial to be fully present and emotionally connected, such as during team-building activities or personal conversations with colleagues. Yet, in tense meetings or amidst conflicts, taking on the observer role might serve you better.

Shift Gears Mindfully: The ability to shift between engagement and detachment is a skill that comes with practice. Be aware of when you're choosing one stance over the other, ensuring it aligns with the situation at hand and the desired outcome.

Avoid Over-Detachment: While being an observer can shield you from impulsive responses, remember that being perpetually detached can make you seem distant or uninterested. Such a stance can hamper your ability to form strong relationships and might leave others feeling like they aren't being truly seen or valued by you.

Self-Check Regularly: Reflect periodically on your interactions. Are there patterns of always leaning more towards engagement or detachment? Regular self-assessments can guide adjustments and refinements in your approach.

Seek Feedback: From time to time, consider seeking input from colleagues you trust. Their perspectives can clue you in on whether you're coming off as overly aloof or excessively involved, guiding you towards a more balanced demeanor.

In essence, the finesse of harmonizing engagement and detachment lies in fluidity – the ability to gracefully transition between the two roles based on the demands of each situation. Achieving this balance ensures both effective communication and personal well-being in the workplace.

Challenges and Limitations

While adopting the observer role can be beneficial, you should also understand its limitations and potential pitfalls to ensure a balanced and effective use. Here are some challenges you might face:

Risk of Emotional Disconnection: If you find yourself consistently leaning into the observer role, be mindful of a growing sense of detachment from your feelings. Over time, this can make it challenging for you to fully experience and navigate your emotions, possibly leading to a sense of emotional inertia.

Misinterpretation by Colleagues: Using the observer role too frequently might cause those around you to interpret your behavior as indifferent or lacking enthusiasm. This could put a damper on teamwork, the trust you've built, and collaborative efforts at work.

Over-Reliance: While the observer stance is undoubtedly a handy tool, it shouldn't be your go-to for every situation. Depending on it excessively can impede the growth of other crucial interpersonal skills you need, like empathy, engaged listening, and assertiveness.

Potential for Avoidance: Be vigilant that you're not using the observer role as a barrier to dodge confronting your own emotions or tough situations. You'll need to discern if your detachment is genuinely serving a constructive purpose or if it's just a means of evasion.

Difficulty in Shifting Roles: For some, once they've grown comfortable in the observer's shoes, it can become a challenge to shift back into a more engaged role when it's needed. Such rigidity can affect your ability to adapt to diverse situations in your professional environment.

Limits to Objective Perspective: Even though detachment can grant clarity, remember that no viewpoint is entirely unbiased. Even when you're in the observer role, your personal experiences and inherent biases could still shape how you perceive and interpret things.

To successfully navigate these challenges, make self-awareness and introspection a habit. Regularly connect with yourself, solicit feedback when appropriate, and remain open to fine-tuning your approach. This will help you harness the benefits of the observer role while minimizing potential drawbacks in the workplace.

Conclusion

Navigating the intricacies of professional life calls for versatile approaches. The observer role offers a distinct lens to view situations, fostering clarity and resilience. Yet, it's essential to remember that no single approach fits all scenarios. Balance is key. Whether you're immersing yourself wholeheartedly or taking a step back to assess, staying attuned to your feelings and the context is paramount. Your professional journey is uniquely yours; embrace the tools at your disposal and adapt them to serve you best.

Are You a Perfectionist Yourself?

Earlier, we discussed how a perfectionist boss might employ manipulative techniques to drive their employees to work harder. But what if the perfectionist isn't just your boss, but you yourself? Perfectionism can be both a blessing and a curse. On the one hand, striving for excellence can lead to outstanding achievements and personal satisfaction. On the other hand, setting excessively high standards for oneself can result in stress, burnout, and a sense of never being good enough. And still, our quest for excellence pushes us to the brink of exhaustion. Time and again, we find ourselves falling into patterns that are clearly detrimental to our well-being. High standards are set as the norm in both our personal lives and the professional world. The clear loser in this perilous game is our soul.

Oh, and one more thing: perfectionists are particularly vulnerable to manipulation, as their intense desire to meet high standards can be exploited by others. A manipulator can easily prey on a perfectionist's fear of failure or criticism, steering them into actions or decisions that serve the manipulator's interests rather than their own. This dynamic can be seen in both personal and professional relationships, where the perfectionist may find themselves going above and beyond to please a friend or boss, even to their detriment.

Also, the constant striving for perfection can make one susceptible to specific types of manipulation related to their perfectionism. For instance, manipulators may use gaslighting tactics, making the perfectionist doubt their capabilities or worth, ultimately causing them to work harder to prove their worth. Such manipulative tactics can leave the perfectionist feeling trapped, as their drive for perfection can be turned against them, leading to a vicious cycle of manipulation and self-doubt. By acknowledging the vulnerability of perfectionists to manipulation, we can begin to identify and address these harmful dynamics and foster a more supportive and empowering environment.

In this section, we will explore what it means to be a perfectionist and how self-imposed perfectionism can impact your life, both positively and negatively. Let's have a closer look.

Understanding Self-Imposed Perfectionism

Perfectionism is commonly defined as the desire to be flawless and the pursuit of extremely high standards, often accompanied by critical self-evaluations and concerns regarding others' evaluations. However, it's important to note that not all perfectionism is detrimental.

Typical Characteristics of Perfectionism are:

- A strong desire to avoid failure
- An intense focus on achieving flawlessness
- An overemphasis on precision and organization
- A tendency to be highly self-critical

It's important that you're aware of the difference between healthy striving and detrimental perfectionism. Healthy striving is a positive form of perfectionism where individuals set high, yet achievable standards and use them as motivation to reach their goals. This form of perfectionism can lead to increased satisfaction, improved performance, and a sense of accomplishment.

On the other hand, detrimental perfectionism, also known as maladaptive perfectionism, involves setting excessively high or unrealistic standards that are almost impossible to meet. This type of perfectionism can lead to feelings of inadequacy, fear of failure, and even mental health issues such as anxiety and depression. The distinction between these two forms of perfectionism is essential, as they have very different impacts on an individual's life and well-being.

The Impact of Perfectionism on Individual Well-Being

When perfectionism takes control of your life, it can have significant effects on your psychological, physical, and social well-being. Let's dive deeper into each of these aspects and reflect on how they might be influencing your daily experiences and relationships.

Psychological Effects: Do you often find yourself feeling anxious or stressed out because you're not meeting your own high standards? This is a common experience for perfectionists. The constant pursuit of flawlessness can lead to anxiety, depression, and even burnout. When you set unrealistic expectations for yourself, the inevitable failure to meet these expectations can result in feelings of inadequacy and self-doubt. You feel that you are never good enough, regardless of your efforts and achievements. Take a moment to consider how your perfectionism might be affecting your mental health.

In addition to the stresses and self-doubt that can arise from self-imposed high standards, perfectionists often experience the frustration of chasing an ever-moving goalpost. Just as you reach what you thought was the pinnacle of achievement, the benchmark for success seems to shift. There is always someone who appears to be doing better, achieving more, or living a seemingly perfect life. This constant comparison with others can exacerbate feelings of inadequacy and fuel the fire of perfectionism, as you push yourself even harder to reach the unattainable goal of being the best. It's crucial to recognize this destructive cycle and take steps to break free from the comparison trap, as it only serves to undermine your confidence and mental well-being.

Physical Effects: The psychological stress caused by perfectionism can also manifest physically. Do you sometimes feel physically exhausted, not from a workout, but from the pressure you put on yourself to be perfect? This exhaustion can lead to other health problems, such as headaches, digestive issues, and sleep disturbances. Also, perfectionists often push themselves to the point of exhaustion in their pursuit of flawlessness, further jeopardizing their physical health. Reflect on any physical symptoms you might be experiencing as a result of your perfectionism.

Social Effects: Perfectionism can strain relationships, as individuals may have unrealistic expectations not only for themselves but also for those around them. Do you find yourself frequently criticizing your loved ones or feeling frustrated when they don't meet your expectations? This can lead to conflicts and feelings of resentment. In addition, perfectionists may isolate themselves from others out of fear of judgment or criticism, further exacerbating feelings of loneliness and inadequacy. Think about how your pursuit of perfection might be affecting your social life and the people you care about most.

In each of these areas, it's important to recognize the toll that perfectionism can take on your well-being and to take steps to mitigate its impact. Remember, striving for excellence is a commendable goal, but it's also crucial to set realistic and achievable standards for yourself and to practice self-compassion when things don't go as planned.

Causes and Triggers of Perfectionism

No one enters the world with the wish of being perfect. Perfectionism is made. It can stem from various sources, each intertwining with one another to shape your perceptions and behaviors. Understanding the root of your perfectionism can be a crucial step in managing it. Let's delve into some common causes and triggers.

Personality Traits: Certain personality traits, such as being highly conscientious, detail-oriented, or averse to risk, can predispose someone to perfectionism. Reflect on your own personality traits and consider how they might contribute to your perfectionistic tendencies.

Cultural and Societal Influences: The culture and society we live in can also play a significant role in shaping our expectations and values. Social media, for instance, often portrays an idealized version of life, which can exacerbate feelings of inadequacy and the desire to be perfect. Similarly, certain cultures or societies may place a high value on achievement and success, further fueling perfectionism. Think about the external influences that might be affecting your quest for perfection.

Past Experiences and Upbringing: Our past experiences and how we were raised can significantly impact our self-esteem and expectations. For instance, growing up with overly critical parents or experiencing traumatic events can lead to a heightened need for control and perfection as a way to cope with these experiences. Reflect on your upbringing and past experiences and consider how they might have contributed to your perfectionism. In particular, think about the role that achievement played during your childhood. Were there rewards or punishments associated with performance? Were your parents overly excited, proud, and rewarding when you got good grades at school and overly critical when you didn't?

In identifying the causes and triggers of your perfectionism, it's important to remember that you are not alone and that there are ways to challenge and change these patterns. By gaining insight into the origins of your perfectionism, you can begin to develop a more balanced and self-compassionate approach to your goals and aspirations.

Strategies to Overcome Detrimental Perfectionism

If you think you might be harboring perfectionist traits that are more harmful than helpful, you're not alone. Here are some proven strategies to help you turn the tide and find a healthier balance:

Reflection and Self-Awareness: Start by reflecting on your perfectionist tendencies and the impact they have on your life. Ask yourself questions like: "What are my perfectionist beliefs?" and "How does perfectionism affect my day-to-day life?" By developing self-awareness, you can start to recognize patterns and triggers of your perfectionism.

Challenging and Changing Perfectionist Thoughts: Once you identify perfectionist thoughts, challenge them. Are these thoughts rational? Are they helpful? Try to reframe these thoughts in a more balanced and realistic way. For example, change "I must do this perfectly" to "I will do the best I can within reasonable limits, understanding that not everything requires perfection."

Embracing Imperfection and Learning from Failures: Understand that perfection is an unrealistic standard. Embrace imperfections and recognize that making mistakes and experiencing failures are normal and valuable parts of learning. Each mistake or failure is an opportunity to grow and improve. Ask yourself, "What can I learn from this experience?"

Practicing Self-Compassion and Kindness: Be kind to yourself. Understand that you are human, and it's okay not to be perfect — practice self-compassion by treating yourself with the kindness and understanding you would offer a friend. Remember, self-compassion is not a sign of weakness but rather a strength that can help you build resilience and thrive in the face of challenges.

By adopting these strategies, you can start to shift your mindset and move towards a healthier, more balanced approach to perfectionism. Remember, overcoming detrimental perfectionism is a journey, and it's okay to seek support from friends, family, or a therapist along the way.

Case Study: Ingrid's Journey from Perfectionism to Self-Acceptance

Ingrid was a patient who sat in front of **Claudia**, tears streaming down her face as she came to terms with the toll her constant pursuit of perfection was taking on her life. This was a pivotal moment for

Ingrid, one that laid bare the cost of always trying to meet impossibly high standards.

Reflecting on Ingrid's journey, it serves as a powerful case study of the detrimental impact perfectionism can have on our lives and the path towards self-acceptance and a more balanced approach to life's challenges.

Ingrid's story illustrates the life of a successful professional who appeared to have a perfect life on the surface. Yet, she experienced constant pressure to be perfect in every aspect of her life — from her career to her relationships. This pressure was not only exhausting but also left her feeling overwhelmed, anxious, and burned out.

During one session, Claudia suggested that Ingrid conduct a self-experiment. For one week, she was to attempt to do everything perfectly — her work, her relationships, her diet, everything. At the end of each day, Ingrid was to reflect on her experiences, noting what she did, how she felt, and any challenges she encountered.

The Lessons Learned:

At the end of the week, Ingrid had a series of important realizations. She recognized that it was okay to read an email just once before sending it instead of obsessively checking it multiple times. She realized the value of delegating tasks to others and how this helped alleviate her feelings of overwhelm. Most importantly, she discovered that by loosening her grip on perfection, she had more energy and enthusiasm for life.

The Positive Changes Experienced:

As Ingrid began to challenge her perfectionist thoughts and embrace imperfection, she experienced a profound shift in her well-being. She found that she was no longer as exhausted at the end of the day and had more time and energy for the activities and people she loved. Her relationships improved as she let go of the pressure to be the perfect partner, friend, or family member.

Conclusion:

Ingrid's journey from perfectionism to self-acceptance is a testament to the transformative power of self-awareness and intentional change. By recognizing the cost of her perfectionist tendencies, challenging her perfectionist thoughts, and embracing imperfection, Ingrid was able to break free from the shackles of perfectionism and live a more balanced and fulfilling life.

Just as Ingrid learned to let go of her pursuit of perfection, so can you. Remember, you are not your achievements or failures. You are valuable and worthy just as you are. Treat yourself with kindness, embrace your imperfections, and celebrate your successes, no matter how small they may be.

You are NOT Your Achievements or Failures

You are Valuable and Worthy Just as You are

Treat Yourself with Kindness, Embrace Your Imperfections

Are You a People Pleaser?

Being a supportive colleague is a valuable trait, but if your desire to please consistently outweighs your own needs and desires, you might be caught in a people-pleasing cycle. A comprehensive article written by psychotherapist and coach Agnes Kucharska, titled "Breaking the People Pleasing Habit: Recognizing Signs, Unveiling Consequences, and Mastering Lasting Transformation," provides significant insight into this phenomenon.

The Roots of People-Pleasing

According to Kucharska, people-pleasing often originates from an emotionally troubled childhood, where individuals learn to prioritize the needs of others in a subconscious bid for value and acknowledgment. People-pleasers might find it hard to assert themselves, fear conflict, overcommit to tasks, and regularly seek approval from others. Unfortunately, these behaviors can lead to resentment, exhaustion, and a fragile sense of self-identity and self-worth.

The Impact on Professional Life

Manipulative bosses can recognize and exploit these tendencies, making people-pleasers vulnerable to unreasonable work demands and disregarding their professional boundaries. They often employ manipulation techniques specifically tailored to leverage the accommodating nature of people-pleasers, such as guilt-tripping them into taking on extra work or using vague promises of future rewards to extract more effort and loyalty. This exploitation not only places an undue burden on people-pleasers but also encroaches upon their personal time and well-being, leading to a cycle of over-commitment and, ultimately, professional burnout.

The psychological impact on individuals with people-pleasing tendencies can be profound and detrimental. Constantly striving to meet the ever-expanding expectations of a manipulative boss can lead to chronic stress and a significant decrease in self-esteem, as their professional worth becomes intertwined with their ability to appease others. This relentless pressure to perform and please can result in feelings of inadequacy and failure, particularly when the goalposts for success are continually shifted. Recognizing these dynamics is crucial for people-pleasers to begin asserting their boundaries and reclaiming their professional agency.

Strategies for Transformation

Kucharska suggests various therapeutic methods that can aid in breaking the cycle of people-pleasing. Dialectical Behaviour Therapy (DBT) and Rapid Transformational Therapy (RTT®) can be incredibly effective. These approaches help individuals challenge and reframe negative beliefs, improve emotional regulation and interpersonal effectiveness, and address past experiences that contribute to people-pleasing tendencies.

Further, mindfulness practice and harnessing the power of neuroplasticity — the brain's ability to adapt and change in response to new experiences — are also crucial in overcoming people-pleasing habits. Individuals can rewire their brains and promote healthier interactions by mindfully reinforcing new behaviors. In conjunction, setting personal boundaries and practicing self-care are pivotal in cultivating a robust sense of self.

> "If you are a giver, know your limits because takers do not have any."
>
> *- spark.co.at*

A Case Study: Jane's Journey from People-Pleaser to Self-Assured Professional

Jane, a dedicated project manager at a busy marketing firm, prided herself on being the go-to person for any crisis. Known for her reliability, she often found herself juggling multiple tasks beyond her job description. Her willingness to always say "yes" earned her temporary praise but perpetuated a cycle where colleagues would delegate their responsibilities to her, leading to late nights and forfeited weekends.

The turning point came during a particularly taxing project where Jane's health began to suffer due to stress. Dark circles had become permanent features under her eyes, and a perpetual weariness became her constant companion, signaling that her lifestyle was unsustainable. It was then that a close friend, observing Jane's deteriorating state, helped her realize she had an unhealthy compulsion to please others at the expense of her own needs. Jane sought professional help and learned that her desire to please stemmed from a deep-rooted fear of rejection. This insight was the catalyst for Jane to seek change.

The Therapeutic Journey:

With guidance from a cognitive-behavioral therapist, Jane began to challenge her limiting beliefs. She attended DBT sessions to improve her emotional regulation and learned through ACT to align her actions with her values, which did not include overworking herself to illness.

One of Jane's first steps was to start saying "no" to tasks that interfered with her primary responsibilities or personal time. She practiced assertive communication, expressing her concerns without fear of conflict. Gradually, her colleagues started to respect her boundaries, and her workload became more manageable.

The Lessons Learned:

Jane discovered that assertiveness does not equate to selfishness. By valuing her time and needs, she could still be a valuable team member without compromising her well-being. She learned the power of delegation and the importance of trusting her team's capabilities. And perhaps the biggest takeaway for Jane: cherish your friends and hear them out.

The Positive Changes Experienced:

As Jane implemented these changes, her work-life balance improved dramatically. Her health recovered, her stress levels dropped, and her satisfaction with her work soared. Her relationships with colleagues improved as they now engaged with her more respectfully.

Conclusion:

Jane's journey from a chronic people-pleaser to a self-assured professional illustrates the transformative power of self-awareness and personal growth. It shows that with the right strategies and support, it's possible to break free from unhealthy patterns and create a more balanced and rewarding professional life.

Seek Clarity Through Professional Support

If the situation with your manipulative boss is taking a significant toll on your mental health and well-being, considering professional assistance is a wise move. Therapists and counselors are trained to help individuals navigate difficult relationships and develop coping strategies to face challenging situations. And let us be clear: seeking professional guidance is not a sign of weakness but rather a testament to strength and self-awareness. It reflects a commitment to prioritize your well-being and to arm yourself with the best tools and strategies for the challenges at hand. There's absolutely no shame in seeking expert perspectives; on the contrary, it's a commendable step towards personal growth and resilience.

The range of tools professionals offer spans from traditional therapy to various therapeutic alternatives:

Traditional Therapy: A licensed therapist or counselor can help you process your emotions, develop effective communication strategies, and provide guidance on setting boundaries with your boss. They can also help you identify patterns of behavior that may be contributing to the toxic work environment and suggest ways to break these patterns.

Cognitive Behavioral Therapy (CBT): This form of therapy focuses on identifying and changing negative thought patterns and behaviors. A CBT therapist can help you develop healthy coping mechanisms and improve your emotional resilience in dealing with a manipulative boss.

Mindfulness-Based Therapy: Techniques like mindfulness meditation can help you manage stress, increase self-awareness, and enhance emotional regulation. Mindfulness-based therapy, like Mindfulness-Based Stress Reduction (MBSR) and Mindfulness-Based Cognitive Therapy (MBCT), can teach you how to practice mindfulness in your daily life.

Rapid Transformational Therapy (RTT®): RTT® is a hybrid therapy that combines elements of hypnotherapy, neuro-linguistic programming (NLP), and cognitive behavioral therapy. It aims to help individuals identify and change subconscious beliefs that may be contributing to their emotional distress. RTT® can be particularly helpful in addressing issues related to self-esteem, confidence, and assertiveness.

Eye Movement Desensitization and Reprocessing (EMDR): EMDR is a psychotherapy treatment designed to alleviate the distress associated with traumatic memories. It involves the patient recalling distressing images while receiving one of several types of bilateral sensory input, such as side-to-side eye movements. EMDR can be particularly effective for individuals who have experienced trauma and can help in processing and integrating traumatic experiences in a healthier way.

Group Therapy or Support Groups: Joining a group therapy session or a support group can provide you with a safe space to share your experiences and learn from others who have dealt with similar situations. This can be an excellent way to gain insights, develop coping strategies, and receive emotional support.

Online Therapy: With advancements in technology, there are now various online platforms that offer therapy sessions through video calls, chat, or email. This can be a convenient and accessible option for those who may not have the time or resources to attend in-person therapy sessions.

By seeking professional help and exploring different therapeutic options, you can better manage the impact of a manipulative boss on your mental health and well-being. Remember, it's essential to prioritize your well-being and seek support when needed.

As you build resilience and develop coping strategies, remember that maintaining your well-being is vital. These coping strategies can act as your first line of defense, but it's also crucial to supplement them with regular self-care and stress management practices. In the upcoming chapter, we will delve into these aspects in greater detail, exploring ways to care for yourself physically, emotionally, and socially. This focus on holistic well-being will serve as your shield and buffer against the stress caused by manipulative behaviors in the workplace.

Key Takeaways

- Define your limits regarding workload, working hours, and personal values, and communicate these boundaries assertively to your boss.

- Build a strong support network both inside and outside of work, including allies, mentors, and friends who understand and support your situation.

- Engage in self-care and prioritize activities that maintain your physical and mental health to protect against the negative effects of workplace manipulation.

- Cultivate a growth mindset by embracing challenges as opportunities for learning and growth. Focus on effort and resilience rather than perfection.

- Adopt the observer role and practice viewing workplace dynamics from a detached perspective to make more objective decisions and reduce emotional reactivity.

- Find the right balance between being emotionally involved and maintaining an objective stance, depending on the situation.

- Regularly assess if adopting the observer role is leading to feelings of detachment from your emotions or colleagues.

- Identify if perfectionist tendencies affect your well-being and learn strategies to embrace imperfection and self-compassion.

- If you tend to prioritize others' needs over your own, recognize this pattern of People Pleasing and work on setting healthier boundaries and asserting your needs.

- Consider therapy or counseling to develop healthier coping mechanisms, especially if workplace manipulation is significantly impacting your mental health.

"I am worthy"
"I am enough"

8

Self-Care and Stress Management

In the previous chapter, we discussed personal coping strategies and resilience-building techniques. Now, we turn our attention to an equally significant topic – self-care and stress management. In dealing with manipulative behavior, maintaining your well-being is as crucial as asserting boundaries and developing resilience. These practices will lay the foundation for the next critical step in our journey: developing emotional intelligence and communication skills.

After discussing the potential impact of manipulative behavior on your mental well-being, we'll now focus on helping you create a personalized and holistic self-care routine that encompasses various aspects of well-being, including physical, emotional, social, and spiritual self-care. This will include practical tips for incorporating self-care activities into your daily life, such as exercise, nutrition, mindfulness practices, hobbies, social connections, and sleep hygiene. Our goal is to emphasize the importance of maintaining a balanced and consistent self-care routine to promote overall well-being in the face of a toxic work environment.

> "We cannot become what we want by remaining what we are."
>
> - *Max Depree*

Lastly, we'll delve deeper into specific strategies and techniques for managing stress in response to manipulative behavior and toxic leadership. This section will cover techniques such as cognitive restructuring, time management, relaxation exercises, deep breathing, progressive muscle relaxation, and grounding techniques. Our objective is to equip you with a toolkit of practical, evidence-based stress reduction methods that can be employed in moments of heightened stress or anxiety resulting from a toxic work environment.

Recognizing the Impact of Manipulative Behavior on Mental Well-Being

It's no secret that toxic leadership and manipulative behavior can severely impact your mental health, leading to stress, anxiety, and even burnout. Numerous scientific studies have confirmed the negative effects of such a work environment on employees' mental well-being. For instance, research by Tepper (2000), as discussed in a review by Schyns and Schilling (2013), found that abusive supervision can lead to heightened levels of stress and anxiety among subordinates. Additionally, a meta-analysis by Verkuil, Atasayi, and Molendijk (2015) revealed that exposure to workplace bullying is consistently associated with reduced mental health, indicating a significant predictor of depression and psychological distress.

One memorable example of the harmful impact of a toxic work environment on mental health can be found in the movie "Office Space." The main character, Peter Gibbons, suffers from constant stress, anxiety, and dissatisfaction due to the manipulative behavior of his boss, Bill Lumbergh. As the movie progresses, Peter's mental well-being deteriorates, further highlighting the consequences of enduring a toxic workplace.

It's essential to recognize the impact that a toxic work environment can have on your well-being and take proactive steps to mitigate its effects. By acknowledging the problem, you are better equipped to identify and implement strategies to safeguard your mental health and ensure a more positive and fulfilling work experience.

Creating a Personalized and Holistic Self-Care Routine

In this section, we will guide you through designing a personalized and holistic self-care routine that addresses various aspects of well-being. We will provide comprehensive information, practical tips, and techniques for implementing effective self-care practices in your daily life.

Physical Self-Care: Exercise, Nutrition, and Sleep

Regular exercise, proper nutrition, and adequate sleep are crucial for maintaining your physical health and resilience. Follow at least two of the following steps, and you will witness a remarkable transformation in your energy levels, mood, and overall well-being, setting the stage for thriving even in a challenging work environment. Here, we love quoting a very simple but accurate slogan that never gets old: JUST DO IT!

- **Exercise**: Aim for at least 150 minutes of moderate-intensity aerobic exercise or 75 minutes of vigorous-intensity aerobic exercise per week. Incorporate strength training exercises at least twice a week. Find activities you enjoy, such as swimming, dancing, or yoga, to make exercise more enjoyable and sustainable.

- **Nutrition**: Eat a balanced diet that includes a variety of fruits, vegetables, whole grains, lean proteins, and healthy fats. Stay hydrated by drinking water throughout the day. Limit processed foods, added sugars, and excessive caffeine intake. Consider meal planning and prepping to make healthier choices more convenient.

- **Sleep**: Prioritize sleep by establishing a consistent sleep schedule, creating a relaxing bedtime routine, and ensuring your sleep environment is comfortable and conducive to rest. Aim for 7-9 hours of sleep per night.

Emotional Self-Care: Mindfulness, Emotional Intelligence, and Mental Health

Managing your emotions and fostering a healthy mindset, you will experience increased resilience, deeper self-awareness, and improved relationships, empowering you to navigate the complexities of a toxic workplace with confidence and grace. Here is what you do:

- **Mindfulness**: Incorporate mindfulness practices such as meditation, deep breathing, or journaling into your daily routine. Mindfulness helps you stay present, focused, and better equipped to manage stress.

- **Emotional Intelligence**: Develop your emotional intelligence by practicing active listening, empathizing with others, and being aware of your emotions. This will not only improve your relationships but also enhance your resilience in the face of adversity. We'll delve deeper into this subject in Chapter 8, exploring how to further develop these crucial skills.

- **Mental Health**: Seek professional help if needed and engage in self-reflection to better understand your thoughts, feelings, and needs. Consider participating in support groups, therapy, or counseling to address emotional challenges and improve your mental well-being.

Social Self-Care: Nurturing Relationships and Seeking Support

On your path to enhancing your ability to cope with workplace challenges, it is vital to maintain strong social connections and to build a robust support network. So, we can only highly recommend following these two simple steps (which can also be quite fun, by the way).

- **Nurturing Relationships**: Invest your heart and soul in cultivating strong relationships with friends, family, and coworkers, and reap the rewards of a more fulfilled and enriched life.

Communicate openly, practice active listening, and offer support to others, whether it's through sharing a laugh, lending a shoulder to cry on, or celebrating their successes. By nurturing these connections, you'll feel more grounded, supported, and ready to face the challenges of a toxic work environment.

- **Seeking Support**: Recognize when you need help, and don't hesitate to reach out to friends, family, or professionals for guidance and support. Consider joining a support group, talking to a therapist, or seeking advice from a trusted mentor. Speaking from personal experience, as a former rehab patient, I, Markus, can attest to the healing and cleansing effect of not only group therapy sessions but also casual conversations with rehab colleagues during lunch breaks or in a WhatsApp chat even after rehab was over. Remember, we all need a helping hand at times, and seeking support is a sign of strength rather than weakness.

Spiritual Self-Care: Connecting with Your Values and Beliefs

Cultivate spiritual self-care to discover inner peace, purpose, and a strong sense of self, providing you with the sound foundation needed to withstand the turbulence of a toxic work environment.

- **Meditation or Prayer**: Incorporate practices such as meditation or – if you resonate with a spiritual or religious practice – prayer as a daily ritual to foster a deeper connection with your beliefs and values. By cultivating a practice that brings tranquility and clarity, you'll be better equipped to handle the demands of a toxic work environment with grace and resilience.

- **Connecting with Nature**: Spend time outdoors and engage in activities such as hiking, gardening, or simply enjoying the beauty of nature to cultivate a sense of inner peace and connectedness. As you reconnect with the natural world, you'll likely find renewed energy and inspiration to tackle the challenges of a toxic work environment.

- **Personal Values**: Aligning your actions with your values can promote a sense of purpose and fulfillment. Take a moment to reflect on your core values and beliefs, and consider how you can weave them into your daily life. Aligning your actions with your values can create a sense of purpose and fulfillment that fuels your motivation and resilience. By staying true to yourself, you'll be better equipped to navigate the challenges posed by a toxic work environment while staying grounded in what truly matters to you.

Question Your Habits

In our quest for well-being, especially within the demanding contexts of our professional lives, the power of questioning and modifying our daily habits cannot be overstated. Habits, those actions we perform almost automatically every day, hold an immense influence over our mental health, productivity, and overall happiness. Yet, it's easy to overlook the cumulative impact of these seemingly innocuous routines. Inspired by my transformative journey, I invite you to re-examine the habits that shape your days. Through this reflection and willingness to change, we can begin to forge paths toward healthier, more fulfilling lives.

Daily Habits I Changed

In my journey from facing a severe mental health crisis and a rehab stay to where I am today — publishing a book aimed at helping others navigate toxic work environments — I made several lifestyle changes. These changes, seemingly small, had a profound impact on my well-being. Here are some of the adjustments I embraced:

Limiting Screen Time: I consciously decided to stop having a Netflix show "in the queue." Previously, any spare moment would tempt me to continue watching the current series, often leading me to watch episodes under the blanket at night so as not to disturb my son with the screen light. I realized that not only was this habit affecting my sleep, but the content, often filled with crime or violence, impacted my mental state. Breaking this cycle helped me regain control over my leisure time and prioritize restorative rest.

Stepping Away from Daily News Consumption: My routine included watching the nightly Austrian news at 10 pm, a habit I believed was essential to stay informed. However, I recognized that the constant exposure to negative stories — ranging from global tragedies to local political scandals — was deeply affecting my outlook and mood. I learned that while staying informed is important, setting boundaries around news consumption to protect my mental health is equally vital. I deeply believe that the human mind isn't built to process an endless stream of distressing information without consequence.

Rethinking Alcohol Consumption: I questioned my usual habit of enjoying a small beer or glass of wine while making dinner, which I initially saw as a harmless way to unwind after a long day. Recognizing the potential impact of even minimal regular alcohol consumption, I switched to non-alcoholic alternatives. This small change preserved the ritual I cherished while eliminating the negative aspects of alcohol, reaffirming that relaxation doesn't need to come at the cost of my health.

None of these changes were tough for me to implement, yet they absolutely transformed my life. They freed up approximately 20 hours every week, which I could then spend on positive activities such as fostering family life, engaging in mindfulness exercises, getting better sleep, and last but not least — writing this book.

Effective Stress Management Techniques: A Toolkit for Resilience

Maintaining your well-being in the face of toxic leadership is paramount, and effective stress management techniques are the key to staying balanced and resilient. In this section, we will explore various evidence-based strategies to manage stress and maintain emotional equilibrium amidst challenging work environments.

Deep Breathing Exercises: The Power of the Breath

Harness the power of deep, slow breaths to activate your body's relaxation response, reducing stress and anxiety. By practicing regular deep breathing exercises, you'll be better equipped to navigate stressful situations, regain control over your emotions, and maintain composure under pressure. Follow this step-by-step guide to get started with deep breathing exercises:

1. Find a comfortable, quiet place to sit or lie down. Make sure your back is straight, and your body is relaxed.

2. Close your eyes and take a few normal breaths to settle in.

3. Place one hand on your chest and the other on your abdomen. This will help you become more aware of your breathing pattern.

4. Inhale slowly through your nose for a count of 4, allowing your abdomen to rise as you fill your lungs with air.

5. Hold your breath for a count of 4.

6. Exhale slowly through your mouth for a count of 4, letting your abdomen fall as you release the air.

7. Repeat this cycle for 5-10 minutes or until you feel more relaxed and centered.

There are also numerous resources available online to help guide you through deep breathing exercises, including audio guides, videos, and apps. Some popular options include:

- Headspace (App): Offers guided breathing exercises, meditation, and mindfulness practices to reduce stress and improve overall well-being.

- Calm (App): Provides a variety of breathing exercises, sleep stories, and guided meditation sessions to help users relax and manage stress.

- YouTube: Search for "deep breathing exercises" or "guided deep breathing" to find a wide range of video tutorials and guided sessions.

By incorporating deep breathing exercises into your daily routine, you'll develop a valuable tool for managing stress and maintaining emotional balance in the face of a toxic work environment.

Progressive Muscle Relaxation: Release Tension and Relax

Progressive Muscle Relaxation (PMR) is a powerful technique that systematically helps you release physical tension and promote relaxation. By tensing and relaxing different muscle groups, you can become more aware of the sensations in your body, identify areas of tension, and train yourself to let go of stress. Here's a step-by-step guide to get started with PMR:

1. Find a comfortable, quiet place to sit or lie down. Ensure your back is straight and your body is relaxed. Close your eyes and take a few deep breaths.

2. Starting with your feet, tense the muscles in your toes and feet for 5 seconds, then release the tension and relax for 10 seconds. Notice the difference between the tense and relaxed states.

3. Move up to your calves, tensing the muscles for 5 seconds and then relaxing for 10 seconds. Observe the sensations as you release the tension.

4. Continue this process with the following muscle groups: thighs, buttocks, abdomen, lower back, upper back, shoulders, arms, hands, neck, and face. Remember to tense each muscle group for 5 seconds and then relax for 10 seconds.

5. Once you have completed the entire body, take a few deep breaths and enjoy the feeling of relaxation throughout your body.

Again, there are numerous resources available online to help guide you through Progressive Muscle Relaxation, including audio guides, videos, and apps. Some popular options include:

- **Progressive Muscle Relaxation** (App): Offers a guided PMR session with step-by-step instructions and soothing background music.

- **Insight Timer** (App): Provides a variety of guided PMR sessions, as well as meditation and mindfulness practices to reduce stress and improve overall well-being.

- **YouTube**: Search for "Progressive Muscle Relaxation" or "guided PMR" to find a wide range of video tutorials and guided sessions.

Incorporating PMR into your regular self-care routine will help you develop a valuable skill for managing stress and maintaining physical and emotional balance in the face of a toxic work environment.

Mindfulness Meditation: Cultivate Present-Moment Awareness

Mindfulness meditation is a powerful practice that focuses on the present moment without judgment, helping you reduce stress and increase emotional resilience. By incorporating mindfulness meditation into your daily life, you can cultivate greater awareness, improve concentration, and develop a more balanced and compassionate approach to dealing with stressors in a toxic work environment. Here's a step-by-step guide to get started with mindfulness meditation:

1. Find a comfortable, quiet space to sit. You can use a chair, cushion, or meditation bench, ensuring your back is straight and your body is relaxed. Close your eyes or maintain a soft gaze.

2. Begin by taking a few deep breaths, inhaling through your nose, and exhaling through your mouth. Allow your breath to return to its natural rhythm.

3. Focus your attention on your breath as it flows in and out of your body. Observe the sensation of the air entering your nostrils, filling your lungs, and leaving your body as you exhale.

4. If your mind begins to wander or you become distracted by thoughts, gently acknowledge the thought and return your focus to your breath.

5. Continue this practice for a set amount of time, starting with 5 to 10 minutes per session and gradually increasing the duration as you become more comfortable with the practice.

There are numerous resources available online to help guide you through mindfulness meditation, including audio guides, videos, and apps. Some popular options include:

- **Headspace** (App): Offers a variety of guided mindfulness meditations and courses, as well as exercises to help you build a regular meditation practice.

- **Calm** (App): Provides guided meditations, sleep stories, and mindfulness exercises designed to help you reduce stress, improve focus, and build resilience.

- **Insight Timer** (App): Offers thousands of guided mindfulness meditations, as well as courses and resources to deepen your practice and cultivate greater well-being.

> "There is no past and no future; no one has ever entered those two imaginary kingdoms. There is only the present."
>
> *- Leo Tolstoy*

Incorporating mindfulness meditation into your daily routine can help you develop a valuable skill for managing stress and maintaining emotional balance in the face of a toxic work environment. By staying present and focused, you'll be better equipped to navigate the challenges that may arise and make more conscious, compassionate decisions.

Time Management: Harnessing Productivity and Reducing Overwhelm

The skill of time management is an essential tool in your self-care kit, particularly when dealing with the pressures of a toxic work environment. Effectively organizing your tasks and prioritizing your workload can minimize feelings of overwhelm and stress, boosting your productivity and enhancing your work-life balance. Here's a step-by-step guide to start developing your time management skills:

Set Clear Goals: Begin by defining what you want to achieve. These goals should be **S**pecific, **M**easurable, **A**chievable, **R**elevant, and **T**ime-bound (SMART).

Prioritize Your Tasks: Not all tasks are created equal. Use the Eisenhower Matrix to categorize your tasks into four quadrants based on their urgency and importance. This helps you focus on what truly matters.

Plan Your Time: Use tools like digital calendars or planners to schedule your tasks. Break down larger tasks into manageable chunks and allocate specific time slots for each task.

Limit Distractions: Identify potential distractions in your work environment and find ways to minimize them. This might involve turning off notifications, creating a quiet workspace, or setting specific "do not disturb" times.

Take Regular Breaks: Research shows that taking short breaks can actually increase productivity. Try techniques like the Pomodoro Technique, which involves working for a set amount of time (e.g., 25 minutes) and then taking a short break (e.g., 5 minutes).

Online tools and resources can be a great help in enhancing your time management skills. Some options include:

- **Trello** (App): A project management tool that allows you to create boards for different tasks and projects, helping you visualize your workload and manage your tasks more effectively.

- **Google Calendar** (App): A digital calendar that can help you schedule and keep track of your tasks and appointments.

- **Forest** (App): A productivity app that helps you stay focused by planting virtual trees that grow as you work. If you get distracted and leave the app, the tree withers.

Improving your time management skills can significantly boost your productivity and help reduce feelings of overwhelm and stress. By taking control of your time, you'll be better equipped to maintain a healthy work-life balance and navigate the challenges of a toxic work environment.

Setting Boundaries (again!): Embrace the Power of "NO!"

Here we go again, talking about setting boundaries, but bear with us — because if there's one thing worth repeating, it's this. In a toxic work environment, asserting clear boundaries and communicating them unambiguously to colleagues and supervisors is a vital step in safeguarding your mental and emotional well-being. Embracing the power of "NO!" can be a game-changer, helping you avoid overextension and diminish the influence of manipulative behavior on your life. These practices are paramount for fostering healthy relationships, both personally and professionally. Open, honest communication about your needs and limits can mitigate misunderstandings, reduce stress, and engender a more balanced dynamic, thus helping you navigate and resist the adverse effects of a toxic work environment.

Follow these steps to start building and maintaining healthy boundaries:

1. **Identify Your Limits**: Reflect on your personal and professional values, and determine what you are and aren't willing to tolerate. This might include setting limits on work hours, the type of tasks you'll take on, or the way you'll allow others to treat you.

2. **Communicate Your Boundaries**: Clearly express your limits to colleagues and supervisors. Be assertive but respectful, and ensure they understand your needs and expectations.

3. **Embrace the Power of "NO!"**: Learn to say "no" when a request or demand crosses your boundaries. It's okay to prioritize your well-being and stand up for yourself, even if it initially feels uncomfortable.

4. **Be Consistent**: Ensure you maintain your boundaries over time and don't hesitate to remind others if they cross them. Consistency is key to ensuring your boundaries are respected.

5. **Reevaluate and Adjust**: As your circumstances change or you gain more insight into your needs, it's essential to reevaluate your boundaries and adjust them accordingly. This ongoing process helps you maintain your well-being in the long run.

I'd like to take a moment here to reflect on a personal experience. During my rehabilitation journey, one theme consistently echoed among therapists and patients alike: the undeniable importance of saying "No." I vividly recall fellow patients grappling with hypothetical scenarios; their apprehensions voiced in statements like, "But if my boss insists...I have to...". These concerns were met with unwavering guidance from therapists. And let's face it, who among us hasn't felt the pressure to always say "yes"? The urge to portray ourselves as super-employees for whom no challenge is too great? The strain of not wanting to disappoint a boss who relies on our help or let down colleagues who are working against a deadline?

"NO, you don't have to do ANYTHING!"

Our therapists would say,

"There's always room to explain yourself and to negotiate."

This advice resonated deeply with me, as it underscored the crucial role of personal boundaries in protecting our well-being. For example, suppose you're asked to take on additional tasks that would keep you working late into the night regularly or that would keep you from working on other topics that need your attention. In that case, it's essential to assertively communicate that you need to maintain a healthy work-life balance and propose alternative solutions such as delegating tasks, extending deadlines, or adjusting your workload.

As you navigate the complexities of a toxic work environment, remember this: setting boundaries is not an act of defiance or disrespect. Instead, it's a courageous act of self-care. You have the right to protect your well-being, and there's always room for negotiation in the face of unreasonable demands. Embrace the power of "No" and stand up for yourself – you're worth it!

These are some helpful resources for setting and maintaining boundaries:

- *"Boundaries: When to Say Yes, When to Say No to Take Control of Your Life (1992)"* by Dr. Henry Cloud and Dr. John Townsend: A book offering guidance on setting healthy boundaries in various aspects of life, including work, relationships, and self-care.

- Assertiveness Training Workshops or Webinars: Programs that teach you how to communicate your needs and boundaries effectively and assertively.

- Support Groups or Therapy: Professional guidance or peer support can be invaluable in helping you build the confidence and skills needed to set and maintain healthy boundaries.

By setting boundaries and embracing the power of "no," you can reduce the negative impact of toxic leadership on your mental health and work performance. With clear communication and consistency, you'll be better equipped to protect yourself and thrive even in the face of manipulative behavior.

Having explored self-care and stress management, we are now equipped with a robust toolkit for maintaining our well-being and managing stress in the face of manipulation. However, dealing with manipulative behaviors also requires interaction and engagement with others. As such, developing emotional intelligence and effective communication skills is the next critical step in our journey. These skills will help us understand and navigate our emotional landscape and interact more effectively with others, including manipulative bosses.

Key Takeaways

- Recognize the impact of manipulative behavior. Understand that it can severely affect your mental health, leading to stress, anxiety, and burnout.

- Create a self-care routine that addresses physical, emotional, social, and spiritual aspects to promote overall well-being in a toxic work environment.

- Incorporate exercise, balanced nutrition, and sufficient sleep into your daily routine to enhance physical health and resilience.

- Practice emotional self-care by utilizing mindfulness and developing emotional intelligence.

- Practice social self-care by strengthening relationships and building a support network to provide emotional and practical support.

- Engage in practices that connect you with your values and beliefs, such as meditation, connecting with nature, or personal reflection.

- Implement stress reduction techniques like deep breathing exercises, progressive muscle relaxation, and mindfulness meditation to maintain emotional balance.

- Develop time management skills to reduce overwhelm and boost productivity.

- Clearly define and communicate your limits to protect your well-being and maintain healthy relationships at work. Say "No"!

- Consider therapy or counseling to develop coping strategies and navigate complicated relationships. Prioritize your mental health!

9

Developing Emotional Intelligence and Communication Skills

In the previous chapters, we delved into personal coping strategies, resilience-building techniques, self-care, and stress management. These skills are crucial for maintaining your personal well-being amidst workplace manipulation. However, to successfully navigate manipulative situations, we must also engage effectively with others at the end of the day. This next chapter, therefore, focuses on developing emotional intelligence and communication skills. These abilities will allow you to understand your emotions and those of others, assert your needs and boundaries effectively, and interact constructively with a manipulative boss or co-workers.

First, we'll delve into the essential components of emotional intelligence and communication skills, exploring how they can empower you to mitigate the effects of toxic leadership and thrive in your career. We'll cover the importance of self-awareness, enhancing empathy and understanding others, building assertiveness and setting boundaries, and offering practical exercises and strategies for skill development.

At the end of each subchapter, we'll provide practical examples to help you achieve the respective goals, illustrating how these concepts can be applied in real-life scenarios. Additionally, we encourage you to visit our website, **www.toxicleadership.info**, where you'll find even more information and tools designed to support you on your journey towards becoming a more emotionally intelligent and effective communicator in the face of toxic leadership.

Understanding Emotional Intelligence

Emotional intelligence is a crucial skill that involves recognizing, understanding, and managing our own emotions, as well as perceiving and influencing the feelings of others. It's not just about being aware of how you feel; it's about applying this awareness to enhance your communication, problem-solving, and relationship-building both within and outside the workplace.

At its core, emotional intelligence comprises four key components:

Self-Awareness: This is the ability to understand your emotions and how they affect your thoughts and behavior. It includes recognizing your emotional triggers, strengths, weaknesses, and values.

Self-Management: This aspect involves controlling impulsive feelings and behaviors, managing your emotions in healthy ways, taking initiative, and adapting to changing circumstances.

Social Awareness: Here, Emotional Intelligence encompasses empathy, or the ability to understand the emotions, needs, and concerns of other people, pick up on emotional cues, and feel comfortable socially.

Relationship Management: This is about developing and maintaining good relationships, communicating clearly, inspiring and influencing others, working well in a team, and managing conflict.

Developing emotional intelligence is not just beneficial for tackling manipulative behavior at work. It plays a significant role in all aspects of life, enhancing personal relationships, improving communication skills, and boosting overall mental well-being. In the following sections, we will explore these components in greater detail, offering strategies and exercises to help you develop and apply these skills effectively in the face of challenging workplace dynamics.

The Power of Self-Awareness

Self-awareness, a theme we've revisited throughout this book, merits deeper exploration. At its core, self-awareness encompasses the conscious understanding of one's thoughts, emotions, and actions. It's about recognizing your innermost desires, motivations, and beliefs and how they influence your behavior. By cultivating self-awareness, you'll be better equipped to navigate the complexities of life, make informed decisions, and foster meaningful relationships.

With heightened self-awareness, you'll be equipped to more easily recognize manipulative tactics and respond proactively, safeguarding your well-being and maintaining your integrity.

A Step-By-Step Guide on How to Gain and Cultivate Self-Awareness

- **Reflect on your Emotions**: Pay attention to your feelings and emotions throughout the day. Recognize the triggers that evoke strong emotions and analyze how you react to them. This will help you understand your emotional responses and develop better-coping mechanisms.

- **Practice Mindfulness**: Mindfulness is the art of being present in the moment without judgment. Incorporate mindfulness techniques, such as meditation, deep breathing, or journaling, into your daily routine to enhance self-awareness and reduce stress.

- **Seek Feedback from Others**: Ask for honest feedback from friends, family, and colleagues to gain an external perspective on your behavior and actions. This will help you identify blind spots and areas for improvement.

- **Set Personal Goals**: Establish clear, attainable goals that align with your values and aspirations. Regularly assess your progress and adjust your strategies as needed. This will keep you focused on your personal growth and development.

- **Identify Your Strengths and Weaknesses**: Recognize your unique talents and areas where you may need improvement. Embrace your strengths and work on your weaknesses to become a well-rounded individual.

- **Analyze Your Decision-Making Process**: Evaluate your choices and the factors that influence your decisions. This will help you understand your thought patterns and make more informed decisions in the future.

- **Develop Empathy**: Put yourself in other people's shoes and try to understand their feelings, perspectives, and experiences. This will enhance your emotional intelligence and improve your interpersonal relationships.

- **Accept Responsibility for Your Actions**: Own up to your mistakes and learn from them. This will help you grow as a person and demonstrate your commitment to self-improvement.

Unlock the Power of Empathy

Empathy – the secret ingredient for forging stronger connections and navigating the intricate landscape of workplace dynamics. By honing your ability to understand and share your colleagues' feelings, you become equipped to transcend your perspective and genuinely grasp the challenges those around you face. Amidst toxic leadership, empathy emerges as your greatest ally, empowering you to rally your team and cultivate a supportive environment where everyone thrives.

Developing empathy is a vital skill that enables you to resonate with the emotions and experiences of others, particularly when dealing with the negative consequences of a manipulative boss. By bolstering your empathetic abilities, you not only establish a nurturing and supportive work atmosphere but also encourage cohesive teamwork to tackle the hurdles presented by toxic leadership. This, in turn, boosts workplace morale and resilience, enabling everyone to collaboratively work towards resolving issues and fostering a positive environment.

Let us return one last time to the movie "The Devil Wears Prada" – undoubtedly a treasure trove of examples when it comes to toxic work environments. This powerful film showcases the transformative effects of empathy in overcoming the challenges of dealing with a difficult boss. Throughout the film, Andy faces a toxic work environment marked by manipulation, unreasonable expectations, and belittlement from her boss. As Andy begins to understand the pressures and complexities that Miranda faces in her personal and professional life, she starts to empathize with her boss. This empathy not only helps Andy navigate the challenging work environment but also allows her to build a stronger relationship with Miranda. By the end of the movie, Andy's empathy plays a significant role in her personal growth and her ability to assert her own values and priorities.

Follow this practical guide below to enhance your empathy skills and create a supportive, collaborative, and thriving workplace environment that rises above the challenges of toxic leadership.

- ☑ **Active Listening**: Pay close attention to your colleagues' words, tone, and body language, and allow them to express their thoughts and feelings without interrupting or imposing your own opinions.

- ☑ **Ask Open-Ended Questions**: Encourage deeper conversations by asking questions that require more than a simple "yes" or "no" answer. This helps you better understand your colleagues' perspectives and emotions.

- ☑ **Put Yourself in Their Shoes**: Imagine how you would feel if you were experiencing their situation and try to relate to their emotions.

- ☑ **Validate their Feelings**: Acknowledge and validate the emotions of your colleagues, demonstrating that you understand and respect their feelings, even if you don't necessarily agree with their perspective.

☑ **Offer Support and Encouragement**: Be there for your colleagues during difficult times, offering a helping hand or a listening ear when needed.

☑ **Practice Empathy in Everyday Interactions**: Make a conscious effort to be empathetic in your daily interactions, both inside and outside the workplace.

☑ **Reflect on Your Own Experiences**: Think about situations where you have felt empathy for others, and identify what contributed to those feelings. Use these insights to help build your empathy skills.

☑ **Educate Yourself on Diverse Experiences and Perspectives**: Read books, watch documentaries, or engage in conversations with people who have different backgrounds and experiences from your own. This broadens your understanding of the world and helps you develop empathy for various perspectives.

☑ **Practice Mindfulness**: Develop self-awareness through mindfulness exercises, such as meditation, journaling, or deep breathing, to help you become more in tune with your emotions and those of others.

Embrace the transformative power of empathy, and together, rise above the manipulations of a challenging boss. Empathy is the key to understanding and resonating with your colleagues' perspectives, empowering you to forge meaningful connections and create a united front against the challenges of a toxic work setting.

Building Assertiveness and Setting Boundaries

Assertiveness is the art of expressing your thoughts, feelings, and needs openly and respectfully while maintaining your integrity and protecting yourself from manipulation. In the face of toxic leadership, assertiveness becomes an essential skill, empowering you to maintain your self-respect and minimize the detrimental effects of a manipulative boss on your mental health and work performance.

Building assertiveness involves mastering the ability to set boundaries, communicate your needs clearly, and stand up for your rights without succumbing to aggression or passivity. By doing so, you establish a healthy balance that fosters mutual respect and understanding within your work environment.

Here are some practical examples to help you build assertiveness and set boundaries in the context of toxic leadership:

- ☑ **Practice "I" Statements**: Instead of using accusatory language, express your feelings and needs using "I" statements. For example, say, "I feel overwhelmed when I receive tasks at the last minute," instead of, "You always dump tasks on me at the last minute."

- ☑ **Learn to Say "NO"**: In a toxic work environment, it's crucial to know your limits and set boundaries. Don't be afraid to say "no" when necessary. For instance, if your boss asks you to work on a project outside of your job description or during your personal time, politely decline while explaining your reasons.

- ☑ **Pause After Speaking**: After delivering an important or potentially controversial message, take a deliberate pause. This allows both you and the listener to fully process the information. By not rushing to fill the silence, you avoid the common trap of justifying your statement unnecessarily. This pause can shift the dynamics of the conversation, encouraging a more measured and thoughtful response from both sides.

- ☑ **Stand up for Your Rights**: If your boss is treating you unfairly or disrespectfully, calmly and respectfully assert your rights. For example, if your boss is undermining your decisions in front of your colleagues, you might say, "I understand that you have a different perspective, but I would appreciate it if we could discuss this privately rather than in front of the team."

☑ **Use Body Language to Convey Confidence**: Maintain eye contact, stand tall, and speak clearly to project assertiveness. Your nonverbal cues can have a significant impact on how others perceive your message.

☑ **Request Feedback**: After asserting yourself or setting boundaries, ask your boss or colleagues for feedback on your communication style. This will help refine your assertiveness skills and demonstrate your commitment to growth and improvement.

By developing your assertiveness and setting clear boundaries, you can effectively navigate the challenges of a toxic work environment, maintain your self-esteem, and reduce the harmful impact of a manipulative boss on your well-being and career.

The Contrast in Empathy (continued)

To illustrate, let's return to the case study from earlier **where I, Markus,** received a WhatsApp message from my former boss, Ethan, during my recovery period. Ethan's approach, which lacked sensitivity to my situation, demanded a response that respected my boundaries while maintaining professionalism. Here's what I wrote:

"Dear Ethan, Thank you for your message. I am not doing particularly well at the moment, so I would prefer not to have a phone call. Perhaps things will look different after some time.

What did you want to discuss? I prefer not to talk about my health condition; I am in contact with our health center and HR regarding that, as well as concerning my return to the bank. I can say that my return is not imminent, and I may know more in the coming weeks. Best regards, Markus"

Looking back at my reaction to Ethan's message today, I must say I could have probably done worse, especially under the circumstances. Switching from WhatsApp to email was a strategic decision that helped formalize the interaction. Email allowed me to thoughtfully articulate my response and maintain a professional tone, which is more challenging in the instant nature of messaging apps. By choosing email, I ensured the conversation remained documented and official, which is important in professional settings, especially when discussing sensitive matters like health and employment status.

In my email, I used "I" statements to communicate my needs and set boundaries clearly. By clearly stating that I was not ready for a phone call and redirecting the conversation towards what Ethan wanted to discuss, I respected my need for privacy and recovery time without completely closing off communication.

At the end, however, it turned out to be the last piece of communication between Ethan and me.

Practice Effective Communication

Navigating the nuances of a manipulative boss requires a comprehensive skill set, with effective communication being crucial. As part of our deep-dive into developing emotional intelligence, it is essential to hone this skill. Effective communication involves being clear, concise, and assertive while maintaining an empathetic stance. The following strategies will aid you in cultivating these competencies:

☑ **Acknowledge Your Rights and Set Boundaries**: Understand that you have a fundamental right to respect and dignity at your workplace. Identify your personal and professional limits and stand firm when they are pushed.

☑ **Foster Self-Awareness**: Understanding your emotions, recognizing your communication style, and being aware of your body language are keys to effective communication. Observe your reactions to different situations and continuously strive to enhance your communication abilities.

☑ **Again: Master the Use of "I" Statements**: Express your sentiments and apprehensions using "I" statements, which can help to prevent blame or accusation. For instance, instead of saying, "You never take my ideas into account," you might say, "I feel disregarded when my suggestions are overlooked."

☑ **Be Concise and Articulate**: In dealing with a manipulative boss, it's essential to deliver your message succinctly and clearly. Steer clear of vague or ambiguous language and specify your needs and expectations.

☑ **Employ Active Listening**: Demonstrate empathy and comprehension by actively listening to your superiors and peers. This involves maintaining eye contact, affirming, and paraphrasing their statements to confirm your understanding.

☑ **Maintain Composure and Confidence**: When standing your ground or addressing concerns, retain a calm and confident demeanor. Avoid being aggressive or submissive, as these behaviors can provoke conflicts and inhibit effective communication.

☑ **Embrace Feedback and Critique**: Regularly request feedback and remain receptive to constructive criticism from your superiors and peers. This approach will enhance your communication abilities and foster a more collaborative work atmosphere.

Through practicing effective communication, you will be able to manage your interactions with a manipulative boss more efficiently, leading to a more positive and productive work environment. This vital skill will not only help you navigate challenging situations but also contribute significantly to your personal and professional evolution.

As we conclude this chapter on developing emotional intelligence and communication skills, remember that these abilities are not just essential for personal growth; they are also powerful tools in responding to manipulative behavior. Armed with the strategies we've learned, we're now ready to take the next big step in our journey: directly responding to manipulative behavior. In the next chapter, you will learn how to use your resilience, self-care practices, emotional intelligence, and communication skills to effectively respond to and counteract manipulation in the workplace.

Key Takeaways

- Key components of Emotional Intelligence are self-awareness, self-management, social awareness, and relationship management.

- Cultivate your self-awareness by developing a deep understanding of your own emotions, triggers, strengths, and weaknesses.

- Practice self-management by learning to control impulsive feelings and behaviors, managing your emotions healthily, taking initiative, and adapting to changing circumstances.

- Enhance your social awareness by developing empathy and the ability to understand the emotions, needs, and concerns of others.

- Enhance your empathy by strengthening your ability to relate to and share your colleagues' feelings. This can significantly boost team cohesion and morale, especially in a difficult work setting.

- Enhance your communication skills by being clear, concise, and empathetic and by employing active listening. This will improve interactions and build healthy relationships with bosses and co-workers.

- Build assertiveness and set boundaries: learn to express your thoughts, feelings, and needs openly and respectfully while standing up for your rights without being aggressive or passive.

- Implement practical exercises such as journaling, active listening, empathy exercises, assertiveness training, and role-playing to further develop your emotional intelligence and communication skills.

- Your emotional intelligence and communication skills will help you detect, understand, and effectively respond to manipulative behavior.

10

Responding to Manipulative Behavior

In the preceding chapters, we've delved into the subtleties of recognizing manipulative behavior in the workplace. While awareness is the first step, the real challenge lies in effectively responding to these tactics. This Chapter is now dedicated to empowering you with practical techniques for addressing various forms of manipulation you may encounter. From gaslighting to emotional blackmail, each subsection provides tailored strategies to help you regain control, maintain your integrity, and safeguard your well-being in the face of manipulation. Whether you're facing subtle undermining or overt control tactics, this chapter aims to equip you with the tools necessary to respond confidently and assertively.

> "Be careful what you tolerate because you are teaching people how to treat you."
>
> *- spark.co.at*

Understanding Your Response Options

In any professional setting, especially when faced with manipulative behavior, the way you choose to respond can have far-reaching implications. Understanding the nuances of different response options is crucial, as each type – passive, aggressive, and assertive – carries its own set of impacts and consequences. The response you select not only shapes the immediate outcome of a specific interaction but also influences long-term workplace dynamics and your well-being.

- **Passive Response**: Opting for a passive response might seem like a way to avoid conflict, but it often leads to internalized stress and resentment. Over time, this can erode your self-confidence and job satisfaction, potentially making you a recurring target for manipulation. A workplace where passive responses are common may become stagnant, with unresolved issues and unexpressed ideas.

- **Aggressive Response**: While an aggressive response can feel empowering at the moment, it typically damages relationships and trust. This approach can escalate conflicts, create a hostile work environment, and harm your professional reputation. In the long term, consistently responding aggressively can lead to isolation and hinder career advancement.

- **Assertive Response**: Assertiveness strikes a balance, allowing you to stand up for yourself respectfully and confidently. This response type not only addresses the issue at hand effectively but also promotes a positive and collaborative work environment. Cultivating an assertive communication style contributes to healthy workplace dynamics and supports your professional growth and mental well-being.

Recognizing these response types and their impact is the first step in developing the skills to navigate complex workplace interactions successfully. As we delve deeper into each response category, we'll explore how you can adopt the most effective strategies to handle manipulative behavior and maintain your composure and integrity in challenging situations.

Passive Response

A passive response in the workplace is often characterized by avoidance of conflict and a reluctance to express one's true thoughts and feelings. While preventing immediate confrontations may seem like a safe choice, it can lead to significant long-term consequences.

Consequences of a Passive Response:

- **Decreased Self-Esteem**: Consistently yielding to others' demands or opinions can erode your sense of self-worth. You may start to question your abilities and judgment, leading to decreased self-esteem.

- **Increased Manipulation**: A passive approach can make you an easy target for manipulative colleagues or bosses who recognize and exploit your reluctance to stand up for yourself.

- **Resentment Build-Up**: Over time, not addressing issues that matter to you can lead to internalized resentment, both towards yourself for not speaking up and towards others for not recognizing your needs.

- **Stagnation in Career Growth**: Passivity might be mistaken for a lack of ambition or ideas, potentially impacting your career progression and opportunities for growth.

Recognizing a Passive Response:

- **Habitual Agreement**: Notice if you habitually agree with others' opinions or decisions, even when they conflict with your views.

- **Avoidance of Confrontation**: Pay attention to your tendency to avoid discussions or situations where conflict might arise, even when the issues are important.

- **Internal Discomfort**: Be mindful of feelings of discomfort or resentment after interactions where you didn't express your true thoughts or feelings.

Aggressive Response

An aggressive response in the workplace is characterized by confrontational and often disrespectful behavior. It's crucial to differentiate between assertiveness and aggression. Assertiveness is about expressing your thoughts, feelings, and needs in a direct, honest, and respectful manner. In contrast, aggression disregards the rights and feelings of others, often involving hostile or domineering behavior.

Differences Between Assertiveness and Aggression:

- **Intent**: Assertiveness aims to communicate effectively and resolve issues, whereas aggression seeks to dominate or win the argument.

- **Impact on Others**: Assertive communication respects others' boundaries and perspectives, while aggressive behavior often violates or disrespects them.

- **Outcome**: Assertiveness usually leads to productive solutions and mutual respect, while aggression often results in conflict escalation and damaged relationships.

Risks Involved with an Aggressive Response:

- **Escalation of Conflict**: Aggressive responses can provoke others, turning a manageable disagreement into a full-blown conflict.

- **Damage to Professional Relationships**: Regular aggression can harm your relationships with colleagues and superiors, leading to a lack of trust and collaboration.

- **Harm to Professional Reputation**: Being perceived as aggressive can negatively impact your professional image, potentially affecting career advancement and opportunities.

- **Increased Stress and Tension**: Aggressive interactions create a hostile work environment, increasing stress and tension for everyone involved.

Strategies to Manage Emotions Leading to Aggressive Responses:

☑ **Pause and Reflect**: Before reacting in a heated moment, take a pause. This break allows you to reflect on your emotions and choose a more constructive response.

☑ **Practice Emotional Regulation**: Techniques such as deep breathing, mindfulness, and meditation can help regulate emotions that lead to aggression.

☑ **Develop Empathy**: Try to understand the other person's perspective. This can help de-escalate potential conflicts and promote a more harmonious interaction.

☑ **Seek Constructive Feedback**: Ask for feedback from trusted colleagues or mentors about your communication style. They can provide insights into moments when you might come across as aggressive.

☑ **Professional Development**: Consider attending workshops or training in conflict resolution and communication skills. These can provide you with tools to express yourself assertively without resorting to aggression.

Assertive Response

Assertive response is the balanced middle ground between passive and aggressive behaviors, especially crucial when dealing with manipulative situations in the workplace. It involves expressing your needs, thoughts, and feelings clearly and respectfully without infringing on the rights of others.

Assertive Rights:

Assertiveness is based on the concept of assertive rights – the fundamental beliefs that underpin assertive behavior. These include:

- **The Right to Express Feelings and Opinions**: Believing that your feelings and opinions are valid and deserve to be heard.

- **The Right to Say No Without Guilt**: Understanding that you have the right to refuse requests or demands without feeling guilty or selfish.

- **The Right to Change Your Mind**: Accepting that it's okay to change your opinion or decision.

- **The Right to Make Mistakes**: Recognizing that making mistakes is a part of being human and doesn't diminish your worth or competence.

- **The Right to Ask for What You Want**: Knowing that it's acceptable to make requests, even if the answer might be no.

Characteristics of an Assertive Response:

- ☑ **Direct and Honest Communication**: Clearly stating your perspective, needs, or concerns in a straightforward manner.

- ☑ **Respectful of Self and Others**: Balancing your rights with the rights of others, ensuring mutual respect in interactions.

- ☑ **Confident and Controlled**: Expressing yourself in a calm and confident manner without being overly emotional or confrontational.

Examples of Assertive Language and Actions:

- In response to being overloaded with work: "I understand the importance of these tasks, but given my current workload, I'll need additional time or resources to complete these effectively."

- When facing unreasonable deadlines: "I want to ensure the quality of the project, so I propose we review the deadline to ensure we can deliver our best work."

- In a situation where your ideas are dismissed: "I feel my suggestions are not being considered. Can we discuss how my ideas might align with the project goals?"

- Addressing disrespectful behavior: "I feel disrespected when interrupted in meetings. I'd appreciate it if we could all listen to each other's points fully before responding."

- When you encounter resistance or differing opinions, acknowledge the other person's stance with, "Respecting that, I can offer you..." followed by a compromise or alternative solution.

Benefits of Assertiveness in Professional Relationships:

- **Preserving Self-Respect**: By standing up for yourself assertively, you maintain your dignity and self-respect, essential for self-esteem and job satisfaction.

- **Balanced Power Dynamics**: Assertiveness contributes to more balanced relationships at work, where neither party feels dominated or dismissed.

- **Enhanced Problem-Solving**: Assertive communication often leads to more effective problem-solving, as it encourages open and honest dialogue.

- **Building Trust and Respect**: Consistent, assertive behavior builds trust and respect among colleagues, as it demonstrates reliability and respect for others.

In practical terms, responding assertively to manipulation involves recognizing the manipulative behavior, addressing it directly, and expressing your needs or concerns without aggression or passivity. This approach allows you to stand your ground respectfully, paving the way for healthier, more productive professional relationships.

Shifting Towards Assertive Behavior:

- ☑ **Self-Reflection**: Begin by recognizing situations where you tend to exhibit passive or aggressive behaviors. Understanding these patterns is crucial for initiating change towards a more balanced, assertive approach.

☑ **Small Steps**: Practice assertiveness in situations with lower stakes where you feel more comfortable. This could mean voicing a different opinion in a meeting or setting boundaries in a polite yet firm manner, whether you're normally inclined to avoid confrontation or to confront too aggressively.

☑ **Assertiveness Training**: Engage in workshops or training sessions that focus on assertive communication. These resources can equip you with effective tools and strategies to express your needs and opinions respectfully and confidently.

☑ **Seek Support**: Discuss your goal of embracing assertiveness with a trusted colleague, mentor, or coach. Their support and feedback can be invaluable as you practice and refine your new communication style.

Remember, transitioning to assertive communication from either passive or aggressive styles is a journey that requires time and consistent effort. Celebrate your progress, no matter how small, and be patient with yourself as you navigate and adapt to this more balanced way of interaction in your workplace.

The Importance of Assertiveness in Responding to Manipulation

Assertiveness is crucial in neutralizing manipulative tactics in the workplace. By confidently and respectfully asserting your reality and needs, you disrupt the manipulator's strategies and reclaim control of the situation. But why is that?

Assertiveness disrupts manipulative tactics because it operates on psychological principles that are fundamentally opposed to manipulation. Manipulative behavior often relies on creating an imbalance of power – the manipulator attempts to assert dominance, whether through confusion, emotional pressure, or fear. Assertiveness, in contrast, is about establishing an equitable power dynamic. It communicates self-respect and respect for others, challenging the manipulator's attempt to establish a one-up position.

When you respond assertively, you demonstrate awareness of your rights and boundaries, and you're less likely to be swayed by guilt, fear, or confusion – the usual manipulation tools. This response signals to the manipulator that their tactics are ineffective, as assertive communication is grounded in honesty and respect rather than control and dominance. Psychologically, this creates a situation where the manipulator's tactics lose their intended impact, as the assertive individual does not engage in the power struggle the manipulator seeks to create.

Additionally, assertiveness involves clear, direct communication, which leaves little room for the ambiguity and misinterpretation often exploited in manipulative interactions. By articulating your needs and perspectives clearly, you disrupt the manipulator's ability to twist words or situations. This clarity is key in maintaining personal integrity and countering attempts at manipulation.

In cases of gaslighting, for example, where your boss might try to distort your perception of reality, an assertive response involves firmly standing by your understanding of the facts. For instance, if your boss falsely claims you didn't complete a task, an appropriate assertive response would be, "I understand your concern, but here's the email that confirms I completed the task by our agreed-upon deadline." Similarly, with emotional blackmail, which often involves using guilt, fear, or obligation to control you, assertiveness helps you recognize these attempts and respond without succumbing to emotional pressures. For example, if a boss implies you're not dedicated because you refuse to work late regularly, an assertive reply might be, "I'm committed to my work, but I also value my work-life balance. Let's find a way to manage these tasks within regular working hours."

Maintaining assertiveness, however, in the face of persistent manipulation can be challenging, especially if the manipulator intensifies their tactics. Strategies for resilience include:

- ☑ **Self-Reflection**: Regularly reflect on your interactions and re-affirm your commitment to assertiveness as a means of self-respect and respect for others.

- ☑ **Seek Support**: Confide in trusted colleagues or a mentor who can provide perspective and reinforcement for your assertive behavior.

- ☑ **Stay Informed**: Educate yourself about manipulation tactics to better recognize and counteract them.

- ☑ **Practice Self-Care**: Engage in activities that bolster your confidence and mental well-being, as a strong sense of self can fortify you against manipulation.

In essence, assertiveness is not just a communication style; it's a defense mechanism against manipulation. By understanding the nature of manipulative tactics and consistently practicing assertiveness, you can maintain your integrity, protect your interests, and contribute to a healthier workplace environment.

And one last thing: when employing assertive communication in response to manipulation, **be prepared for a range of reactions** from the manipulator. Some manipulators may initially be taken aback or react negatively, as assertiveness disrupts their usual dynamic of control. They might respond with further manipulation attempts, increased aggression, or even temporary compliance to regain their footing.

When I, Markus, found myself needing to address very negative feedback from my boss, Ethan, about my performance, I instinctively utilized what I now understand as assertive communication. I meticulously prepared for the follow-up meeting, armed with a clear list of questions and points for discussion. My questions were direct and specific, such as asking for concrete examples where my performance was deemed inadequate or why negative feedback was never directly communicated.

I was determined to remain calm, professional, and polite, consciously keeping my emotions in check. The meeting was challenging, yet it was also revealing. While I couldn't convince Ethan to change his negative assessment, my assertiveness disrupted his usual manipulative tactics, which clearly caught him off guard. He responded with noticeable aggression in his tone, lamenting about the difficulty and annoyance of the situation for him as a leader, subtly trying to assume the role of a victim.

So, did I manage to alter the poor rating or get an acknowledgment of unsubstantiated feedback? Nope. But did I actually expect my boss to admit he was wrong and upgrade my performance rating? Not really. However, I achieved something crucial: I stood my ground, demonstrating that I wouldn't succumb to manipulation or accept an unjust portrayal of my professional abilities. Notably, my approach of sticking to facts, maintaining a respectful tone, and controlling my emotions led Ethan to inadvertently expose his own weakness. He lost his composure, raised his voice, and, once again, resorted to a manipulative tactic to try and 'put me in my place.'

This experience taught me a valuable lesson about the power of assertiveness and the revealing nature of a manipulator's reactions when their usual strategies are effectively challenged.

Reactions like this are part of the manipulator's adjustment process to your new communication style. Stay consistent with your assertiveness, regardless of their initial reaction. Over time, as you consistently employ assertiveness, the manipulator will likely understand that their usual tactics are no longer effective. This can lead to a shift in the dynamic, where more respectful and straightforward interactions replace manipulative behaviors. Remember, the goal of assertiveness is not to change the manipulator but to protect your rights and needs. By maintaining your assertive stance, you establish clear boundaries and a healthier interaction pattern.

Examples of Healthy Assertive Responses

Let's have a look at a few more scenarios to demonstrate how you can assertively affirm your boundaries while fostering constructive collaboration:

When Tasked with a Complex Project Alone:

Envision yourself in a meeting where your boss casually proposes that you tackle a significant project single-handedly. To assert your stance, you might respond with:

"Although I'm flattered by your confidence in my abilities, taking on this project solo wouldn't be feasible within the given timeline without compromising its quality. Let's explore how we can distribute the workload or adjust the deadline to ensure the project's success."

When a Colleague Offloads Tasks:

Now, picture a colleague who consistently tries to pass off tasks to you, claiming you're the 'go-to' person. An assertive reply could be:

"I understand that you're looking for quality outcomes, and I appreciate your trust. However, I need to focus on my tasks at the moment. Let's sit down with the team and figure out a fair distribution of these responsibilities."

When Asked to Work Overtime on Short Notice:

Your boss approaches you late in the day with an urgent request that would require you to stay several hours past your usual time. Instead of caving in or reacting negatively, an assertive response would protect your boundaries:

"I understand the urgency of this request, but I have prior commitments this evening that I can't reschedule. I can come in early

tomorrow or help delegate some of this work to ensure it's completed on time. Let's discuss the best way to move forward without impacting our personal time."

When Faced with Unreasonable Client Demands:

A client is pushing for an unrealistic deadline, and your boss expects you to make it happen. An assertive stance can help manage expectations without sacrificing service quality:

"I'm committed to delivering the best possible outcome for this project. Given the scope of the client's demands, the current deadline could lead to rushed work and oversights. Could we propose a revised timeline that allows us to maintain the high standards we pride ourselves on?"

In each example, the focus is on acknowledging the issue, expressing your limitations or concerns, and offering alternative solutions or seeking compromise. This strategy demonstrates respect for your boundaries and the needs of your boss or client, which is the essence of assertive communication.

Developing Assertiveness Skills

Developing assertiveness is a skill that can be honed over time through practice and self-awareness. Here is a step-by-step guide to help you cultivate assertiveness in your professional interactions:

- **Step 1: Self-Reflection and Awareness**

   Begin by reflecting on past interactions where you felt your response was not assertive. Identify patterns in your behavior and situations that trigger passivity or aggression. Acknowledge your feelings and beliefs about these situations. Understanding your internal dialogue is crucial in shifting towards assertive behavior.

- **Step 2: Understanding Assertive Rights**

  Familiarize yourself with the concept of assertive rights, such as the right to express your opinions, say no, and make mistakes. Affirm these rights to yourself regularly. This can be done through daily affirmations or journaling.

- **Step 3: Role-Playing and Practice**

  Practice assertive communication in low-risk situations or through role-playing exercises. This could involve rehearsing how to express your needs or opinions in a safe environment. Ask a trusted colleague, friend, or mentor to role-play scenarios with you, providing feedback on your assertiveness.

- **Step 4: Gradual Implementation in Real Situations**

  Start implementing assertiveness in real-life situations, beginning with less challenging interactions and gradually progressing to more difficult ones. After each interaction, reflect on what went well and what could be improved.

- **Step 5: Seeking Feedback and Adjusting**

  Seek constructive feedback from others on your assertiveness. Be open to adjusting your approach based on this feedback, understanding that developing assertiveness is an ongoing process.

Addressing Common Barriers to Assertiveness:

- **Fear of Conflict:** Remind yourself that assertiveness is not about conflict but about honest and respectful communication: practice calm and clear expression of your thoughts and feelings.

- **Low Self-Esteem:** Work on building your self-esteem through positive self-talk and by celebrating small successes in assertive behavior.

- **Worry About Others' Perceptions:** Remember that assertiveness is about mutual respect. Others are likely to respect you more for being clear and honest.

Developing assertiveness skills is a journey that requires patience and practice. Remember, each step you take towards assertiveness helps build a foundation for healthier and more fulfilling professional relationships.

The Role of Emotional Intelligence in Responding to Manipulation

In the complex landscape of workplace dynamics, encountering manipulative behavior is an unfortunate reality for many. However, the power of Emotional Intelligence offers a robust toolset for understanding and effectively responding to such challenges. This section delves into the practical application of Emotional Intelligence as a strategic defense against manipulation, emphasizing how its core components can be leveraged to maintain professional integrity and foster healthier interactions.

Leveraging Emotional Intelligence Against Manipulative Tactics

Empathy as Insight

Utilizing empathy, a key element of Emotional Intelligence is crucial in understanding the motives and feelings behind manipulative behavior. This understanding does not justify the behavior but provides a strategic advantage in anticipating and neutralizing manipulative tactics. By empathizing, one can discern whether a manipulator's actions stem from insecurity, a desire for control, or other underlying issues, allowing for a more informed and strategic response.

Self-Regulation in High-Pressure Situations

Manipulators often rely on creating emotional turmoil to unsettle their targets. Here, self-regulation, another aspect of Emotional Intelligence, becomes vital. Practicing self-regulation allows individuals to maintain control over their emotional responses, preventing manipulators from gaining the upper hand. Techniques such as deep breathing, maintaining a calm demeanor, and pausing before reacting can be instrumental in these situations.

Strategic Use of Social Skills

Effective communication and social skills, integral to Emotional Intelligence, are powerful in responding to manipulation. This involves articulating needs and boundaries clearly, without aggression or passivity. Assertive communication, underpinned by Emotional Intelligence, can disarm a manipulator by demonstrating that their tactics are recognized and will not yield the desired outcome.

Problem-Solving with Empathy and Assertiveness

Combining empathy with assertiveness can lead to constructive problem-solving. For instance, addressing a manipulator's behavior by acknowledging their concerns (empathy) and firmly stating your perspective (assertiveness) can pave the way for more productive interactions. This approach ensures your professional boundaries are respected while keeping communication lines open.

By honing these Emotional Intelligence skills, individuals can transform their response to manipulative behavior from reactive to proactive, safeguarding their well-being and promoting a more respectful and effective workplace environment.

Emotional Intelligence in Conflict Resolution

In the context of manipulative behavior in the workplace, conflicts are often inevitable. However, applying Emotional Intelligence can be a game-changer in de-escalating these conflicts. This section focuses on how Emotional Intelligence can be utilized to resolve disputes that stem from manipulation, emphasizing the importance of effective communication and understanding different perspectives.

- **Recognizing Emotional Cues:** One of the first steps in using Emotional Intelligence for conflict resolution is to identify the emotional states of all parties involved, including your own. This involves being attuned to non-verbal cues, tone of voice, and other indicators of underlying emotions. Understanding these emotions can provide critical insights into the reasons behind a conflict, allowing for a more empathetic and targeted approach to resolution.

- **Active Listening and Empathy:** Active listening is a crucial component of Emotional Intelligence that aids in conflict resolution. It involves fully concentrating, understanding, responding, and then remembering what is being said. This practice, combined with empathy, helps in acknowledging the feelings and perspectives of others, even if you disagree with them. It demonstrates respect and understanding, which can be pivotal in reducing tensions and opening up channels for productive dialogue.

- **Self-regulation in Heated Moments:** During a conflict, especially one that involves manipulation, emotions can run high. Here, the Emotional Intelligence skill of self-regulation is essential. It helps to manage and control your emotional response, preventing escalation. Techniques like taking a moment to breathe, pausing to collect thoughts before responding, and maintaining a calm demeanor are vital in these scenarios.

- **Solution-Focused Communication:** Utilize your Emotional Intelligence to shift the conversation from conflict to collaboration. This involves reframing the dialogue to focus on finding mutual solutions rather than dwelling on the problem or individual blame. Phrases like, "How can we resolve this together?" or "What are our shared goals?" can redirect the conversation towards a more constructive outcome.

- **Negotiating and Compromising:** Effective conflict resolution often requires negotiation and compromise. With a strong foundation in Emotional Intelligence, you can better understand the motivations and needs of all parties, allowing for more effective negotiation strategies that acknowledge everyone's concerns while working towards a mutually acceptable compromise.

Navigating Emotional Triggers

Manipulative behaviors in the workplace often trigger strong emotional responses. Effectively navigating these triggers is crucial for maintaining your composure and responding assertively. The first step in managing emotional triggers is to recognize and understand them. Reflect on past experiences to identify which behaviors or situations evoke strong emotional reactions so you can anticipate and prepare for them in the future.

Self-awareness, empathy, and assertive communication are key aspects of Emotional Intelligence that are crucial for managing emotional triggers. We encourage you to revisit Chapter 9, "Developing Emotional Intelligence and Communication Skills," for more in-depth guidance.

One last piece of advice: When dealing with manipulative bosses and managing emotional triggers, it can be significantly helpful to reframe your perspective. Instead of seeing a manipulative attempt as a personal attack, view it as a reflection of the manipulator's own issues or insecurities. Training yourself to make this perspective shift can take time, but once it's achieved, it will greatly reduce the emotional impact of what once triggered you.

Assertiveness and Emotional Intelligence in Action

This section presents a series of brief real-world scenarios to provide practical insights into the dynamics of manipulation and the effectiveness of assertiveness and Emotional Intelligence. Each case study illustrates a different type of manipulative behavior encountered in the workplace and demonstrates how assertive responses, underpinned by Emotional Intelligence (EI), can effectively address these challenges.

Case Study 1: Overcoming Gaslighting in Team Meetings

- **Scenario:** Emily, a project manager, frequently experienced her boss, Mark, twisting her words and questioning her memory of events during team meetings, a classic case of gaslighting.

- **Assertive Response:** Emily started documenting key discussions and decisions. In the next meeting, when Mark attempted to gaslight her, she calmly referred to her notes, providing clear and factual counterpoints to his claims.

- **EI Element:** Emily's response showcased her self-regulation in managing her emotions and maintaining composure, as well as her assertiveness in standing up for her truth.

Case Study 2: Addressing Emotional Blackmail from a Supervisor

- **Scenario:** John, a software developer, found his supervisor, Sarah, using emotional blackmail, such as guilt-tripping him about workload and deadlines, to get him to work overtime regularly.

- **Assertive Response:** John respectfully communicated to Sarah the impact of this constant pressure on his well-being and work-life balance, suggesting alternative solutions for managing the workload.

- **EI Element:** John's approach displayed empathy towards Sarah's pressures as a supervisor while assertively communicating his boundaries and needs.

Case Study 3: Resisting Micromanagement and Control Tactics

- **Scenario:** Linda, a marketing specialist, was struggling with her manager, Tom, who micromanaged every aspect of her work, leaving her feeling undervalued and stifled.

- **Assertive Response:** Linda requested a one-on-one meeting with Tom, where she discussed her need for autonomy in her role, highlighting her past successes and how autonomy would further improve her productivity and job satisfaction.

- **EI Element:** Linda's self-awareness about her work style and needs, coupled with her assertive yet respectful communication, helped address the micromanagement issue effectively.

Case Study 4: Countering Divide and Conquer Strategy

- **Scenario:** In a sales team, Alex noticed his boss, Rachel, employing a "divide and conquer" strategy, pitting team members against each other to maintain control.

- **Assertive Response:** Alex organized a team meeting without Rachel, fostering open communication among colleagues to break down misunderstandings and create a united front.

- **EI Element:** Alex used his social skills to facilitate better team dynamics and empathy to understand and address his colleagues' concerns, fostering a more collaborative environment.

These case studies exemplify how a combination of assertiveness and Emotional Intelligence can be utilized to effectively respond to and counter manipulative behaviors in the workplace, leading to healthier work relationships and a more positive work environment.

Responding to Narcissistic and Machiavellian Bosses

Earlier in Chapter 3 of this book, we talked about the psychology of manipulative bosses and identified various toxic character traits that can permeate leadership styles. Among these, narcissism and Machiavellianism were highlighted for their prevalent impact on workplace dynamics. These traits are the focus here due to their distinct influence on manipulation strategies — narcissists often leverage their charisma and grandiosity, and Machiavellians their cunning and strategic deception. When bosses exhibit these characteristics, they can create particularly insidious environments due to their ability to charm, deceive, and exploit others for personal gain. So, before we delve into responding to specific manipulation techniques, let's have a look at the unique challenges posed by such individuals and what strategies can preserve your well-being and professional integrity.

Quick Fact: The Dark Triad

If your boss not only embodies both narcissistic and Machiavellian traits but also qualifies as a psychopath, you hit the jackpot. You are dealing with a representative of what psychologists refer to as the "Dark Triad". This term encompasses a trio of personality traits — narcissism, Machiavellianism, and psychopathy — known for their malevolent qualities.

Narcissism is characterized by grandiosity, entitlement, and a thirst for admiration. Machiavellianism manifests in manipulative tactics, a cynical disregard for morality, and a focus on self-interest and deception. Psychopathy, the most detrimental trait, combines

---

a lack of empathy and remorse with impulsive behavior and callousness.

In a professional setting, individuals with Dark Triad traits can be particularly damaging. They're often skilled at climbing the corporate ladder through intimidation, charm, and exploitation but leave a trail of conflict and destabilization.

Understanding the Underlying Psychology

Narcissists have an inflated sense of self-importance and crave admiration. They may view themselves as superior and entitled to special treatment. On the other hand, Machiavellians are strategic and often deceitful, using manipulation to achieve their ends without regard for others' welfare. Grasping these motivations helps you predict their actions and prepare your responses accordingly.

Recognizing the Behavior

Recognizing the behavior of narcissistic and Machiavellian bosses involves observing how they interact with you and your colleagues. Narcissists often require constant praise and get irritated if they don't receive it. They may take credit for your work or dismiss your contributions. Machiavellian bosses are more calculating, often pitting employees against each other to maintain control. They use information as currency and may retract support if it benefits them. Identifying these behaviors is key to understanding when you're being manipulated.

Practical Strategies for Response

Here are specific strategies to navigate the challenges of working under such bosses:

☑ **Boundary Setting:** Establish what you are and are not willing to tolerate. Be clear about your limits and communicate them calmly and assertively. Assertiveness conveys confidence and self-respect, which can discourage further manipulation.

☑ **Document Interactions:** Keep a record of your communications. This can serve as evidence in case disputes arise about what was agreed upon.

☑ **Neutral Responses:** When praised excessively or criticized unfairly, respond neutrally. Avoid giving a narcissistic boss the emotional reaction they seek.

☑ **Build Alliances:** Cultivate relationships with colleagues who share your perspectives. There's strength in numbers when addressing systemic issues.

☑ **Seek Mentorship:** Find a mentor outside your direct reporting line for guidance on how to handle difficult situations with your boss.

☑ **Professional Development:** Continue to develop your skills and maintain your professional network. This keeps your career options open should the situation become untenable. If your boss's behavior stifles your growth or causes undue stress, it may be worth considering a change in departments or even seeking opportunities elsewhere.

☑ **Well-Being First:** Prioritize your mental health. Engaging with a therapist or counselor can provide coping strategies for the stress associated with such toxic environments.

The key in dealing with bosses who have narcissistic or Machiavellian tendencies is to protect your interests, maintain your professional integrity, and not allow their behaviors to undermine your confidence or work-life balance. While you can implement strategies to minimize the impact of their behavior, it's also important to recognize situations where the best course of action is to remove yourself from a toxic environment to preserve your mental health and career trajectory.

Case Study: Overcoming Machiavellian Tactics in Deadline Management

Linda, a software developer, faced constant challenges with her boss, Marcus, known for his Machiavellian approach. Marcus would set unachievable deadlines, often shifting blame to Linda's team for any delays while taking full credit for successes. Recognizing this pattern, Linda meticulously documented all project timelines, communications, and Marcus's unrealistic expectations.

With solid evidence in hand and after consulting with a senior colleague, Linda arranged a meeting with Marcus. She calmly presented her findings, highlighting the team's diligence and the impracticality of his deadlines. She suggested a collaborative method for setting achievable timelines, emphasizing the importance of realistic goals for quality output and team morale.

Taken aback by Linda's well-prepared confrontation, Marcus conceded to her proposed method. This new approach led to improved project performance and team satisfaction. Linda's strategy of detailed documentation and assertive negotiation successfully mitigated Marcus's manipulative behavior, fostering a more constructive work environment.

Conclusion: Successfully navigating the workplace in the presence of narcissistic and Machiavellian bosses requires a blend of understanding, recognition, and tactical response. The strategies and insights shared in this subchapter illustrate that while challenging, it is possible to assert your professional integrity and safeguard your well-being against toxic leadership. Remember, the goal is not only to endure but to thrive by asserting boundaries, seeking support, and prioritizing personal development and mental health. Ultimately, this journey reinforces the importance of building resilience and making informed decisions about your career path in the face of manipulative behaviors.

Responding to Gaslighting

Gaslighting is a manipulative tactic where the perpetrator attempts to make you question your reality, memory, or perceptions in order to gain power and control. This manipulation can significantly impact your confidence, well-being, and job performance. Recognizing and responding effectively to gaslighting is crucial in maintaining a healthy work environment and personal mental health.

Understanding the Underlying Psychology

Gaslighters often possess a need for power and control, using psychological tactics to destabilize their targets. This behavior can stem from various underlying issues, including narcissism, insecurity, the desire to deflect accountability, or the inability to handle criticism or conflict. By inducing doubt and confusion, the gaslighter asserts dominance over their victim's perceptions and decisions.

Recognizing the Behavior

Recognizing gaslighting in the workplace is essential but can be challenging due to its subtle nature. Be alert to signs like inconsistent statements, where a gaslighter might contradict what they previously said, causing you to question your memory. Another red flag is the trivializing or dismissing of your thoughts and opinions, aimed at undermining your confidence.

Gaslighters also often twist facts to fit their narrative, creating confusion and self-doubt. Blame shifting is common too, where they avoid responsibility for their mistakes by placing the blame on others. Additionally, isolation tactics may be employed, subtly cutting you off from colleagues and support networks, increasing your dependency on the gaslighter, and reinforcing their control. Awareness of these signs will help you identify and address workplace gaslighting.

Practical Strategies for Response

When you suspect you're being gaslighted, use these strategies to respond effectively:

- ☑ **Trust Your Perceptions:** Reinforce your confidence in your memory and judgment. If you feel something is amiss, trust that instinct.

- ☑ **Seek Validation:** Confide in trusted colleagues or friends about your experiences. Their outside perspective can help validate your reality.

- ☑ **Document Everything:** Keep a detailed record of interactions that you find manipulative. This documentation is vital for identifying patterns and serves as evidence if needed.

- ☑ **Communicate Assertively:** If safe to do so, address the behavior directly with the gaslighter. Use clear, specific examples, and express how their actions impact you. Be direct but respectful.

- ☑ **Set Boundaries:** Define clear boundaries with the gaslighter. Let them know what behavior is unacceptable and what consequences they will face if they continue.

Case Study: Navigating Gaslighting in Team Meetings

As a marketing coordinator, Sarah frequently experienced gaslighting from her supervisor, Tom. In team meetings, Tom would contradict statements he had previously made to Sarah privately, causing her to question her memory. Sarah started documenting these instances and sought feedback from her peers, who confirmed her recollections. With this support, Sarah arranged a private meeting with Tom, where she calmly presented her documentation and expressed how his actions were affecting her work. This assertive approach led to Tom being more mindful of his interactions, and Sarah's confidence in her work was restored.

> **Conclusion**: Effectively responding to gaslighting involves a combination of self-awareness, assertive communication, and seeking support. By trusting your perceptions, validating your experiences, and setting clear boundaries, you can counteract the effects of gaslighting. Documenting incidents and having open discussions can also be powerful tools in restoring your confidence and maintaining a healthy work environment.

Responding to the Exploitation of Guilt and Fear

Manipulation through the exploitation of guilt and fear is a subtle yet powerful manipulation tactic in the workplace. Recognizing when your feelings of guilt or fear are being leveraged by others is key to maintaining control over your professional choices and well-being.

Understanding the Underlying Psychology

Manipulators use guilt and fear as emotional levers to control and influence others. By instilling these feelings, they create a sense of obligation or dread, steering behavior to their advantage. Often, this method is chosen as it allows for indirect control without the need for overt confrontation. Understanding this can be empowering, as it helps you to see the manipulation for what it is - a tactic to sway your actions without legitimate professional justification.

Recognizing the Behavior

Guilt exploitation often manifests in ways that make you feel indebted or inadequate – like being made to feel guilty for not staying late or taking on extra work or receiving subtle suggestions that you owe your boss for past favors. **Fear exploitation**, on the other hand, can be seen in actions like threats of job loss or negative performance reviews to coerce certain behaviors, creating an atmosphere of fear and uncertainty about job security or career progression.

After **I, Markus**, started working part-time, my boss, Ethan, adeptly utilized tactics of guilt and fear exploitation. He frequently reminded me of the "company's support" during my family crisis, often implying that I owed them for the flexibility they had allowed me. Statements like "We are investing in you now, and someday you will pay us back" were common. This approach was not just about creating a sense of indebtedness; it was a clear attempt to make me feel guilty, especially whenever I couldn't meet his high demands.

Simultaneously, Ethan's method of invoking fear was subtler yet equally manipulative. Though not overtly threatening, remarks like he expected me to "pay them back" one day for working part-time left a looming question over the true nature of this 'debt' and its implications for my future at the company. It led me to ponder: How will I have to *pay them back*, and what happens if I don't *pay them back*, especially since I believe I was morally and probably even legally entitled to work part-time?

This constant reminder served as a tool to exploit both guilt and fear, skillfully maintaining a sense of obligation that extended beyond professional boundaries and ventured into personal indebtedness.

Practical Strategies for Response

☑ **Assertive Communication:** Express your discomfort with the manipulative behavior. Make your boundaries clear, stating what is acceptable and what is not in professional communication.

☑ **Seek Clarity:** If vague threats or implications are used, ask for explicit explanations of expectations and consequences. This approach often helps demystify manipulative statements.

☑ **Document Incidents:** Maintain a record of instances where guilt or fear is exploited. This documentation can be a critical asset if you need to escalate the issue.

Case Study: Overcoming Guilt in Project Deadlines

Jane, a graphic designer, often faced unrealistic project deadlines. Her manager's tactic to ensure compliance was guilt-tripping, implying Jane wasn't dedicated if she didn't meet these deadlines. Over time, this led to a significant imbalance in her work-life equilibrium and began to affect her mental health. Realizing the toll it was taking, Jane documented these instances and approached her supervisor to discuss her concerns. She communicated her willingness to work hard but within realistic and fair boundaries. This open communication helped to reset expectations and reduced the instances of guilt-tripping from her boss.

Conclusion: Navigating through manipulation in the workplace, especially when it involves the exploitation of guilt and fear, requires awareness, assertiveness, and sometimes the courage to seek support. Remember, you have the right to work in an environment that respects your emotional boundaries and professional dignity.

Responding to the Undermining of Confidence and Self-Esteem

When manipulators target your confidence and self-esteem, it can be particularly insidious. Such tactics are often subtle and can gradually erode your self-worth and professional confidence.

Understanding the Underlying Psychology

This form of manipulation often stems from the manipulator's insecurities and desire for control. By weakening your self-esteem, they create a scenario where you become more dependent on their approval and less likely to question their authority or decisions. Understanding this can shift the power dynamic as you begin to see these actions as a reflection of their insecurities, not your capabilities.

Recognizing the Behavior

Undermining confidence and self-esteem in the workplace can manifest in various forms. It might involve continuous, unfounded criticism that causes you to question your abilities or backhanded compliments that leave you feeling undervalued. Key signs to watch out for include consistent negative feedback, disregard for your ideas, or constant comparisons to other colleagues. Micromanagement can also be a classic example of this tactic. In my experience with my former boss, Ethan, his excessive scrutiny was not only about control but also a deliberate strategy to undermine my confidence in my professional abilities.

Practical Strategies for Response

☑ **Building Resilience:** Strengthen your self-esteem through positive affirmations and focusing on your achievements. Remind yourself of your skills and successes regularly.

☑ **Seeking Feedback Elsewhere:** If you only receive negative feedback from one source, seek out other perspectives. This can provide a more balanced view of your performance and worth.

☑ **Professional Development:** Engage in activities that build your skills and knowledge. Continuous learning can boost your confidence and reduce the impact of negative feedback.

Case Study: Reclaiming Self-Esteem in a Critical Environment

David, an IT specialist, was constantly belittled by his boss, who often criticized his work in front of his peers. This consistent negative feedback started affecting his confidence. Realizing the impact, David began to document these instances while also seeking feedback from his colleagues and mentors. This external validation helped him realize that the criticism was not reflective of his actual work quality. Additionally, he enrolled in a professional development course, which not only improved his skills but also his confidence. With time, David learned to separate constructive criticism from unwarranted negativity, regaining his professional self-esteem.

Conclusion: Dealing with tactics that undermine your confidence and self-esteem requires a proactive approach. It's about building your resilience, seeking balanced feedback, and continuously developing your skills. Remember, your self-worth is not defined by one person's opinion but by the collective acknowledgment of your abilities and accomplishments.

Responding to Neurolinguistic Programming (NLP)

While NLP itself is not inherently problematic and can be used to enhance personal growth, when used manipulatively, especially in the workplace, it can be a subtle yet effective tool for influencing and controlling employee behavior. Understanding how to recognize and respond to such tactics will help you maintain autonomy over your decisions and mental well-being.

Understanding the Underlying Psychology

NLP, when used manipulatively, exploits the power of language to influence thought processes and behaviors. Manipulators using NLP techniques may be aiming to subtly guide your decisions or change your perceptions to suit their agenda. This tactic can be particularly challenging to identify and counteract because it often operates below the conscious level of awareness.

Recognizing the Behavior

Manipulative NLP often manifests as language patterns designed to subtly influence your thinking and decision-making. This could include suggestive phrases that implant ideas, repetitive language that reinforces a specific point of view, or rhetorical questions that guide you to a predetermined conclusion. Be alert to conversations that seem to lead you in a specific direction or evoke emotional responses designed to sway your actions.

Practical Strategies for Response

☑ **Critical Thinking:** Regularly question the intent behind the language used by others. This helps identify underlying motives and resist subtle manipulation.

☑ **Studying Common NLP Tactics:** Equip yourself by learning about common NLP phrases and techniques. This knowledge allows you to identify manipulative tactics as they occur. For an in-depth look flip to the Appendix where we've put together for you a checklist with "Common NLP Phrases and Tactics".

☑ **Assertive Communication:** If you feel you're being led down a particular path, assert your views and opinions firmly. Don't be afraid to voice disagreement or seek clarity on ambiguous statements.

☑ **Seeking Second Opinions:** Discuss important conversations with trusted colleagues or mentors. Getting a second opinion can help you see different perspectives and identify potential manipulation.

Case Study: Navigating NLP in Sales Meetings

Maria, a marketing executive, noticed that during meetings, her boss often used suggestive language to push for his preferred strategies, subtly framing them as the only viable options. This use of NLP made Maria feel as if her ideas were less valuable. To counter this, Maria began preparing thoroughly for meetings, ensuring her ideas were backed by solid data. She also started openly questioning the implications and assumptions behind her boss's suggestions. This approach not only helped Maria regain her confidence in her ideas but also encouraged a more open and balanced discussion in meetings.

When I, Markus, once had my yearly performance review, my boss, Ethan, employed a tactic I later recognized as "anchoring." As I entered his office for the review, I was immediately confronted with a large display of a family photo I had once shared with my colleagues after my second son was born. This image, naturally associated with my happiest personal memories, was deliberately used by Ethan at the start of a critical professional discussion. It seemed to be a strategic move to emotionally disarm me, anchoring the positive feelings evoked by the family image to the ensuing conversation. This subtle yet powerful use of a personal and emotional anchor in a professional setting was a clear example of how NLP techniques can be manipulated for controlling purposes in the workplace. And it wasn't until later, reflecting on the meeting, that I fully grasped what Ethan had done. Seeing that photo of my lovely family absolutely made me feel happy during most of our talk, but, much to Ethan's likely disappointment, that good vibe couldn't stick around. It all came crashing down with the surprisingly harsh rating he gave me at the end of an otherwise friendly chat.

> **Conclusion**: In the face of manipulative NLP tactics, it's essential to maintain a critical mindset, communicate assertively, and seek external perspectives. These steps will aid in safeguarding your mental autonomy and ensure that your professional decisions are truly your own, not influenced by covert manipulation.

Responding to Emotional Blackmail

Emotional blackmail is a powerful manipulation tactic where a person uses guilt, fear, or obligation to control someone else's actions. It can be particularly damaging in the workplace, affecting both your personal well-being and professional relationships.

Understanding the Underlying Psychology

Emotional blackmailers seek to control and often prey on the victim's desire to maintain harmony or avoid conflict. Understanding this can help you recognize that these manipulative tactics are more about the blackmailer's needs and insecurities than your behavior or performance.

Recognizing the Behavior

Emotional blackmail can be insidious, often manifesting as subtle threats or comments designed to induce guilt. This can take the form of guilty appeals, where blackmailers imply that you're not committed enough or let the team down if you don't comply with their demands. Another tactic is the silent treatment or withdrawal, where they use the absence of communication or support as a tool to influence your decisions. Blackmailers might also resort to fear tactics, such as imposing threats of job loss, demotion, or other negative consequences, to manipulate your actions. They may also remind you of past favors or sacrifices they've made, creating a sense of obligation and indebtedness. Additionally, playing the victim is common, where they portray themselves as the injured party, thereby making you feel responsible for their well-being or happiness. Recognizing these indicators is essential for effectively responding to and managing emotional blackmail in the workplace.

Practical Strategies for Response

- ☑ **Stay Objective:** When confronted with emotional blackmail, focus on the facts and logic of the situation. Remind yourself of the actual circumstances and requirements of your job, separate from any emotional narratives being imposed. This objective stance will help you make decisions based on practical considerations rather than emotional pressure.

- ☑ **Maintain Emotional Distance:** You must emotionally detach from the blackmailer's tactics. Recognize their attempts to manipulate your feelings and consciously choose not to let these tactics dictate your reactions or decisions. This emotional distancing will allow you to maintain clarity and avoid being swept up in unnecessary emotional turmoil.

- ☑ **Assertive Communication:** Clearly and calmly communicate your stance. Express that while you understand their perspective, emotional blackmail is not an acceptable method of communication, and you expect a more professional approach.

- ☑ **Set and Enforce Boundaries:** Establish what you are and are unwilling to tolerate. Be clear about your limits, and if they are crossed, enforce these boundaries with appropriate actions, such as involving HR or declining to engage in manipulative discussions.

- ☑ **Document Incidents:** Keep a record of instances of emotional blackmail. Documenting specific events, dates, and what was said or done can be invaluable, especially if you need to escalate the situation.

Case Study: Handling Blackmail Over Project Deadlines

Martin, a project manager, faced emotional blackmail from his boss, who threatened to give poor performance reviews if Martin didn't meet unrealistic deadlines. Martin's boss also implied that his team's job security depended on these deadlines. Recognizing this as emotional blackmail, Martin documented these interactions and set up a meeting with his boss. In the meeting, he presented a realistic timeline for the project, emphasizing quality and team well-being. Martin also discretely sought advice from HR to prepare for potential fallout. His assertive yet respectful approach led to a renegotiation of deadlines and a reduction in manipulative behavior from his boss.

> **Conclusion**: Responding to emotional blackmail requires clarity, assertiveness, and sometimes external support. By understanding and recognizing these tactics, you can take steps to protect yourself and foster a healthier work environment. Remember, it's essential to prioritize your mental and emotional health and seek support when needed.

Responding to Triangulation

Triangulation is a manipulative tactic that involves using a third person to influence or control a situation. It's a common technique used by manipulators to create confusion, sow discord, and maintain power. This tactic allows the manipulator to maintain control and avoid taking responsibility for their actions.

Understanding the Underlying Psychology

Triangulation is rooted in avoidance and control. It allows the manipulator to avoid direct confrontation and maintain control over the narrative and relationships within the team. This indirect approach can create dependencies and alliances that serve the manipulator's agenda, not the team's overall health.

Recognizing the Behavior

Triangulation often appears as indirect communication, where messages or opinions are relayed through others instead of directly between the involved parties. It can manifest in various forms, such as a boss using a colleague to relay critical feedback instead of speaking to you directly or colleagues spreading rumors rather than addressing issues openly. If you're receiving conflicting messages from different sources, it could be a sign of triangulation. Also, if you're intentionally left out of discussions or decision-making processes, the manipulator may be using triangulation to control the situation.

Practical Strategies for Response

☑ **Direct Communication:** Seek direct conversations with the people involved. If you hear something concerning from a third party, go to the source for clarification.

☑ **Address the Issue Openly:** If you suspect triangulation, address it openly in a team meeting or with the individuals involved, emphasizing the value of direct communication.

☑ **Establish Clear Communication Protocols:** Advocate for transparent communication channels within the team, where direct interaction is encouraged and expected.

☑ **Empower Yourself and Others:** Encourage yourself and your colleagues to communicate directly and not rely on third parties. This empowerment reduces the manipulator's ability to control the narrative.

Case Study: Breaking the Triangle in Team Meetings

In a marketing team, Laura noticed her manager often communicated negative feedback through other team members, creating distrust and confusion. Laura decided to address this by asking for direct feedback in team meetings and encouraging open and transparent discussions. By fostering a culture of direct communication, the team became more cohesive and less susceptible to manipulative tactics.

> **Conclusion**: Triangulation is a powerful manipulation tactic that can cause confusion, conflict, and emotional distress. Addressing triangulation requires a commitment to direct and transparent communication. By recognizing this manipulation and fostering an environment where open dialogue is valued, you can help dismantle these unhealthy dynamics and promote a more positive and collaborative workplace.

Responding to Manipulators Who Play the Victim

Manipulators who play the victim use this tactic to deflect blame and gain sympathy, making it challenging to address their behavior directly. Playing the victim is a manipulation strategy aimed at evading responsibility and controlling others through sympathy.

Understanding the Underlying Psychology

The roots of this manipulative tactic often lie in a desire for attention and validation and sometimes as a defense mechanism to cover up inadequacies or wrongdoings. Recognizing this is crucial in effectively responding to such tactics. It helps you maintain your boundaries and prevent your boss's (alleged) emotional state from dictating your actions.

Recognizing the Behavior

Victim playing in the workplace is a manipulative behavior where a person consistently portrays themselves as the injured party in every situation, often disregarding the facts. This can manifest through constant complaining, where your boss might frequently lament their problems and hardships, typically exaggerating the severity of these issues. They might also avoid taking responsibility for their mistakes or failures, instead shifting blame onto others or external circumstances. In their quest for sympathy, they often seek constant support for their perceived hardships, sometimes exaggerating or distorting facts to gain this sympathy. Additionally, they may resort to emotional manipulation tactics like guilt trips, passive-aggressive behavior, or emotional outbursts, all designed to control others and manipulate situations in their favor. Recognizing these patterns is crucial in dealing with such behavior effectively.

Practical Strategies for Response

- ☑ **Maintain Objectivity:** Stick to the facts and resist being drawn into emotional narratives. Focus on objective criteria and evidence in discussions.

- ☑ **Set Clear Boundaries:** Establish and communicate clear boundaries regarding acceptable behavior and responsibilities. Don't enable the victim-playing behavior by constantly conceding or sympathizing.

- ☑ **Encourage Accountability:** Gently but firmly encourage individuals to take responsibility for their actions. Offer constructive feedback that focuses on actions and consequences.

Case Study: Addressing Victimhood in Performance Reviews

Michael, a team leader, noticed that every time he provided constructive feedback to one of his team members, Clara, she portrayed herself as a victim of unfair treatment. Realizing this pattern, Michael began documenting specific instances of Clara's work needing improvement. In their next performance review, he presented these examples, focusing solely on the work and the expected standards, thereby avoiding any personal blame or emotional entanglement.

> **Conclusion**: Responding to manipulators who play the victim requires a balanced approach to maintaining objectivity, setting clear boundaries, and fostering an environment of accountability. By focusing on facts and encouraging personal responsibility, you can navigate these challenging interactions more effectively.

Responding to Divide and Conquer Tactics

Divide and conquer tactics in the workplace involve creating or exploiting divisions among team members to maintain control or avoid accountability. Recognizing and countering these tactics is vital for preserving team cohesion and ensuring a fair working environment.

Understanding the Underlying Psychology

A boss who employs divide-and-conquer tactics typically seeks control by sowing discord among team members. This behavior often stems from a desire to maintain authority and distract from their inadequacies, creating an environment where they are seen as the indispensable mediator. Recognizing this motivation is essential in effectively responding to and mitigating such manipulative tactics in the workplace.

Recognizing the Behavior

Divide-and-conquer strategies in a workplace setting are often subtle yet impactful. They may manifest through favoritism and exclusion, where a manager or leader shows preferential treatment to certain employees, creating a rift within the team. Another common form is the deliberate spreading of rumors or misinformation intended to pit team members against each other and create an atmosphere of distrust. Additionally, these tactics can involve the manipulative exacerbation of small disagreements or conflicts among team members, often for the manipulator's personal gain. Recognizing these patterns is crucial to addressing and countering them effectively.

These tactics stem from a desire to control or manipulate situations to the advantage of the manipulator. By keeping team members in conflict or distrust, the manipulator can play a central role, often positioning themselves as the necessary mediator or the "reasonable" party.

Practical Strategies for Response

- ☑ **Promote Open Communication:** Encourage honest and transparent communication within the team. Address any misinformation or rumors directly and seek to clarify misunderstandings.

- ☑ **Foster Team Unity:** Focus on team-building activities and shared goals that reinforce unity. Highlight the importance of collaboration and mutual support.

- ☑ **Address Favoritism:** If it is evident, it may be necessary to discuss it with HR or higher management, especially if it affects team morale or performance.

- ☑ **Encourage Conflict Resolution:** Advocate for healthy ways to resolve conflicts and misunderstandings. This can involve team mediation sessions or conflict resolution training.

Case Study: Overcoming Division in a Sales Team

In a sales team, the manager often sets team members against each other by selectively sharing information and playing favorites. This created a competitive and hostile work environment. Realizing the negative impact on their performance and morale, the team collectively decided to address the issue. They organized a meeting with HR to discuss the manager's tactics and its effects on the team. This intervention led to a change in the manager's approach and implementing more transparent and fair practices.

> **Conclusion**: Dealing with divide-and-conquer tactics requires a concerted effort to strengthen team unity, promote open communication, and address underlying issues of favoritism and misinformation. By fostering an environment of collaboration and mutual respect, you can effectively counteract these divisive strategies.

Responding to Micromanagement and Control

Dealing with a boss who micromanages you or exerts excessive control can be a significant challenge. This behavior not only undermines your competence and hinders your autonomy but can also stifle creativity and decrease job satisfaction.

Understanding the Underlying Psychology

The reasons why a boss micromanages or exerts excessive control can be diverse. This behavior often stems from the boss's insecurities, a need for control, or fear of failure. It could also be due to a lack of trust in the team's abilities or difficulty in delegating responsibilities. In more concerning scenarios, it might even be a deliberate tactic to demotivate employees or make them question their abilities. By recognizing the range of these underlying motivations, you can approach the situation with a blend of empathy and caution, facilitating more constructive conversations.

Recognizing the Behavior

Micromanagement is characterized by a boss's overly detailed involvement in your work. This might include frequent unnecessary check-ins, a reluctance to delegate tasks, and a tendency to prioritize minor details over the big picture. These bosses often require constant updates and may redo your work because it doesn't meet their exact standards. Recognizing these behaviors is the first step in addressing the stress and frustration they can cause.

Practical Strategies for Response

- ☑ **Assertive Communication:** Engage in a candid yet respectful conversation with your boss about the impact of micromanagement on your performance. Express your need for autonomy and how greater trust could enhance your productivity and job satisfaction. Frame the conversation around finding a balance that works for both of you.

- ☑ **Demonstrating Competence:** Show your reliability and capability by consistently delivering high-quality work and adhering to deadlines. By proving your competence, you can build trust and gradually negotiate for more independence in your tasks.

- ☑ **Setting Boundaries:** Politely but firmly communicate your preferred ways of receiving feedback and supervision. Clearly define the level of autonomy you need to perform effectively, balancing it with your boss's need for oversight.

- ☑ **Proactive Updates:** Preemptively provide updates on your progress and accomplishments. Regular, voluntary communication can reassure your boss of your commitment and potentially reduce their urge to micromanage.

- ☑ **Seeking Clear Expectations:** Ensure you thoroughly understand what your boss expects from you. When expectations are transparent, the likelihood of micromanagement due to miscommunication or uncertainty can be significantly reduced.

Case Study: Overcoming Control in Project Management

Sarah, a project coordinator, found herself constantly second-guessed and micromanaged by her boss. Her boss would often redo her work, leaving her feeling undervalued and demotivated. Realizing the need for change, Sarah initiated a conversation with her boss, where she expressed her feelings and proposed a new system for project updates and feedback. She emphasized her desire for more autonomy and trust in her capabilities. Gradually, her boss began to step back, allowing Sarah more freedom in her work and improving her overall job satisfaction.

> **Conclusion**: Dealing with a micromanaging or overly controlling boss requires patience, clear communication, and the establishment of professional boundaries. By understanding the psychology behind such behavior and proactively addressing it, you can foster a more balanced and respectful working relationship. Remember, it's about creating an environment where you can thrive professionally while maintaining a positive dynamic with your supervisor.

Responding to Playing on Emotions

Manipulators often play on emotions to exert control or influence in the workplace. This tactic can be particularly challenging to counteract, as it involves navigating complex emotional landscapes.

Understanding the Underlying Psychology

Manipulators playing on emotions often seek to create a sense of obligation, guilt, or indebtedness. They might be looking to exploit your empathy or desire for harmony in the workplace. Understanding these motivations allows you to approach these situations more objectively and maintain control over your responses.

Recognizing the Behavior

Emotional manipulation in the workplace often manifests in various subtle forms. One common tactic is the use of emotional appeals, where your boss or colleague might use personal stories or emotional scenarios to sway your decisions or opinions. Another tactic is guilt-tripping, where you are made to feel guilty for not complying with requests or aligning with certain views. Additionally, flattery might be employed excessively, with the intent of making you more compliant or lowering your defenses against particular requests or agendas. Recognizing these tactics is vital in preparing an effective response and maintaining your professional integrity.

Practical Strategies for Response

- ☑ **Maintain Emotional Boundaries:** It's crucial to differentiate between genuine emotional expressions and manipulative tactics. Keeping your professional and emotional boundaries intact will help you respond objectively.

- ☑ **Seek Clarification:** When faced with emotional appeals, ask for clear, rational reasons behind requests or decisions. This helps to shift the conversation from emotional to logical grounds.

- ☑ **Verify Claims:** If your emotions are being played on through stories or scenarios, take time to verify the facts. Don't immediately act on emotional appeals without understanding the full context.

- ☑ **Rely on Policies and Procedures:** Refer to established workplace policies and procedures to guide your actions, especially when emotions run high.

Case Study: Navigating Emotional Appeals in Team Assignments

Sarah, a project manager, noticed that a team member, Mark, often used emotional stories about personal hardships to avoid complex tasks or to gain extensions on deadlines. Initially sympathetic, Sarah soon realized that these stories were affecting team efficiency and morale. She started requesting factual reasons for any requests for extensions and began cross-verifying Mark's claims. Sarah also reinforced team policies on task assignments and deadlines, making decisions based on equitable workload distribution rather than emotional appeals. By doing so, she was able to maintain a fair and productive team environment.

Conclusion: Responding to emotional manipulation requires a balance of empathy and objectivity. By recognizing manipulative tactics, understanding their psychological underpinnings, and employing practical strategies, you can protect yourself from undue emotional influence and contribute to a more rational and professional workplace environment. Remember, maintaining emotional boundaries is key to professional resilience in the face of manipulative tactics.

Responding to Exploiting Power Dynamics

The exploitation of power dynamics in the workplace occurs when someone in a position of authority, like a boss or senior colleague, uses their power to influence, control, or intimidate others.

Understanding the Underlying Psychology

At the heart of exploiting power dynamics is a desire for control and dominance. It often stems from the individual's insecurities or need to assert authority. Sometimes, it might also be driven by an organizational culture that inadvertently endorses or overlooks such behavior.

Recognizing the Behavior

Exploitation of power dynamics can take various forms, ranging from subtle to overt. It might involve a boss who regularly uses their authority to override your decisions without justification or a senior colleague who frequently delegates their responsibilities to you, exploiting your lower position. It can also manifest in more direct forms, such as using their power to threaten your job security or professional growth if you don't comply with their demands. Recognizing these actions as abuse of power is the first step in formulating a response.

Practical Strategies for Response

☑ **Assert Your Professional Worth:** Stand firm on your professional capabilities and contributions. Clearly and confidently articulate your role, responsibilities, and achievements when necessary.

☑ **Establish Boundaries:** Clearly communicate your professional boundaries. Let your boss or colleague know diplomatically when their actions overstep.

☑ **Document Incidents:** Keep a record of instances where power is being exploited. This can be crucial if you need to escalate the matter or seek advice from HR or a mentor.

Case Study: Navigating Power Dynamics Through HR

Emily, an account manager at a marketing firm, began to notice a pattern with her supervisor, Derek. He consistently delegated his responsibilities to her, claiming it was for her professional development. However, it became clear that this was an exploitation of power dynamics, as he used his authority to offload work and pressure her into compliance with unrealistic deadlines.

After carefully documenting instances of Derek's behavior, including specific tasks, deadlines, and any relevant communications, Emily decided to address the issue directly. She presented her compiled evidence to Derek, hoping for a constructive resolution. However, Derek dismissed her concerns, insisting that the additional responsibilities were for her benefit.

Realizing that a direct approach with Derek was futile, Emily escalated the matter to HR, providing them with the same documentation. HR conducted a review, which included discussions with both Emily and Derek, as well as with other team members, for additional context. The evidence Emily provided painted a clear picture of the situation, leading HR to intervene. They implemented changes to ensure a fairer distribution of workload and established more precise guidelines for task delegation within the team.

This intervention not only alleviated Emily's undue burden but also signaled to the rest of the team that the company took issues of power exploitation seriously. For Emily, escalating the matter to HR was crucial in affirming her professional worth and establishing a more equitable work environment.

> **Conclusion**: Navigating the exploitation of power dynamics requires a balance of assertiveness, strategic thinking, and, sometimes, formal intervention. Remember, while you may be unable to change the person exploiting their power, you can control how you respond to it and take steps to safeguard your professional well-being.

Key Takeaways

- Your choice between passive, aggressive, and assertive responses to manipulation can significantly affect both immediate outcomes and long-term workplace dynamics. Opting for assertiveness is key to maintaining your integrity and well-being.

- Passive responses can lead to increased manipulation and resentment, aggressive responses may damage relationships and reputation, while assertive responses promote respect and effective problem-solving.

- Emphasizing assertive communication lets you express your needs and boundaries clearly and respectfully, fostering a positive work environment and deterring manipulative tactics. Say no without guilt, change your mind, make mistakes, and ask for what you want, reinforcing self-respect and balanced interactions.

- Use assertive language and actions in challenging situations, such as when being overloaded with work, facing unreasonable deadlines, or dealing with disrespectful behavior, to effectively assert your boundaries while seeking collaborative solutions.

- Manipulative behaviors often stem from a desire for control or from the manipulator's insecurities.

- Whether facing gaslighting, exploitation of guilt and fear, or micromanagement, documenting instances provides a factual basis for addressing these issues and can support your case, especially if escalation becomes necessary.

- Across various scenarios, maintaining clear professional boundaries and responding assertively is vital to preserving your integrity and well-being. This includes stating your needs, refusing unreasonable demands, and expressing discomfort with manipulative behaviors.

- Employing components of Emotional Intelligence, such as empathy, self-regulation, and effective communication, empowers you to respond to manipulation with insight and maintain control over your emotions.

- Building alliances with colleagues and seeking mentorship can strengthen your position and provide additional perspectives on handling manipulation. Promoting a culture of open and direct communication within your team will counteract tactics designed to isolate or undermine.

- Engage in professional development and prioritize your mental health. If necessary, don't hesitate to seek external advice or therapy, or consider changes within your professional environment.

11

——

Advocating for a Healthy Workplace Culture

Transitioning from the tactics of responding to manipulation discussed in Chapter 10, we now want to look at the broader canvas of workplace culture. In this chapter, we contemplate the significant influence of organizational values and leadership styles on our daily work lives. We'll explore the subtle signs of toxic team dynamics and the importance of fostering open communication and collaboration. We'll also delve into how you can effectively support colleagues navigating manipulative situations. Join us in this reflective exploration of how we can contribute to creating a healthier, more supportive workplace.

The Impact of Organizational Values and Leadership Styles

In any organization, the values it upholds and the leadership styles it embraces are not just abstract concepts; they are dynamic forces that significantly shape the workplace culture. They do not only influence the day-to-day operations but also the mental and emotional well-being of employees, the financial health of the organization, and the overall productivity of the team.

Organizational values act as a compass, guiding the decisions, behaviors, and interactions within a workplace. They are the bedrock upon which the company's culture is built. Similarly, leadership styles – whether authoritative, participative, transformational, or others – play a pivotal role in molding the work environment. The interplay between these values and leadership styles can either cultivate a positive atmosphere conducive to growth or lead to a toxic environment that stifles progress and harms employees.

When organizational values and leadership styles are aligned and positive, the benefits are manifold:

☑ **Enhanced Employee Morale:** A leadership style that values employee input and fosters respect leads to higher job satisfaction and morale.

☑ **Increased Productivity:** Leaders who inspire and motivate rather than control tend to have teams that are more innovative, cooperative, and productive.

☑ **Lower Turnover Rates:** Companies that prioritize integrity, fairness, and employee well-being often enjoy lower staff turnover, saving costs related to recruitment and training.

Conversely, a mismatch between proclaimed values and actual leadership behaviors can have detrimental effects:

☹ **Mental Health Decline:** Toxic leadership styles that promote fear, overwork, or constant competition can lead to increased stress, anxiety, and even depression among employees.

☹ **Rising Sick Leave and Healthcare Costs:** The mental strain caused by an unhealthy work environment often translates into physical health issues, leading to increased sick leave and higher healthcare costs for the company.

☹ **Financial Repercussions:** A toxic work environment can lead to reduced productivity, higher employee turnover, and damage to the company's reputation, all of which have direct and indirect financial implications.

"The intersection of organizational values and leadership styles is **where the heart of a company's culture lies**. Leaders and organizations must not only define their values but live by them."

Identifying Toxic Team Dynamics

In any team, dynamics play a pivotal role in shaping the well-being and productivity of its members. However, when these dynamics turn toxic, they can inflict harm not only on individuals but also significantly undermine the team's overall effectiveness. Recognizing these signs is the first step towards initiating positive change. So, let's delve into how you can identify signs of toxic team dynamics in the first place.

These are some of the most **common signs of toxic team dynamics**. If you encounter any of these at your workplace, beware:

- **Persistent Negative Communication:** Look for patterns of gossip, hostile jokes, or constant criticism. This includes consistent negative comments, disparaging remarks, or a general tone of cynicism. It's not just about the occasional bad day; it's a pattern where negativity becomes the norm, impacting team morale and individual self-esteem. This atmosphere can stifle creativity and make the workplace feel hostile.

- **Cliques and Exclusion:** Be aware of groups within the team that isolate or exclude others. Sometimes, groups within a team form tight-knit circles, often at the expense of others. These cliques can lead to feelings of isolation for those not included, negatively impacting collaboration and fairness. It's important to foster inclusivity and ensure everyone feels valued and part of the team.

- **Lack of Trust and Support:** Notice if team members are reluctant to share information or help each other. A healthy team environment thrives on mutual trust and support. When team members withhold information, fail to assist each other, or show a lack of interest in their colleagues' success, it can create an environment of competition rather than collaboration. This dynamic can hinder teamwork and affect overall productivity.

- **Unchecked Bullying or Harassment:** Pay attention to behaviors that intimidate or belittle team members. Behavior that intimidates belittles or unduly criticizes team members might manifest as verbal abuse, spreading rumors, or even sabotaging someone's work. Bullying creates a toxic environment where people feel unsafe, and it can lead to serious mental health issues and high staff turnover. It's crucial for such behaviors to be addressed immediately and firmly.

- **Discouragement of Personal Interactions:** When leadership actively discourages personal interactions or private conversations among team members, it can create a cold and impersonal work environment. This approach not only reduces team cohesion and trust but also strips away the opportunity for employees to build supportive relationships, which are essential for a healthy, collaborative workplace.

Encouraging Open Communication and Collaboration

Even if you're not in a leadership position, you have a significant role to play in promoting open communication and collaboration within your team. Your actions and attitude can influence the team's dynamics, encouraging a more inclusive and cooperative work environment. Here are some ways you can contribute:

Tips to Encourage Open Communication:

- ☑ **Being an Active Participant:** Take the initiative to participate actively in team meetings and discussions. Your involvement shows that you value the team's objectives and are committed to contributing. Practice active listening by giving full attention to the speaker, acknowledging their points, and asking clarifying questions. This not only enhances understanding but also builds a respectful and inclusive dialogue culture. Be the pilot, not the passenger!

☑ **Building Relationships:** Foster positive relationships with colleagues through casual conversations, shared coffee breaks, or lunch outings. These interactions, though informal, can strengthen team bonds and trust. Show genuine interest in your colleagues' work and ideas. This can help break down barriers and encourage others to open up, fostering a more collaborative atmosphere.

☑ **Sharing Ideas and Feedback:** Share your ideas and insights during team discussions. Your unique perspective can provide valuable contributions and spark innovative thinking. Also, constructive feedback in a respectful and supportive manner. This helps create a culture where feedback is seen as a tool for growth and improvement rather than criticism.

☑ **Utilizing Collaborative Tools:** Embrace and utilize the collaborative tools available in your workplace, such as shared digital workspaces, project management software, or communication platforms. Encourage others to use these tools by demonstrating their benefits in enhancing team coordination, information sharing, and project tracking.

By following these approaches, you can actively contribute to creating an open, communicative, and collaborative team environment. Your efforts, however small, can make a significant difference in transforming the overall team dynamics and fostering a positive workplace culture.

Supporting Colleagues Experiencing Manipulation

Manipulative behavior in the workplace can often be covert and harmful, impacting not just the direct victim but the team's morale. As a colleague, you can play a crucial role in offering support and creating a more positive work environment. Here's how you can identify and assist those who might be dealing with manipulation at work.

Signs of Manipulation at Your Workplace:

- **Changes in Behavior:** A sudden shift in a colleague's demeanor, such as becoming unusually withdrawn, anxious, or less confident, can indicate they're experiencing distress. These changes could stem from manipulative interactions. Observe if they seem unusually stressed after interactions with certain team members or managers, as this could be a sign of ongoing manipulation.

- **Unfair Workload:** Pay attention if a team member is frequently burdened with unreasonable workloads, subjected to constant criticism, or rarely receives credit for their contributions. These could be signs of targeted manipulation. Note any discrepancies in how tasks and responsibilities are assigned, especially if it seems to disadvantage a particular colleague consistently.

- **Isolation Tactics:** Be aware of any patterns where a colleague is consistently left out of meetings, discussions, or social gatherings. This could be a deliberate tactic to isolate them from the team. Look for signs of information being withheld from them, which can be a subtle form of manipulation to undermine their performance or position in the team.

Ways to Offer Support:

- **Being a Supportive Colleague:** If you notice a colleague who seems to be struggling, reach out to them respectfully and empathetically. Offering a listening ear and acknowledging their feelings can be immensely comforting. Create opportunities for them to share their thoughts in a safe environment, reassuring them that they are not alone and their concerns are valid.

☑ **Sharing Resources:** Inform your colleague about resources available within the organization, such as employee assistance programs, counseling services, or HR policies on workplace behavior. Recommend helpful literature or online resources about coping with workplace manipulation, which can provide them with additional perspectives and strategies.

☑ **Encouraging Reporting When Necessary:** If the manipulative behavior is severe or persistent, suggest that they report the issue to HR or higher management. Emphasize the importance of formally addressing such issues for their well-being and the health of the workplace. Offer to accompany them or provide support during the reporting process if they are comfortable with it. Sometimes, having an ally can make the process less intimidating.

By being vigilant and supportive, you can contribute significantly to helping a colleague navigate through and recover from the effects of workplace manipulation. Your actions can foster a culture of mutual support and respect, ensuring a healthier and more inclusive work environment for everyone.

Key Takeaways

- The alignment of organizational values and leadership styles significantly influences the workplace environment, affecting employee morale, productivity, and turnover rates. Positive alignment can foster a conducive atmosphere for growth, while a mismatch can lead to a toxic environment detrimental to employee well-being and organizational success.

- Leadership that values employee input and fosters respect can lead to higher job satisfaction and morale. Leaders who inspire and motivate rather than control tend to have more innovative, cooperative, and productive teams.

- Toxic leadership styles that promote fear, overwork, or constant competition can lead to increased stress, anxiety, and even depression among employees, negatively impacting their mental health and productivity.

- Identifying signs of toxic team dynamics, such as persistent negative communication, cliques and exclusion, lack of trust and support, unchecked bullying, and discouragement of personal interactions, is crucial for initiating positive change within the team.

- Fostering an inclusive and cooperative work environment is vital. Tips include being an active participant in discussions, building relationships with colleagues, sharing ideas and feedback, and utilizing collaborative tools to enhance team coordination and project management.

- Identify and support colleagues who might be dealing with manipulation at work. This can contribute significantly to creating a positive work environment.

- Even those not in leadership positions can play a significant role in advocating for a healthy workplace culture through their actions, attitudes, and efforts to encourage open communication and collaboration.

- A toxic work environment can lead to reduced productivity, higher employee turnover, and damage to the company's reputation, all of which have direct and indirect financial implications for the organization.

Conclusion

As we reach the close of our journey together, it's time to reflect on the ground we've covered and look forward to the path that lies ahead. Throughout this book, we've navigated the complex landscapes of workplace manipulation, uncovering the nuances of power dynamics, the psychology of manipulative behaviors, and the strategies to protect and empower ourselves and others in professional environments.

We've delved deep into understanding the subtle distinctions between influence and manipulation, and we've exposed the tactics manipulative bosses use to wield power. Armed with psychological insights and practical strategies, you're now equipped to detect and counteract manipulative behavior, establish healthy boundaries, and foster resilience.

The actual value of this journey lies in applying the insights you've gained to real-world challenges. Consider the steps you can take to implement these strategies in your workplace:

- **Regularly assess and reinforce your boundaries.**
- **Share your knowledge with colleagues to create a supportive environment.**
- **Seek continuous learning opportunities to stay informed and adaptable.**

For those looking to dive deeper, exploring additional resources on communication, leadership, and organizational psychology can further enrich their understanding and enhance their effectiveness in fostering positive workplace dynamics.

Remember, the journey doesn't end here. Each day presents new opportunities to apply what you've learned, to grow, and lead by example. You possess the tools and knowledge to navigate the complexities of the workplace with confidence and integrity. Embrace your role as an agent of change, not just in your professional life but in all aspects of your personal growth and development.

Looking forward, let this book serve as a foundation upon which you can build a career that is not only successful but also fulfilling and respectful of your values and well-being. Let it inspire you to advocate for a healthier workplace culture, one where manipulation is recognized and addressed and where every individual is empowered to thrive.

In closing, take pride in the strides you've made and the insights you've gained. The path to empowerment is ongoing, and your journey of growth and positive change is just beginning. Armed with knowledge, resilience, and a commitment to ethical action, you are ready to make a lasting impact. Let's move forward together, embracing the challenges and opportunities that await, and continue to build a more empowering, respectful, and thriving professional world.

A Final Word of Encouragement

As we bring our journey to a close, **I, Markus,** want to leave you with a message of hope and resilience. The creation of this book was inspired by my walk along a precarious high wire, where work became an added weight during a time of personal crisis. But from these challenges, something transformative emerged – an understanding that knowledge and the right strategies can empower us to stand tall against adversity.

Life's unexpected gusts – be it a personal crisis like my son Theodor's severe diagnosis or facing a manipulative, toxic work environment – test our resilience. My story, much like yours, is filled with moments of imbalance. But it's in these moments that we discover our true strength. The journey through my son's health challenges, the toxicity

I faced at work, and Claudia's extraordinary therapeutic approach taught me resilience, a resilience that I now share with you through this book.

In the face of manipulation and toxic leadership, remember that you have the power to reclaim control over your situation. Just as I found solace and strength in my collaboration with Claudia, you, too, can find support and empowerment. Use the knowledge and strategies from this book as your toolkit to navigate and overcome the challenges at your workplace.

> "When one door closes another door opens; but we so often look so long and so regretfully upon the closed door, that we do not see the ones which open for us."
>
> *- Alexander Graham Bell*

Today, as I reflect on my journey and share it with you, I also celebrate the triumphs. The first, of course is the remarkable progress of my son Theodor, who, against all odds, continues to thrive as a symbol of joy and strength. The second is my own personal evolution. In the past eighteen months, I've grown immensely. Working with Claudia as my therapist and later even collaborating with her and researching for this book has not only equipped me with invaluable tools to now navigate confidently through potentially toxic work environments but also fostered a newfound resilience within me. This same resilience and optimism are what I wish for you in your professional journey. Let our experiences be a testament to the fact that even in the toughest times, there is hope and a path forward.

As you step forward from here, do so with the confidence that you are equipped to handle whatever challenges come your way. The strategies and insights in this book are more than just lessons; they are your armor and shield against the winds of manipulation and toxicity. And remember, while we may each walk our own high wire, we don't walk it alone. With the proper support, knowledge, and resilience, we can keep our balance, no matter how strong the winds. Claudia's and my hope is that this book has not only equipped you with the tools you need but also inspires you to walk ahead with renewed confidence and strength.

May this book guide you through the complexities of the workplace. And as you move forward, may you find not just success, but joy and fulfillment in your professional life. Walk ahead with courage, with hope, and with the knowledge that you have the power to change your narrative. Your journey starts now.

Before we go, Claudia and I want to share one last real-life example with you. This time, it's not about a manipulative boss, nor is it about just a bad leader. It's an email sent by a manager, let's call him Rob, of an international company who was newly posted to the Viennese branch of the company. The email was sent to more than 100 employees whom Rob would be overseeing from now on. The email read as follows:

Subject: Hello from Rob – Your New Head of the Vienna Office

Dear Team,

I hope this message finds you well. My name is Rob, and I'm thrilled to be joining the Vienna branch as your new branch manager. Having worked with our international teams for several years, I'm excited about the opportunity to work directly with all of you and to contribute to our continued success.

A little about myself – I'm married with two wonderful sons who keep me on my toes. Our family is passionate about football, and we're die-hard supporters of Liverpool FC. So, don't be surprised if you catch me checking the latest scores or wearing my team's jersey on match days! Besides football, I enjoy hiking, photography, and exploring new cuisines. I believe life is about the experiences we gather, and I'm looking forward to creating new ones here in Vienna.

On a more personal note, family means everything to me. It's the anchor that keeps me grounded and the compass that guides my decisions. With that in mind, I want to share with you that on Wednesdays, I'll be starting the day a bit later than usual to drop my youngest son off at his weekly music class, a passion of his that we wholeheartedly support. Similarly, on Thursdays, I'll be leaving a bit early to attend my older son's football training sessions – a budding athlete in the making!

I share this with you not only to give you a glimpse into my life but also to underscore a belief that's very important to me: the balance between work and family life. I'm a firm advocate for ensuring our jobs enrich our lives and not the other way around. While work is important, it should never come at the expense of our well-being or our time with loved ones.

In the coming weeks, I plan to connect with all of you over a cup of coffee or tea in smaller group settings. I'm eager to learn about your roles and ambitions and how I can support you in achieving your goals.

And remember, my door (virtual or otherwise) is always open for a chat, a question, or even a debate on whether Liverpool will win the league this year (spoiler: they will).

Warm regards,
Rob

We don't think there is much left to say after this. Maybe only that they do exist. They are out there, the bosses who are true leaders, empathetic, understanding, and genuinely invested in the well-being of their teams. Leaders like Rob remind us that the workplace can be a space of growth, respect, and mutual support, where the balance between professional success and personal fulfillment isn't just a dream but a tangible reality.

Warm regards,
Markus and Claudia

Appendix: Workplace Manipulation Behavior Checklist

Evaluate your workplace environment and interactions with your boss using the checklist below. Tick the boxes that apply and jot down any notes or examples you recall. This will help you determine if manipulative tactics are being used against you.

Gaslighting

Is your boss denying or twisting facts, making you question your memory or sanity?

Notes:

Does your boss dismiss your concerns or feelings as overreactions or misconceptions?

Notes:

Exploiting Guilt and Fear

Is your boss using your emotions to pressure you into compliance or silence?

Notes:

Do you feel guilty for asserting your needs or boundaries around your boss?

Notes:

Undermining Confidence and Self-Esteem

Does your boss belittle your accomplishments or ideas?

Notes:

Is constant criticism from your boss making you doubt your abilities?

Notes:

Neurolinguistic Programming (NLP)

Is your boss using specific language patterns or body language to subtly influence your thoughts or actions?

Notes:

Emotional Blackmail

Is your boss threatening to withdraw emotional support or disclose sensitive information unless you comply with their demands?

Notes:

Triangulation

Is your boss bringing a third person into dynamics to create competition or further isolate you?

Notes:

Playing the Victim

Does your boss portray themselves as the aggrieved party to deflect responsibility and gain sympathy?

Notes:

Divide and Conquer

Is your boss creating or exploiting rifts between team members?

Notes:

Micromanagement and Control

Does your boss excessively control your work or decisions, indicating a lack of trust?

Notes:

Playing on Emotions

Is your boss manipulating your emotions to sway your decisions or actions?

Notes:

Exploiting Power Dynamics

Is your boss leveraging their position of authority to coerce, intimidate, or unduly influence your actions?

Notes:

Persuasion Techniques

Is your boss misusing persuasion skills for selfish ends rather than mutual benefit?

Notes:

References

Chapter 1: Why Are So Many Bosses Bad Leaders?

Bennis, W., & Thomas, R. (2008). Crucibles of leadership.*Harvard Business Review*, 80 9, 39-45, 124. https://doi.org/10.2307/j.ctvpg85tk.9.

Day, D., Fleenor, J., Atwater, L., Sturm, R., & McKee, R. (2014). Advances in leader and leadership development: A review of 25 years of research and theory. *Leadership Quarterly*, 25, 63-82. https://doi.org/10.1016/J. LEAQUA.2013.11.004.

Fischer, T., Tian, A., Lee, A., & Hughes, D. (2021). Abusive supervision: A systematic review and fundamental rethink. *The Leadership Quarterly*. https:// doi.org/10.1016/j.leaqua.2021.101540.

Goleman, D., Boyatzis, R., & McKee, A. (2002). Primal leadership: Learning to lead with emotional intelligence. Boston, MA: Harvard Business School Press.

Martinko, M., Harvey, P., Brees, J., & Mackey, J. (2013). A review of abusive supervision research. *Journal of Organizational Behavior*, 34. https://doi. org/10.1002/JOB.1888.

Paulhus, D., & Williams, K. (2002). The Dark Triad of personality: Narcissism, Machiavellianism, and psychopathy. *Journal of Research in Personality*, 36, 556-563. https://doi.org/10.1016/S0092-6566(02)00505-6.

Peter, L. J., & Hull, R. (1969). The Peter principle: Why things always go wrong. New York: William Morrow and Company.

Krasikova, D., Green, S., & LeBreton, J. (2013). Destructive Leadership. *Journal of Management*, 39, 1308 - 1338. https://doi.org/10.1177/0149206312471388.

Kruger, J., & Dunning, D. (1999). Unskilled and unaware of it: how difficulties in recognizing one's own incompetence lead to inflated self-assessments. *Journal of personality and social psychology*, 77 6, 1121-34 . https://doi. org/10.1037/0022-3514.77.6.1121.

Schein, E. H. (2010). Organizational culture and leadership (4th ed.). San Francisco, CA: Jossey-Bass.

Swanson, E., Kim, S., Lee, S., Yang, J., & Lee, Y. (2020). The effect of leader competencies on knowledge sharing and job performance: Social capital theory. *Journal of Hospitality and Tourism Management*, 42, 88-96. https://doi.org/10.1016/j.jhtm.2019.11.004.

Tepper, B. (2007). Abusive Supervision in Work Organizations: Review, Synthesis, and Research Agenda. *Journal of Management*, 33, 261 - 289. https://doi.org/10.1177/0149206307300812.

Chapter 2: About Manipulation

Bowles, H. R., & Gelfand, M. J. (2009). Status and the evaluation of workplace deviance. *Psychological Science*, *21*(1), 49–54. https://doi.org/10.1177/0956797609356509

Buss, D., Gomes, M., Higgins, D., & Lauterbach, K. (1987). Tactics of manipulation..*Journal of personality and social psychology*, 52 6, 1219-29. https://doi.org/10.1037/0022-3514.52.6.1219.

Cleary, M., West, S., McGarry, D., Greenwood, M., &Kornhaber, R. (2019). Manipulation in health care: a positive or negative experience? *Issues in Mental Health Nursing*, *40*(11), 985–987. https://doi.org/10.1080/01612840.2019.1643631

Erikson, T. (2021). Surrounded by bad bosses (and lazy employees): How to stop struggling, start succeeding, and deal with idiots at work. St. Martin's Essentials

Förster, M., Mauleon, A., &Vannetelbosch, V. (2014). Trust and manipulation in social networks. *Network Science*, 4, 216 - 243. https://doi.org/10.1017/nws.2015.34.

Giumetti, G. W., Hatfield, A. L., Scisco, J. L., Schroeder, A. N., Muth, E. R., & Kowalski, R. M. (2013). What a rude e-mail! Examining the differential effects of incivility versus support on mood, energy, engagement, and performance in an online context. *Journal of Occupational Health Psychology*, *18*(3), 297–309. https://doi.org/10.1037/a0032851

Hyde, J., Grieve, R., Norris, K., & Kemp, N. (2020). The dark side of emotional intelligence: the role of gender and the Dark Triad in emotional manipulation at work. *Australian Journal of Psychology*, *72*(4), 307–317. https://doi.org/10.1111/ajpy.12294

Klein, A., & Martin, S. (2011). Two dilemmas in dealing with workplace bullies – false positives and deliberate deceit. *International Journal of Workplace Health Management, 4*(1), 13–32. https://doi.org/10.1108/17538351111118572

Krause, D. (2012). Consequences of Manipulation in Organizations: Two Studies on its Effects on Emotions and Relationships. *Psychological Reports,* 111, 199 - 218. https://doi.org/10.2466/01.21.PR0.111.4.199-218.

Lyons, M. (2019). The dark triad in the workplace. In *Elsevier eBooks* (pp. 137–160). https://doi.org/10.1016/b978-0-12-814291-2.00006-1

Mutsaers, P. (2014). "All of Me": Psychologizing Turkish-Dutch police officers in the Netherlands. *Anthropology of Work Review, 35*(2), 72–83. https://doi.org/10.1111/awr.12041

Nepryakhin, N. (2019a). Classification of vulnerability factors in the process of psychological manipulation. *Network Science.* https://doi.org/10.33422/icarss.2019.03.93

Nepryakhin, N. (2019b). Classification of vulnerability factors in the process of psychological manipulation. *Proceedings of the International Conference on Advanced Research in Social Sciences.* https://doi.org/10.33422/icarss.2019.03.93

Neveu, J., &Kakavand, B. (2019). Endangered Resources: The role of organizational justice and interpersonal trust as signals for workplace corruption. *Relations Industrielles, 74*(3), 498–524. https://doi.org/10.7202/1065170ar

Pugh, J. (2020). Controlling influences. In *Oxford University Press eBooks* (pp. 59–90). https://doi.org/10.1093/oso/9780198858584.003.0004

Rospenda, K. M., & Richman, J. A. (2004). The factor structure of generalized workplace harassment. *Violence & Victims, 19*(2), 221–238. https://doi.org/10.1891/vivi.19.2.221.64097

Tomková, A., &Čigarská, B. (2022). Identification and Assessment of Human Manipulation in the Work Environment. *International Journal of Organizational Leadership, 11*(3), 274–286. https://doi.org/10.33844/ijol.2022.60330

Chapter 3: Understanding Manipulative Behavior and Tactics Employed by Manipulative Bosses

Bailey, C. D. (2013). Psychopathy and Accounting Students' Attitudes towards Unethical Behaviors. *Social Science Research Network.* https://doi.org/10.2139/ssrn.2279976

Erikson, T. (2020). Surrounded by psychopaths: How to protect yourself from being manipulated and exploited in business (and in life). *St. Martin's Essentials*

Giammarco, E. A., & Vernon, P. A. (2014). Vengeance and the Dark Triad: The role of empathy and perspective taking in trait forgivingness. *Personality and Individual Differences, 67,* 23–29. https://doi.org/10.1016/j.paid.2014.02.010

Heym, N., Firth, J. L., Kibowski, F., Sumich, A., Egan, V., &Bloxsom, C. (2019). Empathy at the Heart of Darkness: empathy deficits that bind the dark triad and those that mediate indirect, relational aggression. *Frontiers in Psychiatry, 10.* https://doi.org/10.3389/fpsyt.2019.00095

Kastner-Bosek, A., Dajić, I., Mikus, N., Weidenauer, A., & Willeit, M. (2021). Addicted to Self-esteem: Understanding the neurochemistry of narcissism by using cocaine as a pharmacological model. *Journal of Experimental Psychopathology, 12.* https://doi.org/10.1177/20438087211044362.

Koonar, N. S. (2017). *The influence of narcissism, Machiavellianism and psychopathic personality traits on leader's preferences in followers.* https://doi.org/10.24124/2014/bpgub1608

Kucharska, A. (2023, May 10). Breaking the People Pleasing Habit: Recognizing Signs, Unveiling Consequences, and Mastering Lasting Transformation. LinkedIn. https://www.linkedin.com/pulse/breaking-people-pleasing-habit-recognizing-signs/

Kuftyak, E., Slyusarev, A. S., Palin, A. V., Козлов, М., Ivanitskaya, E. D., Rumyanceva, Y. M., &Bagryancev, G. V. (2023). Relationship between impaired attachment type and dark triad traits in patients with borderline personality disorder (pilot study). *ObozreniePsihiatrii I MedicinskojPsihologiiImeni V.M. Behtereva.* https://doi.org/10.31363/2313-7053-2023-632

Lata, M., & Chaudhary, R. (2020). Dark Triad and instigated incivility: The moderating role of workplace spirituality. *Personality and Individual Differences, 166,* 110090. https://doi.org/10.1016/j.paid.2020.110090

Marcus, D. K., Preszler, J., & Zeigler-Hill, V. (2018). A network of dark personality traits: What lies at the heart of darkness? *Journal of Research in Personality, 73,* 56–62. https://doi.org/10.1016/j.jrp.2017.11.003

Nübold, A., Bader, J., Bozin, N., Depala, R., Eidast, H., Johannessen, E. A., & Prinz, G. M. (2017). Developing a taxonomy of dark triad triggers at work – a grounded theory study protocol. *Frontiers in Psychology, 8.* https://doi.org/10.3389/fpsyg.2017.00293

Nübold, A., Van Gils, S., & Zacher, H. (2022). Daily work role stressors and dark triad states. *Zeitschrift Fur Psychologie-journal ofPsychology*, *230*(4), 311–320. https://doi.org/10.1027/2151-2604/a000505

Schyns, B., Braun, S., & Wisse, B. (2019). Dark personalities in the workplace. *Oxford Research Encyclopedia of Psychology*. https://doi.org/10.1093/acrefore/9780190236557.013.553

Spain, S. M., Harms, P. D., & LeBreton, J. M. (2013). The dark side of personality at work. *Journal of Organizational Behavior*, *35*(S1), S41–S60. https://doi.org/10.1002/job.1894

Wisse, B., &Sleebos, E. (2016). When the dark ones gain power: Perceived position power strengthens the effect of supervisor Machiavellianism on abusive supervision in work teams. *Personality and Individual Differences*, *99*, 122–126. https://doi.org/10.1016/j.paid.2016.05.019

Chapter 4: Detecting Manipulative Tactics

Bowers, L. (2003). Manipulation: searching for an understanding. *Journal of Psychiatric and Mental Health Nursing*, *10*(3), 329–334. https://doi.org/10.1046/j.1365-2850.2003.00603.x

Daniel, T. A. (2017). Managing toxic Emotions at work: HR's unique role as the "Organizational Shock Absorber." *Employment Relations Today*, *43*(4), 13–19. https://doi.org/10.1002/ert.21599

Davidhizar, R. (1989). Participative management: the power of positive manipulation. *Today's OR nurse*, 11 11, 18-25

Davidhizar, R., & Giger, J. N. (1990). When subordinates go over your head. *JONA: The Journal of Nursing Administration*, *20*(9), 29???34. https://doi.org/10.1097/00005110-199009000-00008

Hyde, J., Grieve, R., Norris, K., & Kemp, N. (2020). The dark side of emotional intelligence: the role of gender and the Dark Triad in emotional manipulation at work. *Australian Journal of Psychology*, *72*(4), 307–317. https://doi.org/10.1111/ajpy.12294

Ivan, K., & Natalya, T. (2019). MANIPULATIVE BEHAVIOR IN THE PROFESSIONAL ACTIVITIES OF OFFICE STAFF. Ìnsajt, *1*, 96–101. https://doi.org/10.32999/2663-970x/2019-1-15

Khalid, J., & Ahmed, J. (2015). Perceived organizational politics and employee silence: supervisor trust as a moderator. *Journal of the Asia Pacific Economy*, *21*(2), 174–195. https://doi.org/10.1080/13547860.2015.1092279

Krause, D. E. (2012). Consequences of Manipulation in Organizations: Two Studies on its Effects on Emotions and Relationships. *Psychological Reports*, *111*(1), 199–218. https://doi.org/10.2466/01.21.pr0.111.4.199-218

Lutgen-Sandvik, P. (2003). The communicative cycle of employee emotional abuse. *Management Communication Quarterly*, *16*(4), 471–501. https://doi.org/10.1177/0893318903251627

McAvoy, B. (2003). Workplace bullying. *The BMJ*, *326*(7393), 776–777. https://doi.org/10.1136/bmj.326.7393.776

Myers, C. D., & Tingley, D. (2016). The influence of emotion on trust. *Political Analysis*, *24*(4), 492–500. https://doi.org/10.1093/pan/mpw026

Pa, M. (1996). Manipulation: a manager's perspective..*Seminars in perioperative nursing*, 5, 127.

Skiba, T. S., & Wildman, J. L. (2018). Uncertainty reducer, exchange deepener, or Self-Determination Enhancer? Feeling trust versus feeling trusted in Supervisor-Subordinate relationships. *Journal of Business and Psychology*, *34*(2), 219–235. https://doi.org/10.1007/s10869-018-9537-x

Urda, J., & Loch, C. H. (2012). Social preferences and emotions as regulators of behavior in processes. *Journal of Operations Management*, *31*(1–2), 6–23. https://doi.org/10.1016/j.jom.2012.11.007

Chapter 5: Confronting Your Boss – Or Better Not?

Brown, T. C., McCracken, M., & Hillier, T. (2013). Using evidence-based practices to enhance transfer of training: assessing the effectiveness of goal setting and behavioural observation scales. *Human Resource Development International*, *16*(4), 374–389. https://doi.org/10.1080/13678868.2013.812291

De Dreu, C. K. W., & Gelfand, M. J. (2007). *The Psychology of conflict and conflict management in organizations*. https://doi.org/10.4324/9780203810125

Glomb, T. M. (2002). Workplace anger and aggression: Informing conceptual models with data from specific encounters. *Journal of Occupational Health Psychology*, *7*(1), 20–36. https://doi.org/10.1037/1076-8998.7.1.20

Harari, M. B., Thompson, A. H., &Viswesvaran, C. (2018). Extraversion and job satisfaction: The role of trait bandwidth and the moderating effect of status goal attainment. *Personality and Individual Differences*, *123*, 14–16. https://doi.org/10.1016/j.paid.2017.10.041

Johansson, M., & Andersson, L. E. (2020, August 11). Using a Smartphone App to Assess and Support Transfer of Training of Leadership Skills - a Feasibility Study. https://doi.org/10.16993/sjwop.131

McDonald, G. E., Vickers, M. H., Mohan, S., Wilkes, L. M., & Jackson, D. (2010). Workplace conversations: Building and maintaining collaborative capital. *Contemporary Nurse, 36*(1–2), 96–105. https://doi.org/10.5172/conu.2010.36.1-2.096

McKenzie, D. (2015). The role of mediation in resolving workplace relationship conflict. *International Journal of Law and Psychiatry, 39*, 52–59. https://doi.org/10.1016/j.ijlp.2015.01.021

Overton, A. R., & Lowry, A. C. (2013). Conflict Management: Difficult Conversations with Difficult People. *Clinics in Colon and Rectal Surgery, 26*(04), 259–264. https://doi.org/10.1055/s-0033-1356728

Pérez, J. a. P., Medina, F. J., Arenas, A., &Munduate, L. (2015). The relationship between interpersonal conflict and workplace bullying. *Journal of Managerial Psychology, 30*(3), 250–263. https://doi.org/10.1108/jmp-01-2013-0034

Robinson, J. S., & Garton, B. L. (2008). AN ASSESSMENT OF THE EMPLOYABILITY SKILLS NEEDED BY GRADUATES IN THE COLLEGE OF AGRICULTURE, FOOD AND NATURAL RESOURCES AT THE UNIVERSITY OF MISSOURI. *Journal of Agricultural Education, 49*(4), 96–105. https://doi.org/10.5032/jae.2008.04096

Schuliery, N. M. (1998). The optimum level of argumentativeness for employed women. *Journal of Business Communication, 35*(3), 346–367. https://doi.org/10.1177/002194369803500303

Zweibel, E. B., Goldstein, R., Manwaring, J. A., & Marks, M. (2008). What sticks: How medical residents and academic health care faculty transfer conflict resolution training from the workshop to the workplace. *Conflict Resolution Quarterly, 25*(3), 321–350. https://doi.org/10.1002/crq.211

Chapter 6: Understanding and Changing Core Beliefs

Dozois, D. J. A., &Rnic, K. (2015). Core beliefs and self-schematic structure in depression. *Current Opinion in Psychology, 4*, 98–103. https://doi.org/10.1016/j.copsyc.2014.12.008

Eze, J. E., Ifeagwazi, C. M., &Chukwuorji, J. C. (2019). Core Beliefs challenge and posttraumatic growth: Mediating role of rumination among internally displaced survivors of terror attacks. *Journal of Happiness Studies, 21*(2), 659–676. https://doi.org/10.1007/s10902-019-00105-x

Kaufman, J. J., Allbaugh, L. J., & Wright, M. O. (2018). Relational wellbeing following traumatic interpersonal events and challenges to core beliefs. *Psychological Trauma: Theory, Research, Practice, and Policy, 10*(1), 103–111. https://doi.org/10.1037/tra0000253

Luu, T. T. (2021). Worker resilience during the COVID-19 crisis: The role of core beliefs challenge, emotion regulation, and family strain. *Personality and Individual Differences, 179*, 110784. https://doi.org/10.1016/j.paid.2021.110784

Millings, A., &Carnelley, K. B. (2015). Core belief content examined in a large sample of patients using online cognitive behaviour therapy. *Journal of Affective Disorders, 186*, 275–283. https://doi.org/10.1016/j.jad.2015.06.044

Rosmarin, D. H., Pirutinsky, S., Auerbach, R. P., Björgvinsson, T., Bigda-Peyton, J. S., Andersson, G., Pargäment, K. I., &Krumrei, E. J. (2011). Incorporating spiritual beliefs into a cognitive model of worry. *Journal of Clinical Psychology, 67*(7), 691–700. https://doi.org/10.1002/jclp.20798

Thompson-Brenner, H., Smith, M., Brooks, G., Franklin, D., Espel-Huynh, H., & Boswell, J. (2018). Core Beliefs. *The Renfrew Unified Treatment for Eating Disorders and Comorbidity*. https://doi.org/10.1002/9781119395348.ch10

Thompson-Brenner, H., Smith, M., Brooks, G., Berman, R., Kaloudis, A., Espel-Huynh, H., Franklin, D. R., & Boswell, J. F. (2021). Therapist materials for core beliefs. In *Oxford University Press eBooks* (pp. 181–192). https://doi.org/10.1093/med-psych/9780190946425.003.0012

Chapter 7: Personal Coping Strategies and Resilience-Building Techniques

Christopher, J. C., Christopher, S. E., Dunnagan, T., &Schure, M. B. (2006). Teaching Self-Care through mindfulness practices: the application of yoga, meditation, and qigong to counselor training. *Journal of Humanistic Psychology, 46*(4), 494–509. https://doi.org/10.1177/0022167806290215

Dunkley, D. M., &Blankstein, K. R. (2000). Self-Critical Perfectionism, Coping, Hassles, and Current Distress: A Structural Equation Modeling Approach. *Cognitive Therapy and Research, 24*(6), 713–730. https://doi.org/10.1023/a:1005543529245

Dunkley, D. M., Ma, D., Lee, I. A., Preacher, K. J., &Zuroff, D. C. (2014). Advancing complex explanatory conceptualizations of daily negative and positive affect: Trigger and maintenance coping action patterns. *Journal of Counseling Psychology, 61*(1), 93–109. https://doi.org/10.1037/a0034673

Dunkley, D. M., Mandel, T., & Ma, D. (2014). Perfectionism, neuroticism, and daily stress reactivity and coping effectiveness 6 months and 3 years later. *Journal of Counseling Psychology, 61*(4), 616–633. https://doi.org/10.1037/cou0000036

Dunkley, D. M., Solomon-Krakus, S., &Moroz, M. (2015). Personal Standards and Self-Critical Perfectionism and Distress: stress, coping, and perceived social support as mediators and moderators. In *Springer eBooks* (pp. 157–176). https://doi.org/10.1007/978-3-319-18582-8_7

Dunkley, D. M., Zuroff, D. C., & Blankstein, K. R. (2003). Self-critical perfectionism and daily affect: Dispositional and situational influences on stress and coping. *Journal of Personality and Social Psychology, 84*(1), 234–252. https://doi.org/10.1037/0022-3514.84.1.234

Dweck, C. S. (2006). *Mindset: The new psychology of success. Random House.*

Filyasova, Y. A. (2021). PERFECTIONISM IN THE WORKPLACE: MAIN FEATURES AND CAREER GROWTH MANAGEMENT. *Social'no-trudovyeIssledovaniâ,* 3(44), 157–169. https://doi.org/10.34022/2658-3712-2021-44-3-157-169

Hegney, D., Tsai, L., Craigie, M., Crawford, C., Jay, S. M., & Rees, C. S. (2020). Experiences of university employees of the impact of a mindful self-care and resiliency program on their well-being. *Higher Education Research and Development, 40*(3), 524–537. https://doi.org/10.1080/07294360.2020.1764508

Jiang, F., & Ko, S. (2022). The Impact of Self-Oriented Perfectionism on job Crafting: Focusing on the mediating effect of work engagement and the moderating effect of perceived organizational support. 조직과인사관리연구, *46*(4), 23–45. https://doi.org/10.36459/jom.2022.46.4.23

Kondratowicz, B. B., &Godlewska-Werner, D. (2022). Growth mindset and life and job satisfaction: the mediatory role of stress and self-efficacy. *Health Psychology Report.* https://doi.org/10.5114/hpr/152158

Mirzairad, R., Haydari, A., Pasha, R., Ehteshamzadeh, P., &Makvandi, B. (2016). The Relationship between Perfectionism and Psychological Distress with the Mediation of Coping Styles and Self-Esteem. *International Journal of Mental Health and Addiction, 15*(3), 614–620. https://doi.org/10.1007/s11469-016-9689-8

Ollier-Malaterre, A., Rothbard, N. P., & Berg, J. M. (2013). When Worlds Collide in Cyberspace: How boundary work in online social networks impacts professional relationships. *Academy of Management Review, 38*(4), 645–669. https://doi.org/10.5465/amr.2011.0235

Pierre, K. D. (1986). Enhancing Well-Being at the workplace: *Employee Assistance Quarterly, 1*(4), 19–28. https://doi.org/10.1300/j022v01n04_02

Stamper, C. L., &Johlke, M. C. (2003). The impact of perceived organizational support on the relationship between boundary spanner role stress and work outcomes. *Journal of Management, 29*(4), 569–588. https://doi.org/10.1016/s0149-2063_03_00025-4

Chapter 8: Self-Care and Stress Management

Cloud, H., & Townsend, J. S. (1992). *Boundaries: When to say yes, when to say no to take control of your life.* https://ci.nii.ac.jp/ncid/BB17350165

Irawati, K., Budi, A. W. S., &Haris, F. (2021). Stress Management Training for working, elderly, and health cadre women : RumahPendampingEmakSehat Jiwa. *Indonesian Journal of Community Engagement, 7*(2), 130. https://doi.org/10.22146/jpkm.53612

Klawonn, A., Kernan, D., & Lynskey, J. V. (2019). A 5-Week seminar on the Biopsychosocial-Spiritual Model of Self-Care improves anxiety, Self-Compassion, mindfulness, depression, and stress in graduate healthcare students. *International Journal of Yoga Therapy, 29*(1), 81–89. https://doi.org/10.17761/d-18-2019-00026

Law, R. M., Dollard, M. F., Tuckey, M. R., &Dormann, C. (2011). Psychosocial safety climate as a lead indicator of workplace bullying and harassment, job resources, psychological health and employee engagement. *Accident Analysis & Prevention, 43*(5), 1782–1793. https://doi.org/10.1016/j.aap.2011.04.010

Lee, E. O. (2007). Mind—Body—Spirit Practice and Perceived Self-Efficacy for Mental Health Promotion: An Exploratory study. *The International Journal of Mental Health Promotion, 9*(3), 35–47. https://doi.org/10.1080/14623730.2007.9721841

Lowenstein, K. G. (2002). Meditation and Self-Regulatory techniques. In *Elsevier eBooks* (pp. 159–181). https://doi.org/10.1016/b978-012638281-5/50009-7

Moore, M., Montgomery, L. K., & Cobbs, T. D. (2021). Increasing student success through in-class resilience education. *Nurse Education in Practice, 50,* 102948. https://doi.org/10.1016/j.nepr.2020.102948

Newsome, S., Christopher, J. C., Dahlen, P., & Christopher, S. (2006a). Teaching Counselors Self-Care through Mindfulness Practices. *Teachers College Record, 108*(9), 1881–1900. https://doi.org/10.1111/j.1467-9620.2006.00766.x

Newsome, S., Christopher, J. C., Dahlen, P., & Christopher, S. (2006b). Teaching Counselors Self-Care through Mindfulness Practices. *Teachers College Record, 108*(9), 1881–1900. https://doi.org/10.1111/j.1467-9620.2006.00766.x

Ng, A., &Boey, K. W. (2021). Efficacy of body-mind-spirit oriented psychosocial programme in promoting holistic well-being of students in late adolescence. *Asia Pacific Journal of Counselling and Psychotherapy, 12*(1), 22–37. https://doi.org/10.1080/21507686.2021.1876114

Parshad, O., & Parshad, O. (2004, June 1). *Role of yoga in stress management. The West Indian medical journal*, 53 3, 191-4.

Patel, S., Chauhan, D., & Patnaik, R. (2022). Promotion of psychosocial wellbeing in new mothers through mindfulness-based cognitive therapy. *International Journal of Health Sciences (IJHS)*, 5040–5055. https://doi.org/10.53730/ijhs.v6ns2.6265

Paul, G., Elam, B., &Verhulst, S. J. (2007). A longitudinal study of students' perceptions of using deep breathing meditation to reduce testing stresses. *Teaching and Learning in Medicine, 19*(3), 287–292. https://doi.org/10.1080/10401330701366754

Schyns, B., & Schilling, J. (2013). How bad are the effects of bad leaders? A meta-analysis of destructive leadership and its outcomes. *The Leadership Quarterly, 24*(1), 138–158. https://doi.org/10.1016/j.leaqua.2012.09.001

Verkuil, B., Atasayi, S., &Molendijk, M. L. (2015). Workplace Bullying and Mental Health: A Meta-Analysis on Cross-Sectional and Longitudinal Data. *PLOS ONE, 10*(8), e0135225. https://doi.org/10.1371/journal.pone.0135225

Woods, J. H., &Minniti, M. J. (1987). The Relationship of Stress Management Training to the Experience of Pain in Clients with Intractable Angina. *Journal of Holistic Nursing, 5*(1), 11–13. https://doi.org/10.1177/089801018700500104

Zastrow, C. (1987). Using Relaxation Techniques with Individuals and with Groups. *Journal of Independent Social Work, 2*(1), 83–95. https://doi.org/10.1300/j283v02n01_08

Chapter 9: Developing Emotional Intelligence and Communication Skills

Amir, S. (2021). Teaching emotional intelligence to undergraduate students. *Pakistan Journal of Neurological Surgery, 25*(2), 276–279. https://doi.org/10.36552/pjns.v25i2.562

Ashwin, M. (1992). Working with individuals. In *Elsevier eBooks* (pp. 117–166). https://doi.org/10.1016/b978-0-7506-0185-6.50012-0

Desai, M. (2018). Module 2 Self-Empowerment. In *Rights-based direct practice with children* (pp. 33–68). https://doi.org/10.1007/978-981-10-4729-9_2

Fernandez, C. S. P. (2007). Emotional intelligence in the workplace. *Journal of Public Health Management and Practice, 13*(1), 80–82. https://doi.org/10.1097/00124784-200701000-00013

Guntersdorfer, I. R., &Golubeva, I. (2018). Emotional intelligence and intercultural competence: Theoretical questions and pedagogical possibilities. *Intercultural Communication Education, 1*(2), 54–63. https://doi.org/10.29140/ice.v1n2.60

Herman, I. R. (2018). Teacher's and students personal development needs - Theoretical perspectives. *The European Proceedings of Social and Behavioural Sciences.* https://doi.org/10.15405/epsbs.2018.06.84

Ilie, O., &Metea, I. (2015). Empathic and assertive communication. Efficient communication developments. *Conference Proceedings, 21*(1), 214–217. https://doi.org/10.1515/kbo-2015-0035

Liebrecht, C., &Montenery, S. (2016). Use of simulated Psychosocial Role-Playing to enhance nursing students 'Development of soft Skills. *Creative Nursing, 22*(3), 171–175. https://doi.org/10.1891/1078-4535.22.3.171

Lu, Y. E., Dane, B., & Gellman, A. (2005). An experiential model. *Journal of Teaching in Social Work, 25*(3–4), 89–103. https://doi.org/10.1300/j067v25n03_06

Pedrazza, M., &Boccato, G. (2009). The tension between empathy and assertiveness and its correlation with self-efficacy. *DiPAVQuaderni, 25*, 131–142. https://doi.org/10.3280/dipa2009-025009

Rubin, R. B., & Martin, M. M. (1994). Development of a measure of interpersonal communication competence. *Communication Research Reports, 11*(1), 33–44. https://doi.org/10.1080/08824099409359938

Chapter 10: Responding to Manipulative Behavior

Dooley, J., Shaw, T., & Cross, D. (2012). The association between the mental health and behavioural problems of students and their reactions to cyber-victimization. *European Journal of Developmental Psychology, 9*(2), 275–289. https://doi.org/10.1080/17405629.2011.648425

Epstein, N. B. (1980). Social consequences of assertion, aggression, passive aggression, and submission: Situational and dispositional determinants. *Behavior Therapy*, *11*(5), 662–669. https://doi.org/10.1016/s0005-7894(80)80005-0

Furnham, A., &Rawles, R. (1994). Interpersonal influence and coping strategies. *Personality and Individual Differences*, *16*(2), 357–361. https://doi.org/10.1016/0191-8869(94)90176-7

Gnezdilova, Y., &Author_Id, N. (2021). STRATEGIC AND TACTIC ARRANGEMENT OF EMOTIONAL MANIPULATIVE METACOMMUNICATION. ФізичнеВихованняТаСпорт, *1*, 3–9. https://doi.org/10.17721/folia.philologica/2021/1/1

Heisler, G. H., & McCormack, J. (1982). Situational and personality influences on the reception of provocative responses. *Behavior Therapy*, *13*(5), 743–750. https://doi.org/10.1016/s0005-7894(82)80030-0

Hollandsworth, J. G. (1977). Differentiating assertion and aggression: Some behavioral guidelines. *Behavior Therapy*, *8*(3), 347–352. https://doi.org/10.1016/s0005-7894(77)80067-1

Kosutić, Z. (2018). The importance of assertive communication in school and social functioning of adolescents. *Psihijatrija Danas*, *50*(1), 67–71. https://doi.org/10.5937/psihdan1801067k

Ryan, E. B., Anas, A. P., & Friedman, D. B. (2006). Evaluations of older adult assertiveness in problematic clinical encounters. *Journal of Language and Social Psychology*, *25*(2), 129–145. https://doi.org/10.1177/0261927x06286350

Sodoma, K. A. (2022). Emotional gaslighting and affective empathy. *International Journal of Philosophical Studies*, *30*(3), 320–338. https://doi.org/10.1080/09672559.2022.2121894

Vp, S. (2019a). Assertiveness, Machiavellism, Lack of Protection from Manipulations and Psychological States of Teachers and Students. *Psychology and Psychotherapy: Research Study*, *3*(1). https://doi.org/10.31031/pprs.2019.03.000551

Vp, S. (2019b). Assertiveness, Machiavellism, Lack of Protection from Manipulations and Psychological States of Teachers and Students. *Psychology and Psychotherapy: Research Study*, *3*(1). https://doi.org/10.31031/pprs.2019.03.000551

Yoshioka, M. R. (2000). Substantive differences in the assertiveness of Low-Income African American, Hispanic, and Caucasian women. *The Journal of Psychology*, *134*(3), 243–259. https://doi.org/10.1080/00223980009600865

Руденок, А., Petyak, O., &Ігумнова, O. (2021). Gender aspects of gaslighting as a form of psychological violence in the family. *NaukovijVìsnikSìverŝini. Serìâ: Osvìta, 2021*(2), 137–151. https://doi.org/10.32755/sjeducation.2021.02.137

Chapter 11: Advocating for a Healthy Workplace Culture

Boies, K., Fiset, J., & Gill, H. (2015). Communication and trust are key: Unlocking the relationship between leadership and team performance and creativity. *Leadership Quarterly*, *26*(6), 1080–1094. https://doi.org/10.1016/j.leaqua.2015.07.007

Chilcutt, A. S. (2009). Exploring leadership and team communication within the organizational environment of a dental practice. *The Journal of the American Dental Association*, *140*(10), 1252–1258. https://doi.org/10.14219/jada.archive.2009.0048

Hu, N., Chen, Z., Gu, J., Huang, S., & Liu, H. (2017). Conflict and creativity in inter-organizational teams. *International Journal of Conflict Management*, *28*(1), 74–102. https://doi.org/10.1108/ijcma-01-2016-0003

Sarin, S., & O'Connor, G. C. (2009). First among Equals: The Effect of Team Leader Characteristics on the Internal Dynamics of Cross-Functional Product Development Teams*. *Journal of Product Innovation Management*, *26*(2), 188–205. https://doi.org/10.1111/j.1540-5885.2009.00345.x

Tost, L. P., Gino, F., &Larrick, R. P. (2013). When power makes others speechless: the negative impact of leader power on team performance. *Academy of Management Journal*, *56*(5), 1465–1486. https://doi.org/10.5465/amj.2011.0180

Tsai, Y. (2011). Relationship between Organizational Culture, Leadership Behavior and Job Satisfaction. *BMC Health Services Research*, *11*(1). https://doi.org/10.1186/1472-6963-11-98

Markus Zehentner

With an extensive and varied career over more than two decades, Markus Zehentner has worked in multiple sectors, including the Austrian judicial system, IT consulting, and the finance industry. He earned his doctorate in law in Austria after conducting research at UCLA Law School. He has also served as a portfolio manager in New York City. Currently working as a senior legal counsel, Markus applies his comprehensive professional background and experiences to his role as the author of 'Breaking Free from Toxic Leadership.'

Several years ago, Markus's journey was marked by significant personal and professional challenges. During a particularly demanding phase in his career, exacerbated by a severe family health crisis, Markus reached a crucial turning point while undergoing therapy. It was during this period that he met Claudia Schwinghammer, who was initially his therapist and later became a collaborator. Their professional relationship has since evolved, fostering a collaboration that not only rejuvenated Markus's personal drive but also catalyzed their work on this book.

Markus combines his legal acumen, diverse industry knowledge, and extensive research to equip readers with strategies to recognize, resist, and overcome manipulative behaviors in the workplace. His dedication extends beyond mere professional expertise, involving a thorough investigation into psychological and organizational behavior to enrich his guide.

His story is one of empowerment, dedicated to helping others reclaim their autonomy and thrive despite adversarial conditions. Today, Markus continues to inspire and advocate for healthy workplace dynamics, sharing his insights and experiences to foster environments that promote well-being and resilience.

Claudia Schwinghammer

With a dynamic career that covers more than 25 years across various business sectors, Claudia Schwinghammer has continually evolved to align with her core values and passions. Transitioning from the corporate world to psychotherapy, she was driven by a profound desire to delve into the human psyche and explore the foundations of happiness and personal growth.

Claudia's professional transformation began as she followed her long-standing interest in mental health and personal development. As a certified RTT® therapist and a devoted student of human behavior, Claudia focuses on helping individuals release past burdens and replace limiting beliefs with empowering ones. Her work revolves around key questions of what genuinely brings us happiness and how we can reclaim our personal power.

In her therapy practice, Claudia provides unique, personalized insights, recognizing that each individual's journey is distinct. Her commitment to her clients' growth and her ability to witness their transformation brings her immense gratitude and continuously renews her love for her work.

As the co-author of "Breaking Free from Toxic Leadership," Claudia blends her extensive business experience with her therapeutic expertise to provide a comprehensive guide on navigating manipulative work environments and enhancing personal resilience. Her contributions significantly deepen the understanding of the psychological dynamics of manipulation and the development of healthier workplace relationships.

Beyond her therapeutic practice, Claudia is the driving force behind SPARK, an award-winning company she founded to enhance mental health in business settings through workshops, training programs, and personalized support services. This venture underscores her dedication to improving both individual and organizational health.

Characterized by a compassionate grasp of the complexities of human experiences, Claudia is an invaluable guide for anyone seeking to thrive in both personal and professional realms.